NOUVEAU IS BETTER THAN NO RICHE AT ALL

OTHER BOOKS BY MARYLIN BENDER

The Chosen Instrument
At the Top
The Beautiful People

NOUVEAU
IS BETTER
THAN NO
RICHE
AT ALL

MARYLIN BENDER with
MONSIEUR MARC

G. P. PUTNAM'S SONS
New York

The authors gratefully acknowledge permission from
George Weidenfeld & Nicolson Ltd., London, to reprint
excerpts from *Chips*, the diaries of Sir Henry
Channon edited by Robert Rhodes James,
published in 1967.

Designed by Richard Oriolo

Library of Congress Cataloging in Publication Data

Bender, Marylin.
  Nouveau is better than no riche at all.

  1. Fashion—United States. 2. Marc, Monsieur. 3. Beauty
operators—United States—Biography. 4. Upper classes—
United States. 5. United States—Social life and customs.
I. Marc, Monsieur. II. Title.
GT615.B46 1983   391'.00973   83-9731
ISBN 0-399-12867-0

Printed in the United States of America

CONTENTS

Illustrations follow page   128.

PREFACE

One must go back to the court of Louis XVI to find the first insider's view of top society life penned by a hairdresser. In the memoirs of Léonard, *coiffeur-valet de chambre* to Marie Antoinette and to *le grand monde*, we have a primary source of information about fashion, foibles and the mentality of that extravagant period.

Like most autobiographies, Léonard's is self-serving and, as the editors who published it stress, riddled with factual error. Its value lies in the fact that Léonard was a participant in the high life at Versailles and the chic *quartiers* of Paris as well as in the failed plan for escape from the revolution that ultimately ended in the execution of the royal couple.

As coiffeur-artist, Léonard bears direct responsibility for the excesses of dress that stamped the image of the queen. Apart from his activities at the court, he was also a highly successful businessman and a great lover. What more could a cultural historian ask of a source?

To establish the significance of hairdressing in costume and in myth, one should go back much further. Egyptians during the reigns of the Pharaohs were endlessly inventive with wigs and makeup as were the ancient Greeks in sculpturing hair. Coiffure illuminates the study of nearly every era, with the possible exception of the Middle Ages, when women's hair disappeared beneath veils, wimples and steeple headdresses.

Before the eighteenth century, hairdressing for the most part was divided along lines of gender—females tended to women's tresses, male barbers (also considered surgeons) took care of men's. Léonard Autié was a young wigmaker with a growing reputation in the theater for his spectacular coiffures when he came to the attention of Madame du Barry, one of the favorites of Louis XV. She recommended him to the dauphin's fifteen-year-old bride, newly arrived from Austria.

Léonard recorded his first impressions of Marie Antoinette: "She was neither beautiful, pretty or even seductive—only promises of beauty. Extremely thin, ash blonde hair, azure blue eyes, a high forehead, aquiline nose too pronounced, small mouth, thick lips." Such is the candor of the professional beautician. Léonard also drew a portrait of the inner woman: "Gentle character but imperious, virtuous in principle but forced to be loose. It was hard for her to resist desire."

Marie Antoinette was afraid of catching cold in the drafty palace, but she disliked wearing hats. Léonard braided her hair with strips of silk to give her "a piquant look" she liked. Compliments flowed and from then on she gave him *carte blanche*.

Four years later, her husband ascended the throne. But it was Léonard of whom it was said, "He came and he is king." He created coiffures at the rate of one a week and sometimes daily, exhausting the fashion reporters who kept tabs on the court. He collaborated with Rose Bertin, a milliner and dressmaker of the rue Saint Honoré who was also in the service of the queen.

In the portraits of his royal client by Madame Elisabeth Vigée-Lebrun, we can see some of his concoctions of ribbons and plumes and rely on the caricaturists of the time for the rest. Léonard erected towers of hair on the heads of the poor queen and her ladies-in-waiting. In some he incorporated still lifes and vignettes. Duchesses were seen entering their carriages on their knees, the only way to accommodate Léonard's scaffold hairdos.

In retrospect, his best work was the short, curly coiffure he designed for the queen after her hair began to fall out during pregnancy.

Flouting previous custom, Marie Antoinette insisted that Léonard maintain a private clientele in the city along with his service at court in Versailles. He grew wealthy and mingled with high society, married an Italian actress and also taught younger hairdressers.

He was more than a hairdresser to the queen and her husband. In 1791 he was involved in the plot for them to flee the country. Léonard went ahead to make contact with foreign emissaries. What happened is unclear, but Louis and Marie Antoinette were apprehended at Varennes and taken back to Paris where two years later they were sent to the guillotine. Léonard escaped, quite possibly with some of the royal jewels, and made his way to Germany and to Moscow where he sat out the next twenty turbulent years, returning to France in 1815 with the Bourbon restoration.

There have been several Léonards in this century, hairdressers who placed their imprint on fashion, made a business of their art, consorted with the upper crust and also wrote their autobiographies. Among the notables were Antoine and Alexandre of Paris and Vidal Sassoon of London whose cockney persona took on a southern California glaze after a successful transplant to American soil.

Alexandre and Sassoon made their mark in the Sixties, a decade of generalized ferment in which the spheres of fashion, society and commerce coalesced. The locomotives of social change were dubbed the Beautiful People, a title that indicated their superficial charm but underestimated their long-range influence.

In the first section of this book, I track them to the present and their evolution in the Reagan years, a period characterized thus far by a singular regard for personal wealth from which all other benefits and values seem to flow.

Without exaggerating the parallels between late-eighteenth-century France and the United States in the last years of the twentieth, one recognizes the social vantage point occupied by a hairdresser like Monsieur Marc, who counts the First Lady and other bicoastal celebrities among his clients.

The second section of the book is his commentary. Unlike Léonard, Marc de Coster is amiable and kind, a sportsman who would rather be in a duck blind at 5:00 A.M. than at an A-list party at 10 P.M. However, because of his social experiences in New York, Paris and various gilded playgrounds, his artistry and his cultivated taste, he is a legitimate authority on elegance, that attribute of a less brutal time which women and men seem bent on acquiring again.

—MARYLIN BENDER

BOOK ONE

THE
NOUVEAU
RICHE

Like the antecedents of so many of those it defined, its origins were not easy to pin down. A pop archaeologist spotted it in a needlecraft boutique on Worth Avenue in Palm Beach, the Florida resort that thrives in a perpetual state of *arriviste* renewal, during the first Christmas season of the Reagan administration. Subsequently, it appeared on Madison Avenue in New York, in shops frequented and often owned by European émigrés from socialism who found the last bastion of free enterprise a merrier place in which to play and invest their capital. It was announced through a medium dear to the hearts of bicoastal society and their cousins in corporate country-club America: those plump little pillows without which no bed was well made, no sofa properly dressed. The motto of the 1980s was emblazoned in grospoint: NOUVEAU IS BETTER THAN NO RICHE AT ALL.

Women's Wear Daily, chronicler of fashions in garments and *moeurs*, relayed the message in headlines: HOT NOUVEAU for the collection of Calvin Klein, a Seventh Avenue Midas; RICH BI-CH for the offerings of designers like Bill Blass and Oscar de la Renta, who catered to the First Lady and her circle. "These are clothes that are meant to intimidate and to look every penny they cost," said *WWD*.

And finally, there was Diana Vreeland, dowager empress of American fashion, explaining why she had chosen the first fourteen years of the twentieth century as the subject of an exhibition at the Costume Institute of the Metropolitan Museum of Art that was to be a highlight of the frenzied New York social season in the fall of 1982. "*La Belle Époque*," she proclaimed, was "the moment of the *splendeur* of the *nouveau riche*."

The new rich, a term connoting a vulgar show of prosperity, formerly merited scorn as best expressed in French, an elitist language. But when the oracle spoke (Vreeland had given the name the Beautiful People to the social standard-bearers of the Sixties), implying that money of recent vintage ostentatiously displayed was praiseworthy, the meaning of the term was turned upside down.

One hundred fifty years ago, Alexis de Tocqueville observed that social life in the United States was based on wealth above all, and that the rules and classifications were neither absolute nor permanent. A nation of immigrants tried to construct a class system based on ethnic and religious superiority and on such arbitrary measurements as the size of Mrs. William Waldorf Astor's ballroom, which could accommodate 400. None of these exclusionary tactics were as rigid as the bloodlines and feudal land grants of the Old World, and in the end the source of privilege always reverted to money. As a broker for Sotheby Parke Bernet's real-estate division specializing in properties of $1 million or more remarked, "Wealth is our aristocracy."

However, wealth was supposed to be seasoned before it could gain social acceptability, redeemed by the passage of time and, with the help of considerate tax laws, by massive charitable gifts. Thus were robber barons transformed into hallowed philanthropists.

The American frontier provided constant supplies of new rich to whom the *nouveaux* of yesterday might condescend. Railroad and steel magnates gave way to oilmen and automobile moguls, who yielded to electronics and cosmetics fortune-makers and Wall Street proxy fighters. Of late, it has been the turn of high-technology wizards and, as always, real-estate developers.

Each wave of parvenus had to submit to a social testing period, but now it seemed no such trial was necessary. To be *nouveau riche* in the Eighties was to be in style.

As always, fashion was only reflecting a shift in the culture at large. In the Sixties, fashion did not invent the demographics; half the U.S. population was under twenty-five. Nor did it create student unrest in the Latin Quarter of Paris, the resistance of draft-age Americans to their country's involvement in Vietnam, or the take-over of British art and music by youngsters from working-class backgrounds. Fashion capitalized on the primacy of youth and extended its authority beyond clothing. Everything from refrigerators to intellect was fashionably packaged to sell.

When the mood of the Seventies turned narcissistic and there were profound changes in sex roles and moral values, fashion turned them to commercial advantage, too. That *nouveau riche* failing, conspicuous consumption, became a patriotic duty. Whenever the economy showed signs of slowing down, consumers were hailed as the engine of recovery, their purchases fueled by bank credit.

In the Eighties, fashion interprets the pervasive evidence of new wealth. More than 200,000 Americans are counted as millionaires, the ranks having more than doubled in fifteen years. The striver who succeeds in fulfilling the American dream of amassing his first million dollars feels like the

Red Queen Alice met on the other side of the looking glass, running to stay in place. As a guest at a mixer for male millionaires and suitable playmates observed, "A million dollars is practically middle-class these days."

Double-digit millions are needed to qualify as rich. The real-estate booms and the merger mania of American business in the Seventies created flocks of *nouveaux*, and the same acquisitive fever rages unabated in the Eighties. The Forbes Four Hundred, an apocryphal list of Croesuses compiled by a business magazine, placed such *nouveaux* nabobs as Marvin Davis, an investor in oil, gas and the stock of 20th Century-Fox, in the same billionaire class with the venerable shipping and real-estate king Daniel K. Ludwig, the two-generation Pritzker dynasty of Chicago, and with David Rockefeller and Paul Mellon, whose assets have been accumulating for three generations.

Increasingly, newer fortunes eclipsed the old. The eponymous Rothschilds were reportedly shrunken in wealth to just under $1 billion. Averell Harriman, son of the railroad baron and a venture capitalist in his own right, was said to be reduced to tending a mere $100 million, one-fifth of the estimated value of the Lauder family's cosmetics empire built in the last twenty years. Gloria Vanderbilt, whose $4-million railroad inheritance had seemed so vast in the depressed Thirties when she was the principal in a custody suit, went on the road selling blue jeans to maintain her accustomed life-style and to earn the title of one of America's twenty-five most influential women as determined by the *World Almanac* in 1981. As the motto pillows asserted, to be new rich was better than any alternative.

In 1981 more than 4,000 Americans had annual incomes in at least seven figures. Among them were twenty-five corporation executives who each received compensation in excess of $1.5 million. Their earnings were dwarfed by the multimillions raked in during the course of a single year by TV entertainers like Alan Alda and Johnny Carson, by country and rock musicians like Kenny Rogers and Paul McCartney, and by Steven Spielberg, the guiding genius behind the movie *E.T.* about a homesick creature from outer space. Analysts said *E.T.*'s appeal was based on its ability to take audiences' minds off bankruptcies and 10-percent unemployment. The executive vice-president of the oil-drilling-equipment company who grossed $5,658,000 in a twelve-month period was overshadowed by Calvin Klein, who received $7 million as his personal share from just one of his licensees, Puritan Fashions, manufacturers of blue jeans bearing his name.

While the rich were multiplying and getting richer, on their own initiative but also with the help of the White House and the tax legislators in Congress, their splendor contrasted with the bewilderment of another group, the newly impoverished. Hundreds of thousands of jobless and homeless were ejected from the middle class across the poverty line, where more than 30 million Americans have annual family incomes below $9,287.

Still others, uncounted by statisticians, reckoned themselves among the *nouveaux pauvres*. They were the ones whose real income had declined in the inflation-ridden Seventies and, not being corporate executives with the power to vote themselves 15.9-percent annual increases in bad years as well as good, and multimillion-dollar "Golden Parachutes" if they lost their jobs in a take-over battle, they felt poor in the Eighties. So did families who didn't have two robust earners; retirees on pensions that seemed ample in earlier times; those engaged in occupations that traditionally offered prestige rather than financial rewards; and even scores of single-digit millionaires who were inhibited in keeping up with the Joneses.

They couldn't blame it all on inflation. Some of it was due to market forces—too many foreigners and other *nouveaux* bidding up the price of necessary luxuries. The $7.25 *prix fixe* lunch at La Grenouille and the $27 one-ounce bottle of French couturier-labeled perfume had almost quadrupled in fifteen years. New York cooperative apartments, condominiums on the Gold Coast of Florida, and undistinguished houses in the canyons of Los Angeles had reached the point where no one blinked at million-dollar asking prices.

While the $100 bill became a unit of currency at the supermarket and cocaine at $150 a gram the bourgeois drug of choice, bicoastal society was drinking Dom Perignon at $40 a bottle as *vin ordinaire*, Concorde-ing to Europe and back for $4,255 and paying $1,000 a couple for tickets to charity balls benefiting cultural institutions. In the climate of Reagan voluntarism, radical chic was passé. The rich were saving landmarks rather than funding Black Panthers. Civil rights had lost cachet. The *Wall Street Journal* noted that the blacks in television sitcoms were living as plutocrats, though affluence was not restricted to one racial category. In prime time, the businessman's newspaper observed, "rich is every bit as in as poor was 10 years ago."

As for victims of sex discrimination, they had been seduced by the corporation. Once-radical feminists were now striding smartly in high-heeled pumps and man-tailored suits, a firm grip on their attaché cases, to become rich and powerful superwomen.

Everyone was moving upscale. Adult education courses were offered in wine tasting, *haute cuisine*, social climbing and its related subject, "How to Marry Money." At Dartmouth's Amos Tuck Graduate School of Business, a noncredit course in ballroom dancing was added to the curriculum for M.B.A.'s, an acknowledgment that "social graces count a lot in the game of high finance," the game that many of the brightest graduates of elite universities chose to play, postponing more idealistic pursuits for another decade.

The emphasis in marketing shifted from mass to class, as consumer-research experts advised business to fix its sights on the maturing baby-boom generation, now aged twenty-five to forty-five, the fastest-growing age group in America, and potentially the most affluent. Supermarkets converted to gourmet food emporiums, magazines readdressed themselves to readers with incomes of $50,000 to $100,000, the minimum that publishers promised to deliver to advertisers. It had been noticed during the Christmas 1982 season that the rich were immune to recession, witness brisk sales of $30-a-pound chocolates, Mercedes-Benz sedans with $35,000 sticker prices, and $3,000 evening dresses.

Mostly books about self-improvement—how to become healthier, sexier and wealthier—made the best-seller lists. Whatever prestige had formerly attached to non–money-making endeavors in the arts and academe had vanished along with the assumption, derived from the New Testament and other literature, that riches were the root of unhappiness and evil. As Russell Baker noted, "The Reagan Government has finally dissipated those old myths about the curse of wealth and once again made it fashionable and respectable to be rich."

Though he avoided disclosing his exact worth, Ronald Reagan's personal fortune was estimated at between $4 million and $5 million, which he had made as a spokesman for big business after his career as an actor had waned and from judicious investments in real estate. Wealthier friends had staked his political campaigns, and 200 generous donors had contributed to "the new luxury," as the Reagan advent in Washington came to be called, by donating a tax-deductible $700,000 to refurbish the personal quarters of the White House. A private foundation came up with $200,000 for the new china Nancy Reagan deemed essential.

"The preponderance of these people is self-made. They followed the American dream," said Charles Z. Wick, one of the president's California backers whom he had appointed director of the International Communications Agency. "During the Depression when people were selling apples and factories were still and guys were jumping out windows because they lost everything, people would go to the movies," he added. "They loved those glamour pictures showing people driving beautiful cars and women in beautiful gowns, showing that people were living the glamorous good life."

America's chief propagandist overlooked the fact that the White House was occupied in those grim days by a Hudson Valley landowner. Franklin D. Roosevelt, whom Ronald Reagan was fond of selectively quoting, lived in typically *vieux riche* style. His wife, Eleanor, a dowdy dresser, set a meager table; when the king and queen of England visited the family estate at Hyde Park, New York, the Roosevelts offered them hot dogs.

Actually, a comparison with the Kennedy White House would have been more to the point; it was the only period in the century when a couple with movie-star glamour resided at 1600 Pennsylvania Avenue. Jacqueline Kennedy was the idol of the fashion press, a model for millions of American women who imitated the little-nothing look of her wardrobe and stole the hat perched on the back of her bouffant hairdo.

Yet the significance of her liaison with the American fashion industry pales in comparison to Nancy Reagan's, a walking advertisement for the California couturiers like James Galanos and Jean Louis and for Seventh Avenue celebrity designers such as Bill Blass and Adolfo.

Nancy Reagan, a fastidiously groomed woman never seen with a hair out of place, was criticized for her expensive clothes, which, in the first year of her husband's administration, were revealed to have been largely in the nature of gifts. The $10,000 Galanos dress she wore to the Inaugural Ball was donated to the Smithsonian Institution and a plan was afoot to send other items of her wardrobe to museum collections. But the scheme had to be aborted, partly because it was announced at the same time the government was arranging to distribute surplus cheese to the hungry poor; the *nouveau riche* dazzle of her clothes and her bicoastal society chums went down badly among the *nouveaux pauvres*.

In fact, the brouhaha had a hypocritical side. The freebee to the celebrity, whether in clothes, personal services or restaurant meals, is a privilege enjoyed by entertainers, socialites, public figures and even by certain members of the castigating press.

It was hardly coincidental that the anointment of the *nouveaux riches* should have come from the fashion sector, for some of the most astonishing examples of new riches arise out of Seventh Avenue. Just when the nation's heavy manufacturing core—steel, automobiles and industrial machinery—was pronounced moribund, obsolete or perilously ill, the formerly second-class "rag trade" produced megamillionaires to rival America's basic industrialists of yore.

Previously, some modest fortunes had been made in the needle industry, but more often in the real estate under the showrooms and factories than in the seasonal caprices of manufacturing women's dresses, suits and coats. Whatever big bucks were reaped from the clothing business had been in sturdy, inexpensive body coverings like Levi Strauss's blue denim jeans and overalls, which enabled his descendants, the Haas family of San Francisco, to enjoy the fruits of old money. A more recent example is Louis Russek, a New Yorker, who sold his Health-Tex children's wear company to Chesebrough-Pond's in 1973 in a $200-million exchange of stock. His daughter, Isabelle Leeds, circulates in fashion society.

The spigot from which the new wealth flowed was opened just at the point when Seventh Avenue began concentrating on selling images and fantasy rather than actual clothing per se, through the promotion of fashion designers as celebrities and the building of licensing networks for their labels.

In the 1960s, a marriage abetted by the press—between Seventh Avenue and willing New York socialites—linked up with the wider pop culture and its instant stars. Women achieved fame by the clothes they wore, the designer names they eagerly dropped to reporters and the regularity with which their photographs appeared in *Women's Wear Daily* and the publications that followed the lead of its publisher, John Fairchild, who gloried in the role of starmaker.

Seventh Avenue had observed how the Paris couturiers recouped some of the losses from their prestigious but cost-inefficient dressmaking operations through the marketing of perfume and accessories invested with the magic of their names. The *maison de couture* traded the use of its glamorous label to the manufacturer of the fragrance, scarf or handbag in return for a percentage of the wholesale value of the merchandise, usually a 4- to 6-percent royalty.

As long as Paris set world fashion trends, decreeing whether women in New York, Tokyo and Rio de Janeiro shortened or lengthened their skirts, nipped in their waists or let their bodies disappear under tentlike chemises, the revenues from franchises were relatively insignificant. Only after the French *haute couture* lost its authority in the mid-Sixties—challenged by young ready-to-wear designers in London and New York, and under cross fire from various democratizing forces that destroyed the marketable value of what Paris knew best how to sell, elitist elegance—did the exploitation of designer names gather momentum.

Pierre Cardin drew the blueprint. As a couturier, he was somewhat suspect, the ideas from his design laboratory too avant-garde. So Cardin crossed the sexual frontier to revolutionize men's wear with a period-piece silhouette copied from England. This successful venture led to an international franchise empire, the exact dimensions of which he obscures with a typically European reticence about disclosing financial details. Cardin branched out further into real estate. He bought Maxim's restaurant, which he is extending into licensed operations, and he is also a sponsor of the arts.

Reliable sources estimate that royalties of about $30 million a year are paid on half a billion dollars' worth of wholesale goods labeled with the Cardin name, everything from neckties and ball gowns to calculators and telephones. (What does a telephone designed by Pierre Cardin look like? A business writer for the *New York Times* posed the rhetorical question. The answer: like a telephone with the Pierre Cardin signature.) Cardin's annual personal income from his various interests is said to run in the millions of dollars.

Other French couturiers who own their own businesses and collect enough royalties from lending their names to be described as annual millionaires are Hubert de Givenchy and Yves Saint Laurent. Karl Lagerfeld—a German free-lance designer for French and Italian ready-to-wear houses, most notably Chloé, Chanel and Fendi, as well as German and Japanese firms—and Valentino, the Roman couturier, do at least as well.

The French may have had a head start in panning gold from franchising but the Americans have more than caught up. The $85 billion in clothing sold at retail in the United States is saturated with brand and designer labels, initials and other emblems that Harry Reasoner, the TV correspondent, had dubbed human graffiti. Signs of consumer resistance to such merchandise, which carries higher price tags than anonymous items, were detected in the recessionary selling climate of 1982, but a thriving subindustry of off-price retailing developed to meet the challenge. The merchant buys the goods at less than normal wholesale prices from overstocked manufacturers and resells it at correspondingly lower-than-normal prices to a public "educated" by massive advertising and publicity to recognize designer names and styles.

Among the names with the highest recognition factor are Calvin Klein and Ralph Lauren, who together accounted for about $1.5 billion in sales of designer-labeled products. They personally pull down sums in the low double-digit millions—more than the compensation of chief executives of the nation's top industrial companies—from revenues of their own clothing manufacturing companies but mostly from international license fees.

Though Klein designs pricey clothes such as $500 coats and $1,000 dresses, the greater part of his fame and fortune derives from the blue jeans presented in a memorable television commercial by the precocious teenage model Brooke Shields, guilelessly murmuring, "What comes between me and my Calvins? Nothing."

Lauren is a brilliant merchandiser of American folkloric themes and the Establishment style known as "preppy."

On a lesser scale, but still on the magnitude of millions, are the annual licensing fees generated by Bill Blass and Oscar de la Renta, whose skills at social promotion outweigh any originality they may have once displayed at the drawing board.

Halston, known at first by the hats he made for Jacqueline Kennedy during her White House years (she has never been seen wearing one since then, and he abandoned millinery to design dresses), is adored by both society women and rock and film luminaries like Liza Minnelli, whom he escorts to parties. He operates under the corporate wing of Norton Simon, Inc., a conglomerate assembled from a base of Hunt canned foods and Wesson vegetable oil. In 1973 Norton Simon bought Halston's business for $7 million in stock, since considerably eroded in value, in order to fasten the Halston name to a fragrance to be produced by the Max Factor cosmetics division. In a market crowded with no less than forty-seven designer-labeled scents, the fragrance "Halston" remains a consistent leader.

The fashion world has always believed in living well, display being its *métier*, Puritan restraint its *bête noire*. One pinched pennies or took out a loan in order to wear Hermès handbags and Lobb shoes and to sleep between Porthault sheets. Now that they can afford their facades, the fashion megamillionaires are behaving in the expected *nouveau riche* manner, flaunting their prosperity and stirring predictable vexation among the older-rich settlers in the posh communities where they alight.

"These people made all their money themselves so they don't have to feel guilty," said the beneficiary of one American fortune still quietly nourishing a third generation of descendants.

Rolls-Royces clogging once quiet country lanes and the din from private jets and helicopters, those symbols of power formerly reserved for presidents and shahs, now ferrying *nouveaux* to their weekend estates and Caribbean resorts, are particularly annoying. "You can't hear yourself think," said a winter resident of Montego Bay, Jamaica, who arrived twenty years ago when it was a tranquil, British-accented colony with Noel Coward and Adele Astaire for star neighbors. David Mahoney, chairman of Norton Simon, and Ralph Lauren are among the jet-powered newcomers to the area. Lauren bought the property of the late investment banker Clarence Dillon and arranged to have it extensively renovated by Angelo Donghia. He also has a Donghia-proofed duplex on Fifth Avenue, a ranch in Colorado, a house in the Hamptons and his very own Hawker-Siddeley jet for commuting.

Lauren tries to live circumspectly, as just a very wealthy family man with a wife and three children. Calvin Klein's style, by contrast, is sybaritic and as publicized as an Italian auto magnate's, down to the kidnapping of his daughter, which, fortunately, had a quick, happy ending before it was splashed on the front pages of newspapers. Klein has a duplex overlooking Central Park furnished with a greenhouse and a gymnasium, houses in Fire Island Pines and Key West and a spread in Connecticut. Renting a jet spares him the spectacle of masses of vacationing travelers of all sizes and shapes, with his name on their denim-sheathed rumps, squeezing into the narrow seats of a wide-body plane.

The most famous designers have abdicated their historic role as innovators of style. Instead, they salute the independence of American women, who refused in the Seventies to abandon miniskirts for longer lengths and took the easy way out into pants and separates. Bill Blass, one of the champions of this let-them-wear-ruffles school of fashion, maintains that "to design clothes today, you have to know how your customer lives, what she wears and needs." He and other designers who cater to affluent women of middle age and older take to the road several times a year, staging fashion shows that would put nightclub entertainers to shame. They get to know local society leaders, who buy their dresses to wear to the charity benefits at which the designers make their personal appearances.

More than clothes, the designers are selling their identities to women who may be unsure of their own. The contemporary byword is that fashion makes a statement about the wearer. If one is inarticulate, one lets a fashion designer do the talking.

In order to franchise their labels, designers must construct glamorous personalities for themselves, immediately comprehensible to American country clubbers, to shoppers on New Bond Street in London, to Japanese housewives. In a Bill Blass boutique on the Ginza in Tokyo, a photograph of "King Blass" looms large next to pictures of two women who are identified with his clothes, Faye Dunaway, the actress, and Nancy Kissinger, wife of the former secretary of state.

The mystique of the designer name must be so compelling that a woman (or a man) will want to wear Bill Blass's initials, back-to-back B's, instead of their own; spend a couple of thousand dollars or more for a dress, certain that several other women at the party will be wearing the same model, and, when that happens, not feel disappointed but elated as though she had been recognized as a member of a secret society. "See, I made the society column in your dress," a woman tells Blass gleefully in a segment filmed for a Barbara Walters television report on "20/20" that was watched by 19 million viewers.

Buy Blass, or another star designer, and have a piece of the American dream—which, if television and the print media are telling the truth, is about being rich, powerful and hobnobbing with superachieving celebrities.

Blass seems to have fulfilled his youthful fantasies. At sixty, he looks back without affection to a Spartan boyhood in Fort Wayne, Indiana, from which he fled to New York as soon as he received his high-school diploma. Like so many designers, he formed his values in movie theaters on Saturday afternoons, studying the sophisticates of the silver screen—the exquisitely gowned sirens like Garbo, Dietrich, Lombard, and the nattily dressed heroes like Fred Astaire and Herbert Marshall.

Later, as an apprentice on Seventh Avenue, he hung around the Stork Club, El Morocco and other haunts of café society, le beau monde of the prejet era. A voyeur, he acquired the style and mannerisms he perfected in the Sixties when he was a bachelor escort to society women, with whom he still maintains friendships. "When I had my children, Bill was always at the hospital," Mrs. Thomas Bancroft, Jr., told WWD. Blass squired the former Melissa Weston during her postdebutante days when she modeled on Seventh Avenue. He has traveled to Europe with another chum of long standing, Louise Melhado, a Seventh Avenue real-estate heiress.

Once a year, he picks up the $30,000 tab for a party to benefit a music school, and the ladies turn out in their Blasses. He donates $10,000 for a benefit for the New York Public Library, an annual event that draws a mix of old money, financially successful authors and dignified celebrities (one of the few fund raisers to which Jacqueline Onassis lends her presence), and the contribution entitles him to play host to a literary lion at his table. Blass draws John Irving, author of *The World According to Garp*.

WWD refers to Blass as "Gentleman Bill" and comments on the elegance with which he wears his dinner jacket, five nights a week in season if the newspaper columnists are to be believed. Invariably, he is quoted as saying he is bored by his social obligations and longs to be alone with his golden retrievers at his house in Connecticut.

There's a macho edge to his gentility. Blass is a hybrid, a cross between Cole Porter and Clark Gable. *Yeahs, damns, ain'ts* and the requisite English *bloody* pepper his conversation. "Why not get your ass in a Blass?" he jokes with Barbara Walters when she asks about the Bill Blass blue jeans he is wearing at his country estate.

A cigarette dangles from his lips. At a fashion show, he loosens his necktie; if it's at a resort, he may appear sockless in polished loafers. According to Patricia Buckley, number one New York hostess of the Reagan circle, Blass is "filled with sex appeal." A rival designer calls him "the last of the movie stars."

The First Lady gives him the special hug she reserves for especially good male friends when they meet rather frequently in New York and Washington. Mrs. Reagan has been seated between him and Oscar de la Renta at Manhattan dinner parties, and both designers have attended state dinners at the White House.

In a *New Yorker* cartoon, the chatelaine of a high-rise apartment says to her buttoned-up spouse, "But if there *were* a Secretary of Clothing, I'd nominate Bill Blass."

The ladies are photographed in multiples at society soirees in Bill Blass designer dresses retailing at $1,000 to $6,000. His name is attached to thirty-five other product lines in a $206-million-a-year franchising empire that ranges from bathing suits, down coats, men's dinner jackets and bedsheets to the interior of an automobile and chocolates.

"Would the world understand Bill Blass chocolates?" wondered Joan Glynn, vice-president of marketing for Bloomingdale's, the matchmaker between the designer and Godiva Chocolates, a spin-off of a Belgian candy company acquired by Campbell's Soup Company, which then sought to put elegant distance between its plebeian self and its tony acquisition.

Contrary to the widely held opinion that designers give little more than their names to their licensed products, Blass contributed firm ideas about chocolate (make the taste less bitter, the texture more crunchy and chewy, he advised) and its packaging. What had always been gold and white became Art Deco-ish black, gold and silver. A fourteen-ounce box of Bill Blass chocolates sells for $12.

Bloomie's threw a party in the store for Bill and his candy; and the ladies and Jerry Zipkin, the chief nondesigner escort of the Reagan circle, attended. Not only did they understand Bill Blass chocolates but some of the guests made away with the displays. "Darling, they are raping the table. Nancy Kissinger can't get any chocolates," Zipkin complained to Glynn.

One observer was puzzled. Didn't most of the ladies have 750-calorie-a-day silhouettes? "Gorge and purge," an authoritative voyeur replied. *Nouveau* society is bulimic.

While Blass plays the sophisticated gentleman with a touch of tough guy, Oscar de la Renta's charm has a softer European side. *WWD* christened him "fashion's Dominican Casanova."

Hebe Dorsey, a jet-set journalist, composed a rhapsody in print for the readers of *Vogue* about his physical charms. Likening his skin to pale amber, his slanted eyes to ebony and his teeth to a perfection of porcelain, she marveled in detail at the erectness of his posture. Dorsey termed his stutter "exquisite" and marveled at how rich Oscar de la Renta was from all those licensed umbrellas, jewelry, sheets, furs, and a fragrance, "Oscar," that has regularly placed among the top ten best-selling scents since its introduction in 1977.

Born Oscar Renta in Santo Domingo to an insurance salesman and his wife who had a feeling for fine clothes, he escaped to Madrid at age twenty to study art and submit sketches to local couturiers. In Paris, he was apprenticed to Antonio del Castillo at the House of Lanvin, whose clientele of wealthy South Americans was in constant need of extravagant ball gowns. During those years he added the *de la*, which he says was part of his family name way back when. In 1963 Oscar de la Renta arrived in New York and took a route similar to Blass's as a Seventh Avenue society designer. He hired a social-registered press attaché and escorted C. Z. Guest, the wife of a Phipps steel heir, to parties. His output has always been geared to conservative women who like to sparkle at night and who feel galvanized by taffeta, brocade and ruffles.

There is no reason to believe he would have run out of such women to dress or ceased to serve as man-about-town, but the boost to his career as something more than a dress manufacturer came about through his marriage in 1967 to Françoise de Langlade, who died in June 1983, a former editor of French *Vogue*. A twice-divorced, hard chic woman of many talents, she was described even by admirers as ruthless in her social maneuvering. (*Ruthless* is one of those newly positive words like *nouveau riche*.) Bolstered by her drive, her contacts among the European *beau monde* and her skills as a hostess, the de la Rentas wield something like the power of Elsa Maxwell, partygiver *extraordinaire* to café society in the Thirties and Forties.

But whereas Elsa Maxwell entertained in public facilities such as hotel ballrooms and nightclubs, and her coterie was largely dilettante, the de la Rentas' stage setting was their apartment, decorated in whatever style

Françoise anticipated as a trend (currently a hothouse of Second Empire furnishings and Orientalist paintings). *Nouveaux* are not content to shine through their designer clothes; their environment and the food they consume, however sparingly, must be sensational as well. The hand-me-down decor and the fare of roasts and cooked-through vegetables of the old rich are incomprehensible to a social caste that was born yesterday. *Nouveau* socialites, as their chroniclers relentlessly inform the public, are superachievers to whom work constitutes pleasure and social credentials.

An article in the *New York Times* magazine in December 1980 headlined "Living Well Is Still the Best Revenge" (another pillow motto) predicted the de la Rentas' prominence in the Reagan social scheme. Written by a *nouveau* journalist, it identified them as power brokers in the intensely competitive new-rich society, which, lacking few ancestors to boast about, screens candidates for proof of power and fame as well as money. By these standards, fashion designers like de la Renta and Blass are seen as international businessmen whose prestige confers status upon those with whom they choose to associate.

Like Mollie Parnis, the only Seventh Avenue hostess to rival Françoise de la Renta in aggressiveness and success (though Parnis's power base has Democratic overtones, having been erected in the Johnson administration when she used to send dresses for Lady Bird to try on at her suite at the Hotel Carlyle), Françoise de la Renta gave a meticulously thought-out party. The guest list was apportioned among corporate leaders, high government officials in lucrative retirement, fashionable intellectuals, a rich blue-blooded couple and representatives from the entertainment world such as a movie producer and a sexy actress to serve as rara avis in a salon specializing in high-minded discourse. And, of course, several media celebrities.

It could never be said of the de la Rentas, as it was of the late Alice Roosevelt Longworth, one of America's royal princesses and a top hostess in success-driven Washington, that it was possible to also meet failures at her table.

During the Sixties, the press served as matchmaker between Seventh Avenue and society in the creation of the Beautiful People. By the Eighties, the scribblers had elevated themselves from the grubby charm of the fourth estate to the first in *nouveau* society. The ranks of the nobles, which had always included such millionaire media lords as Katharine Graham, chairman of the Washington Post Company, which also owns *Newsweek* magazine, and William Paley, founder of CBS, opened to take in star journalists from both videoland and print, including old-time gossip columnists, some of whom moonlight in TV.

Partly, this was the result of the glamour achieved by two young and unknown reporters for the *Washington Post*, Robert Woodward and Carl

Bernstein, whose investigation of the Watergate break-in in 1972 eventually drove President Richard Nixon from the White House. Their dogged independence earned them substantial royalties from a best-selling book about their work, which was subsequently made into a movie in which they were played by Robert Redford and Dustin Hoffman, and their editor, Benjamin Bradlee, by Jason Robards.

Reporters who cover society, on the other hand, have always been notoriously susceptible to co-optation. But even after their beats became commercially prized by their publishers, and a mocking style of writing was found to boost advertising as well as circulation, the writers had a vested interest in not being declared persona non grata by their subjects. That was hardly ever a serious possibility, however. The Oscar Wilde epigram "There is only one thing in the world worse than being talked about, and that is not being talked about" is *nouveau* creed.

A further boost to the status of journalists came from the widespread impression they sowed that the *nouveau* social circuit controls the levers of national and international power. Just look at the guest lists. If Bill Blass and Oscar de la Renta are present, can Henry Kissinger be far behind? Or the First Lady? Or even the president of the United States?

The definition of gossip widened even as its purveyors became socially respectable. Newspaper people used to say that in their poorly paid calling they met such interesting people—other newspaper people—and now they have succeeded in getting that point across to the public.

The amiable Liz Smith, syndicated columnist for the *New York Daily News* and a featured regular on the local NBC television news broadcast, chitchats about movie folk and her fellow toilers in communications vineyards.

James Brady's "Page Six," a potpourri of gossip about show biz, publishing and the Beautiful People, was the best-read feature in Rupert Murdoch's combative evening daily, the *New York Post,* and was syndicated by the *Los Angeles Times* under the title "Eavesdropping." Brady, who pioneered fashion gossip in the Sixties when he was publisher of *WWD,* now gossips in print for *Advertising Age* and for CBS television in New York. A regular on TV talk shows, where he promotes the novels he turns out every eighteen months, Brady has become a celebrity himself.

There's no danger of catching their death of cold from standing vigil in the street for *nouveau* society correspondents who figure prominently in the "media events" they are called upon to report. Nor has the post-Watergate pressure for full disclosure overtaken their columns.

Aileen Mehle, who writes under the byline Suzy for the *Daily News,* perpetuates the tradition of society gossip as established by the Hearst newspapers in their Cholly Knickerbocker columns. She frequently alludes to Charlotte Curtis of the *New York Times* as breaking bread at the same dinner parties she attends. Reporting on the identical gathering, Curtis may refer to Mrs. Mehle without identifying her position with a rival morning daily.

According to Curtis's account of a party given by Alice Mason, a Manhattan real-estate broker who competes with the de la Rentas, it was Mrs. Mehle who cut in on General Alexander M. Haig's lecture on the MX intercontinental ballistic missile—over the main course of pork and apricots—to divert the conversation to less serious topics. The former secretary of state then revealed that he had locked former president Jimmy Carter out of his private bathroom aboard *Air Force One* on the flight to Anwar el-Sadat's funeral.

Mrs. Mason seats her guests at fashionably round tables of eight and had surrounded her guest of honor with the women journalists, Mike Wallace of CBS and Henry Anatole Grunwald, editor in chief of *Time*, thus assuring that her achievements as a superhostess and Haig's plans to write his memoirs would be duly disseminated.

When Curtis, an associate editor of the *Times*, was removed from her powerful post as editor of the Op-Ed page to an ambiguous assignment as columnist, she gave "a nice, private dinner party" at Le Cirque, which *WWD* covered down to the place cards inscribed in her private-school handwriting. It was a show of *nouveau* and Establishment power. The Mike Wallaces, Henry Grunwald and Barbara Walters, escorted by celebrity economist Alan Greenspan, were there. Bill Blass and Mollie Parnis represented Seventh Avenue. Marietta Tree, a Boston Brahmin and former Democratic salon keeper, appeared in an Oscar de la Renta fur shawl. Rounding out the A-list were Mildred Hilson; Kitty Carlisle Hart; Thornton Bradshaw, chairman of RCA; Felix Rohatyn, of Lazard Frères and chairman of the Municipal Assistance Corporation, whose wife, Liz, wears designer clothes; Jerry Zipkin, the Reagan circle's leading extra man, and Arthur Ochs Sulzberger, Curtis's no longer quite so supportive publisher of the *Times*.

"I can't wait to get back to the streets," *WWD* quoted Curtis as saying. "It's really the only way to report, to find out what's going on."

Eugenia Sheppard, doyenne of fashion journalists, is reticent about her personal relationships, even when they impinge on her work. In the Fifties, she began identifying women in her "Inside Fashion" column in the *New York Herald-Tribune* by the designer labels in their clothes and thereby created the impetus for the new fashion society. The *New York Times* and other newspapers followed suit and, with *WWD's* photographers heading the pack, promoted a stampede of intrepid reporters stalking women at society balls to pose the question "Whose dress are you wearing?" Those who responded "My own" were doomed to social insignificance.

It was just this mélange of Seventh Avenue and New York *Social Register* that broke down the walls previously estranging rag traders from polite society. Designers are forever in Sheppard's debt and they also appreciate her refusal to wash dirty linen in her columns.

Wearing her blond hair in a mass of ringlets gives this tiny woman the look of a Shirley Temple doll. Though she moves more slowly than she did when she came to New York from Columbus, Ohio, in the Thirties, she still has the grace and energy of a Ginger Rogers on the dance floor, where she is likely to be in the arms of her closest associate, Earl Blackwell.

They are an inseparable couple, dividing their time among his penthouse on West 57th Street, her apartment nearby and his house in the Bahamas, where they write novels together. He is a confirmed bachelor, she twice divorced and once widowed. Her third husband, the military historian Walter Millis, died in 1968. Sheppard has been a newspaperwoman for more than forty years, Blackwell a society publicist and promoter for a comparable length of time. His Celebrity Service, a listing of individuals whom press and business might wish to be put in touch with for one reason or another, is the umbrella for his other activities. Blackwell's particular forte is in organizing an exclusive club to which social climbers will yearn to belong. He provides the core membership from his stable of pedigreed individuals and carefully maintains the balance of old and *nouveaux* necessary to keep the enterprise desirable. Doubles, a dining club in the Sherry-Netherland Hotel, is one such enterprise; the Nine O'Clocks Ball another. Both institutions regularly appear in Sheppard's column, which is syndicated from the *New York Post*, and Blackwell is listed as a guest without further identification.

Budd Calisch, owner of a public-relations and advertising agency and one of fashion society's handsomest bachelor escorts, frequently is mentioned in Sheppard's and Mehle's columns without his professional handle. Calisch has twice escorted Mary Lou Whitney, the boundlessly energetic socialite, to Bangkok when her husband, Cornelius Vanderbilt Whitney, was feeling under the weather. Mrs. Whitney's chum, Queen Sirikit of Thailand, organizes international society reunions to publicize her interest in Thai handcrafts.

John Fairchild, chairman and publisher of *Women's Wear Daily*, is extremely selective about his appearance at *nouveau* society functions. An old-money type himself, Fairchild, a Princeton graduate and scion of a trade publishing family, prefers to send his editor, Michael Coady, and to exercise power from a distance through the pages of *WWD*, and even more so, through *W*, its glossy satellite biweekly. With a circulation of 200,000—one in six a millionaire, its advertising salesmen vouch—*W* has stepped beyond *WWD*'s garment-center boundaries to depict "a lush tapestry of life-style" in slick four-color reproduction. The decision whether to cover a party can hold a social reputation in the balance. Fairchild's list of Ins and Outs published in *W* in January is eagerly scanned by designers, restaurateurs and hostesses. In January 1983 Fairchild decreed gray hair,

La Grenouille, Orsini's and Swedish antiques to be "in" and jogging, steak, Jacqueline Onassis and Jerry Zipkin (by veiled references) "out."

The media manufacture celebrities, performing this function almost as efficiently as Detroit, in the heyday of U.S. industrial supremacy, turned out automobiles, with annual model changes and enforced obsolescence to keep the assembly lines moving.

Celebrities feed the voyeurism that afflicts America in the Eighties. A craving to know is reinforced by a compulsive desire to tell—private horrors, buried shames, unspeakable sufferings. Nothing is taboo except that which is passé, such as virginity and monogamy. Alcoholism and mastectomy verge on old-hat. Everything is considered a fit topic for revelation: widowhood, drug addiction, rape, incest. The furthest frontiers of sexual deviation must be crossed.

Tattle creeps into conservative newspapers. Even the *Wall Street Journal* finds it pertinent to an account of the financial woes of a broadcasting company that its chief executive "whose close associates describe . . . as intensely private" is involved with his former secretary.

The stronger stuff is on network television. Group therapy at 9:00 A.M. with Phil Donahue, the confessional at 9:00 P.M. with Merv Griffin. At 10:00 P.M. on "20/20" Barbara Walters, the correspondent with the million-dollar contract, vies with her celebrity subjects, dressing up or down as the occasion warrants. If the interviewee is an actress, Walters outglitters her. For a chat behind bars with Jean Harris, who had just lost her appeal from a conviction for second-degree murder, she affected olive drab.

The trial of Mrs. Harris, headmistress of the Madeira School near Washington, one of those institutions that used to educate the daughters of the old rich but can no longer be so choosy about the source of funds, was fraught with social significance. The lover whom she killed, Dr. Herman Tarnower, a physician practicing in an upwardly striving suburb, Scarsdale, New York, had become a millionaire celebrity by writing a book on dieting. Mrs. Harris was a self-supporting divorcée, a cultured woman and a Christian who had found love and diversion with a Jew who was not the marrying kind. She had been supplanted in the doctor's attention by a younger woman. It appeared that the jury, originally sympathetic to her plight, was swayed in the opposite direction by her snobbish tone when she testified in her own behalf.

The interview began with Mrs. Harris coming through the barred door separating the cellblock of the Bedford Hills Correctional Facility from the visitor's room. She was wearing a cableknit sweater over a tailored shirt and pants, the classic sportswear look that spectators remembered from her courtroom appearances, when every fashion detail was reported by the press. Walters threw out the predictably investigative questions: Let's hear about drugs and female homosexuality behind prison walls. Harris was minimally responsive. Then Walters inquired solicitously, "Tell me, do you miss him?"

Defenses crashing, Harris wept. The video lens zoomed in for the close-up as cruelly as Richard Avedon, the fashion photographer, did in the Seventies with his still camera on his dying father's cancer-ridden face. Harris tried in vain to escape the voyeur's gaze. She shielded her pale blue eyes, wet with tears, with a booklet rolled in her hand.

The previous year, she had been dissected in a best-selling book about her trial. *Mrs. Harris* brought celebrity and the sort of financial return once thought irreconcilable with highbrow endeavor to the critic Diana Trilling, widow of Lionel Trilling of Columbia University, an influential shaper of literary sensibilities in the Fifties. Mrs. Trilling was offended by Dr. Tarnower's *nouveau riche* taste as manifested in his Japanese-style house and pond with an island built for private meditation and by his cosseting of elderly *vieilles riches* female patients. The scholar equated vulgarity with weak moral fiber and suggested that Mrs. Harris was guilty of some unspeakable lapse in putting up with him.

Why did Jean Harris submit to further humiliation on TV? Doomed to incarceration until she is past seventy, was she seeking assurance that she was not forgotten? Did she need the status that celebrity, and even its underside, notoriety, confer?

Celebrities rev up the engines of commerce. The phenomenon is age-old, only the range is new.

Entertainers and star athletes have always been used to endorse products for the mass market, such as sporting goods, automobiles and cosmetics, for which their skills and physical grace have a natural affinity.

Now the grizzled businessman usurps the limelight. Lee Iacocca, an able auto executive of heroic stature, after being fired by Henry Ford II and accepting the awesome challenge of rescuing the number three auto maker from bankruptcy, does a feisty and credible job of selling Chryslers on TV. So does former astronaut Frank Borman, chairman of Eastern Air Lines, for the chronically embattled carrier.

To hawk the merits of his family's poultry business, Frank Perdue develops a TV persona—abrasive and slightly comic like that of New York City's Mayor Edward Koch, whom he resembles. Not content with plucking fowl, Perdue lets viewers see him bare-chested in the shower and knotting his black tie, in order to promote chicken as elegant fare.

John Z. DeLorean posed in blue jeans, boots and styled white hair in front of his stainless-steel sports car for a Goodyear tire advertisement, but his macho presence didn't prevent bankruptcy for his auto company. He was later indicted for conspiracy to sell cocaine to save the enterprise.

It is unclear, except to those familiar with his penchant for self-promotion, what DeLorean's friend David Mahoney is doing on the TV screen touting Avis, the number two car-rental agency. He identifies himself as its chairman. Avis is one of the sicklier parts of his Norton Simon empire, which he doesn't mention. Nor does he allude to the conglomerate's dismal record of earnings and wretched state of executive morale under his stewardship. *Fortune* named him one of the nation's ten toughest bosses. He is also one of the best-paid, in the million-dollar class for annual compensation, and a pillar of *nouveau* society. The pilot of his corporate jet formerly sat at the controls of *Air Force One.*

Some listeners were amazed to hear the voice of Paul A. Samuelson on their radios making a pitch for Allied Van Lines. "I'm Paul Samuelson of MIT. I won the Nobel Prize for my book on economics," he said, establishing his credentials for endorsing a moving company. The professor, a multimillionaire from the royalties of the textbook and his prudent investments in the stock market, was the only academic among the "achievers" selected by Allied for its advertising campaign, the others being a race car driver, a diving champion, a former astronaut and a basketball coach. Samuelson was soon chagrined by the attention he drew and promised never to commit such an unseemly act again, leaving open the question why, except for greed or the gratification of being considered a celebrity, he did it in the first place.

One can scarcely carp at the serpent of avarice in the garden of academe when the arts have been irrevocably commercialized. Pop artists paved the way in the Sixties with their exaltation of the trivia of middle-class existence, brand names and all, and Andy Warhol established the value of publicity in creating a market for the artist's work. Warhol's *Soup Can, 19 cents,* one of his literal renderings of Campbell's products that were bringing prices in the four figures in 1962, fetched $95,000 at auction in 1978.

In the Eighties, a young crop of fiction writers such as Ann Beattie captured the materialistic ennui of the baby-boom generation by establishing character and plot through the listing of their consumer preferences.

Books are merchandised as commodities with national promotion and short shelf lives. Artists and writers find that preselling their work is a condition of survival. Being a celebrity is a forerunner of commercial success instead of the other way around, although one's celebrity quotient may rise in inverse ratio to critical esteem.

A beauty editor who has written her first novel is described by her publisher as "soon to be one of our most dazzling author/celebrities." Writers like Jerzy Kosinski, Norman Mailer, Kurt Vonnegut and his wife, the photographer Jill Krementz, are recognized fixtures on the *nouveau* social circuit.

William F. Buckley, Jr., conservative ideologue, newspaper columnist, novelist and video personality through his television program, "Firing Line," is a paragon of grace. His erudition is unfeigned, his wealth inherited, but he has also made a pile from his intellect. Moreover, he can claim President Reagan as an old friend. Buckley's productive energy is formidable. Since he spends as much time at work or such serious play as sailing the Atlantic in small craft, his stately wife, Patricia, is a ubiquitous figure on the *nouveau* scene, always in designer clothes and often with a "walker" (as *WWD* christened the bachelors available for escort duty).

In the Sixties, the marriage of fashion and society made celebrities out of clotheshorses by virtue of their willingness to drop designer names. For the socially secure, sudden renown for conspicuous consumption turned out to be a panacea for certain kinds of pain. Divorceés, widows, and wives with inattentive spouses no longer had to suffer in loneliness. Fashion provided designer clothes for identity, occasions to wear them and surrogate husbands to take them there. Visibility even led to paid work in fashion, decorating and such fields where a tastemaker image was highly salable or to seats on prestigious philanthropic boards. For the social climber, the instant celebrity conferred by association with parvenu designers proved to unlock previously unbreachable walls.

Seeing one's photograph in the newspapers can become an addictive pleasure, however, with all the hazards of compulsive behavior.

Numerous charter members of the Beautiful People have since withdrawn from the fishbowl. Amanda and Carter Burden were the golden couple to Seventh Avenue and the fashion press. She was the daughter of the elegant Mrs. William Paley, he the heir to Vanderbilt railroad and other millions. The modern art on their walls, the band on her ponytail, every word they uttered was grist for the reporter's notebook.

His political career, shaped in the Kennedy mold, fizzled. They were divorced and married others. Amanda became the wife, for a brief period, of quintessentially *nouveau* Steven J. Ross, chairman of Warner Communications, an entertainment complex he constructed on his first wife's family's mortuary business. Ross lives like a robber baron of old (now with his third wife) in a thirty-seven-room apartment on Park Avenue and an estate in East Hampton, protected by secretaries and bodyguards and transported in his private jet. In 1981 his compensation from Warner, $1,954,-136, made him the best-paid corporate executive.

Baby Jane Holzer became a household name through her lion's mane hairdo. She gravitated to the Andy Warhol netherworld, where she dabbled in films, and when the scene got too "kinky and drug addicted," she quit to lead a balanced and unpublicized life. Holzer was last heard from, if not seen, commenting on another pop fashion superstar of the Sixties, Edie Sedgwick of the New England Brahmin clan, who was rescued from oblivion in a best-selling book of 1982, *Edie*, about her degradation and death from drug abuse. The book was edited by celebrity Jean Stein, an heiress to MCA entertainment millions.

If some of the pioneer B.P.'s have faded into obscurity, there is no dearth of replacements, particularly from one sector of the Old Guard, its lively widows. Among those revered by *nouveau* society are Mildred Hilson, wife of an investment banker; Mary Lasker, who was married to an advertising mogul; and Brooke Astor, whose husband, Vincent, never let his fortune, one of the oldest in New York, stagnate. Though Mesdames Lasker and Astor are exuberantly chestnut-haired, their prominence in the style pages of newspapers is a symbol of the graying of America: The median age has advanced to 30, with 11.4 percent of the population over 65, and female life expectancy at 78.3 years. Philanthropy is the stated reason for their willingness to hobnob publicly with *nouveaux*. Even Blanchette Hooker Rockefeller, whose late husband, John D. III, was the shyest of the five Rockefeller brothers, has learned to enjoy being photographed if it will help raise money for the Museum of Modern Art, of which she is president.

Seeing that charity catches the otherwise aloof socialite's attention, Seventh Avenue and retail merchants have become devoted to good works. Bloomingdale's was the first to float the outrageous idea of giving a benefit party in a department store. In 1971 it staged a cocktail reception for the Film Society of Lincoln Center and, thus emboldened, has stepped up the pace of the festivities. During the last five years, Bloomie's raised $2.5 million for charity in its headquarters and branch stores.

Bloomingdale's tends to concentrate on cultural aspects of the community "except in Philadelphia, which is big on diseases," according to Joan Glynn, vice-president of marketing and the store's social expert. To promote the opening of a new branch in Willow Grove Park, Bloomie's gave a dinner dance in the suburban branch to benefit the Children's Hospital of Philadelphia. For entertainment, it engaged a circus troupe and transported a bevy of designers—Bill Blass, Oscar de la Renta, Mary McFadden and Diane Von Furstenberg—by helicopter to mingle with the local socialites.

Having the parties on the premises saves the cost of renting a hotel or armory and is more efficient; its own employees do the staging. Marvin Traub, Bloomie's chairman, a "hands-on manager" in the tradition of the Harvard Business School, his alma mater, tastes the food and wine.

The business motivation for the retailer is to reach a certain affluent customer who is otherwise unlikely to cross his portals, and to capture some of the socialite luster for the store. "You'd kill for Henry Kissinger at your party," said Mrs. Glynn of Bloomingdale's. She has not had to resort to violence. The former secretary of state and his wife have attended several parties at the Lexington and 59th Street store and he even let his charisma shine on a preview of model-room settings.

The papparazzi, who service celebrity-producers like *WWD*, *People* and the news weeklies and whose picture sales are a barometer of *nouveau* social status, marvel at how obliging Kissinger is. No request to pause and turn the other cheek to the camera is too onerous for him.

Unlike his successor, President Carter's secretary of state Cyrus Vance, who keeps his aristocratic profile low as he tends his Wall Street law practice, to which he commutes by subway, Henry Kissinger assiduously cultivates a *nouveau* style. He draws down hefty consulting fees from industry, banking and TV, pens best-selling memoirs, and hops around the world with friends in their corporate jets. He is a diadem in the Oscar de la Rentas' crown.

According to Diana Vreeland's analysis of contemporary mores, "Now everything is power and money and knowing how to use it. Today, as soon as you see the name Kissinger, you know you're in the right place at the right time."

Less engaged observers believe that Kissinger has simply matured since his bachelor days in the Nixon era when he was seen in the company of Hollywood starlets and confided to an Italian journalist his vision of himself as a heroic cowboy.

Kissinger's wife, Nancy, a tall, angular woman known for her braininess when she worked for Nelson Rockefeller, their mutual patron, has emerged as a fashion oracle. Inexhaustibly supplied with designer clothes, she is an extremely cooperative source for reporters on issues of dress, skin care and socializing.

With so many cuts in federal funding for the arts and education, fund raisers look to fashion designers and their socialite friends for help. A showing of the collection of Koos Van Den Akker, a Madison Avenue couturier, to benefit the Winston Churchill Library in Fulton, Missouri, brought out the bluest bloods, including the British prime minister's onetime daughter-in-law, Pamela, the wife of Averell Harriman, as speaker. One of the European *gratin* at the show remarked, "If Winston Churchill knew there was a fashion show to benefit his library, he would probably have laughed, leaned back and lit a cigar."

Pierre Cardin underwrote the $300,000 cost of installing the Belle Époque exhibition at the Metropolitan Museum of Art and bought four tables of ten guests each for the $500-a-ticket dinner before the preview to benefit the Costume Institute. The event publicized his plan to open a branch of Maxim's in New York.

Purely for self-promotion, Valentino spent an estimated $700,000 to stage a fashion show and dinner in the Temple of Dendur at the museum. Most of that amount was consumed by transportation and hotel expenses for his Rome organization, models' fees and related costs of mounting a fashion spectacular. Only $25,000 went to the museum as a corporate-sponsor contribution.

The museum had hit on the fund-raising ploy of offering its magnificent spaces for parties as a once-a-year-privilege of corporate patronage. Many banks and businesses make use of it for quiet dinners for retiring officers. After the publicity of the Valentino bash and, close on its heels, a fiftieth-anniversary party for Harry Winston in the Charles Engelhard Court of American Sculpture, in which some of the firm's famous jewels were displayed in cases, the museum raised the contribution required for such media events to $50,000.

Tax-deductible social climbing was an American custom that the wealthy foreigners who joined *nouveau* society quickly caught on to. "But they don't want the tax-deductible receipt, they just buy the ticket to go to the party," said Mary Sykes Cahan, a senior public-affairs associate of the museum who converted her expertise as a socialite volunteer raising money through the Beautiful People for worthy causes to a professional job. She thinks up projects like parties and cruises that bring in money to the "desperately poor" institution.

No excuse is too commercial for the émigrés to stomach if it promises social exposure. During the peak fall and spring seasons, the New York calendar is chockablock with luncheons, cocktail parties and soirees of every imaginable stripe, such as the introduction of a designer fragrance or a party by an Italian publisher conferring awards for international elegance and life-style on "The Best."

The latter drew a flock of Texans, titled Europeans and an assortment of celebrities such as Claus von Bulow, a Newport socialite out on $1-million bail pending appeal of his thirty-year sentence for attempted murder of his wife; Cristina DeLorean, whose husband, John, had raised $5-million bail in California while he awaited trial on cocaine conspiracy charges; and Roy Cohn, who has starred in several publicized cases both as attorney and defendant.

Preeminent among the *nouveaux* celebrities is Jerome Robert Zipkin, number one bachelor squire, taste arbiter, and nexus of bicoastal society and the European Concorde set.

Eugenia Sheppard knighted Zip, as he is called by his legion of female admirers, social celebrity of the year 1981 because of his close friendship with the First Lady and for "having spotted her as a winner 20 years ago."

During the mid-Sixties, Zipkin was drawn into the network of wealthy denizens of Beverly Hills who were and remain the Reagans' pals. Ties developed, particularly with the wives. Unlike the men in the group, mostly entrepreneurial types, he had ample time and inclination to devote to their interests by day as well as evening.

He has shared with the First Couple some of the most significant events of their lives in recent years, such as the 1976 Republican convention when Ronald Reagan failed to receive the party's presidential nomination and in 1980 when he succeeded. During the 1982 Christmas vacation the president and Mrs. Reagan spent in Palm Springs at the estate of the megamillionaire publisher Walter Annenberg, Zipkin attended the round of parties that at one point occasioned a motorcade to the El Dorado Country Club. A reporter counted seventeen Cadillacs, five Mercedes-Benzes and one Rolls-Royce.

Zipkin's portly figure, often seen in New York in bespoke tailoring and black tie, was photographed in a checked shirt open at the neck and a blazer. He was conforming with the president's turtleneck and plaid jacket, which, by the California code of evening dress, is permissible when the women are in glitter and silk.

After the election, Nancy Reagan described to a journalist her relationship with Zipkin. During a trip to Kentucky some years before, she said, "Ronnie would go off to meetings and there we'd be—Jerry and I—in our bathrobes, and me with my pincurls in my hair and we'd talk and laugh. He has tremendous enthusiasm. He's bright, articulate, thoughtful and terribly amusing—all these great things." Mrs. Reagan also said, without further clarification, that Zipkin was "a sort of modern-day Oscar Wilde. He has more depth than a lot of people in our lives."

From the testimony of her chum Betsy Bloomingdale and others in their circle, Jerry Zipkin appears to serve as a combination best friend such as women ordinarily have among members of their own sex, big brother such as they may have had to accompany them to their first dances and years later to play indulgent uncle to their children, mother confessor and shopping consultant.

As Truman Capote was for the Most Beautiful Person of the Sixties, the late Barbara ("Babe") Paley, Zipkin is an adviser on the arts. What's worth seeing on Broadway or the West End? What must they read? His digests are brief and rapid-fire, delivered with a Mayfair inflection.

"Jerry is a nerve center of superfluous information," said a man who feels well disposed toward Zipkin. "Where did Douglas Fairbanks get his walking stick? Jerry knows. If you can't get on a flight to London, call Jerry. If someone comes to town and wants to reach Dolly Goulandris, he knows she's in Rome for the weekend and he has the telephone number."

Says a publicity woman for a fashion house, "Jerry is a grapevine. The ladies all trail after him." He escorts them to designer showings, to benefit parties in stores and museums, private dinners in Manhattan, London and Paris, and state dinners at the White House. WWD mischievously blacked him out of photographs for a period, leaving the ladies he was squiring with their arms inexplicably poised in midair. Every now and then John Fairchild decides to take an idol down a peg or two, but dubbing Zipkin "the ghostly walker" had no effect whatsoever on his standing.

On the contrary, insiders say it is Zipkin's disfavor that nouveau society most fears. His blank stare as a woman reaches out to greet him from a table at Le Cirque can be devastating. However gentle and solicitous he may be to his followers, his snubs are considered lethal.

The road Zipkin traveled to attain these heights began in the Washington Heights and Inwood sections of upper Manhattan, which his father, David Zipkin, developed in the Twenties and Thirties with housing for middle-class tenants. He also owned several buildings in other parts of the city, including the one on Park Avenue in which the family had its apartment and where his son still lives.

Jerry Zipkin prepared at private schools for Princeton, which he attended with the class of 1936, majoring in art and archaeology and taking time off in his junior year to travel abroad. He belonged to none of the eating clubs that ordered undergraduate social life in those years. Said a friend familiar with Ivy League cruelties of that era, "And now Jerry can get in where most people can't. He rates the best table at Le Cirque and spends New Year's Eve with the president of the United States." Zipkin is living his youthful fantasies, too.

David Zipkin died in 1945 at the age of eighty. He named his only son executor of his estate and managing agent for his realty. In the years to come, the neighborhoods in which most of the apartment buildings were located changed ethnic composition and deteriorated considerably. But the rents from such unchic addresses as 575 West 175th Street and 152 Dyckman Street, along with the income from a portfolio of blue-chip securities, lubricated Zipkin's social career and allowed him to become a gentleman in the English mold.

Even as he continued to make his home with his mother until her death in 1976 (his sister, Elinor, married and lives in Madrid), he joined the international set that nested on the French Riviera before and after World War II and found safe haven in the U.S. during the hostilities. He played bridge with Somerset Maugham and provided a sympathetic audience for the author's secretary and lover, Alan Searle, during Maugham's dotage. Maugham died in 1965 at ninety-one.

His biographer, Ted Morgan, has speculated that the character of the American expatriate snob, Elliott Templeton, in *The Razor's Edge* may have been based in part on Zipkin. Morgan was certain, however, that another inspiration for Templeton was Sir Henry ("Chips") Channon, an Anglicized Chicagoan of inherited wealth and homosexual tendency who married a Guinness, fathered a son, sat in the House of Commons and became a lion of London society.

Channon's diaries, *Chips*, published posthumously in England in 1967, made delicious reading for bicoastal socialites, whose appetite for London gossip is insatiable. Channon formed enduring friendships at Oxford with royal pederasts and, in middle age, with women like Lady Emerald Cunard and Diana Cooper who assisted his rise in society.

"I am riveted by lust, furniture, glamour and society and jewels," Channon wrote. "I am an excellent organizer and have a will of iron; I can only be appealed to through my vanity."

In another passage that illuminates the ethic of the male social butterfly, he acknowledged that "I have no morals, no ideals, no principles whatsoever—except that of good manners—and that I have had a most enjoyable life. I do not see that morals or religion are at all necessary to our happiness; but one has a richer, more varied life, if one keeps up appearances and a code of distinguished manners."

Nouveau society, like earlier generations of socially aspiring Americans, is gripped by Anglomania. English antique furniture and sporting pictures are mandatory, as are weekends in the country in houses decorated with chintz and large dogs loping about. Russell Page, the English landscape architect, must be commissioned to do the gardens. "Jewelry is out for reasons of security and, besides, the gardens can cost more," said an Old Guard expert on the *nouveau riche*.

Everyone is going to the loo, declaring the hectic social pace to be such a bloody bore and trying to master the British art of being savagely rude and exquisitely polite at the same time.

During the turbulent Sixties and Seventies, when the civil-rights movement and other social upheavals caused cultural barriers to crumble, white Anglo-Saxon Protestants appeared to be an endangered elite in the U.S. Almost any other ethnic group was more sought after for college admissions, executive training programs and TV commercials. Although *nouveau* is a melting-pot society, largely because of these forces, and money rather than genealogy the price of admission to its ranks, the WASP is its aristocrat of choice if a Briton can't be had.

W devoted an issue to the "Wobbly Wasps." It documented the characteristics of the breed (such as a fondness for fly fishing, grilled-cheese-and-tomato sandwiches, very dry martinis) and its afflictions, such as dry skin and wobbly knees, hence the sobriquet. *W* also introduced its English relatives, the Sloane Rangers, so-called after the street in Chelsea where they like to shop, and identified the Princess of Wales as a member in good standing before her marriage.

British television series that cast the indestructible class system in a benign light, such as "Upstairs Downstairs," and the perennially riveting accounts of the romance of Edward and Wallis had long been a staple of public TV in the U.S. In 1981 two new dramatic offerings bemused the fashion industry. A television dramatization of Evelyn Waugh's novel *Brideshead Revisited* and a movie about two university students competing as Olympic runners, *Chariots of Fire*, acquainted audiences with the manners, mores and sartorial splendor of the British upper crust between the two world wars. Though their impact was felt most pronouncedly in men's fashion, these films and others revived a general passion for English-pedigreed classics and further stimulated conversation about a return to elegance.

The groundwork had been laid on Seventh Avenue by designers like Perry Ellis, one of the few authentic WASPs in the industry and, since he was embraced by Manhattan Industries and urged to exploit himself in licensing deals, one of its fledgling million-dollar-a-year earners.

Ellis affects the image of an aging Ivy Leaguer, frozen in a time warp somewhere between 1928 and 1953, with his button-down shirts, unbelted khaki pants and long, broad-shouldered camel-hair coats, all of which are the heart and soul of his collections for both men and women. Ellis roughs up the classics, adds a drop of outrage to the cut or the detail and ends up endowing cashmere cableknit sweaters and baggy pants with a contemporary air. He obviously has fun with Anglo-American tradition.

Ralph Lauren, on the other hand, takes it in dead earnest and both his products and the life he leads appear to be the expression of a personal fantasy. The background music for one of his shows was Neil Diamond singing "Hang on to the Dream," and Lauren is not ashamed to talk about the American dream, such as it must have occurred to a City College boychik from the Bronx who wore white bucks and Bermuda shorts when his friends were sporting motorcycle jackets.

A friend who met him in the Sixties when he was starting out as a necktie salesman recalls Lauren as the ultimate Savile Row blade in double-vented suits and suede shoes. He admits to being inspired by Douglas Fairbanks and F. Scott Fitzgerald. *The Great Gatsby*, with its central figure a parvenu living out his fantasy, was a popular morality play for Seventh Avenue and the costumes in the film another source for copyists.

Lauren chose the sport of British royalty and WASP playboys as the name for his first line of neckties and the men's furnishings that followed. The figure of the polo player is the emblem of his empire.

With proper modesty, Lauren seems reluctant to describe himself as a designer. "I'm inspired by concepts," he told James Brady in a television interview. "I project myself through the clothes."

Says a retailer bred to the preppy style who has watched his rise with grudging admiration, "Ralph Lauren merchandised a concept. He created the definitive WASP, and he sells it to people who believe it is 'the look' without having more information. Never having seen the original, they don't know that L. L. Bean is authentic preppy and less expensive, or that they could go to a tailor and get a jacket made for the same money or a little more."

The models in the advertisements for Lauren clothes feature men, women and children who might have been plucked at random from a yacht club in Greenwich. Eyes are blue, hair sunstreaked blond or mousy brown with nary a hint of curl, and haughty noses straight as plumb lines.

In what might be seen as supreme arrogance, Lauren appears in the advertising series wearing Levi's faded to exhaustion and a denim shirt, as though he were above the need for designer clothes. As he became vastly successful, he graduated from gray flannel to the American Cowboy, an image of the president of the United States.

There is also in English upper-class custom a deep vein of sexual ambiguity to be mined. After heterosexual awakening, gay assertiveness and a general rethinking of gender roles during the Seventies, America was ready for androgyny.

The fashion world, which had always been responsive to homosexual direction, welcomed the opportunity—presented by a stream of revelations in books and films from Britain about the Bloomsbury set and their opposite numbers, the decadent aristocrats of the far Right—to endorse the chic of bisexuality. Less than ten years after his death in 1973, Noel Coward, the personification of wit, urbanity and discreet homosexuality, was rediscovered in the U.S. His diaries were published, his plays revived on Broadway and in regional theaters.

An advertising campaign for Christian Dior's thirty-five American licensees, directed by Richard Avedon, played on the ambiguous relationship among two men and a girl. It was inspired by Coward's 1933 comedy of manners, *Design for Living*.

American designers projected ambiguity both in their life-styles and in explicit advertising with two-channel messages, one for a straight audience, the other for gays. Calvin Klein was seen on the party trail in black tie with Bianca Jagger, the former wife of a Rolling Stone, on his arm. His advertising campaigns feature him in a variety of poses—cropped close-ups in which he stares sullenly at the reader and portraits of him reclining, half-dressed, against a hazy background. Like the advertisements for his men's jeans that show a shirtless youth with rippling muscles, the appeal is unmistakably to male homosexuals.

Bloomingdale's, a pioneer in catering to the homosexual trade through its men's fashion department, but mostly through the styling of the merchandise and word of mouth, was joined by purveyors of luxury products and services who discovered that gay men in the high-earning baby-boom age brackets have a predilection for conspicuous overconsumption. Ideal *nouveaux*, they are trying to prove, said the publisher of a gay publication, that "not only can we live as well as the Joneses; we live a damn sight better."

A spate of films about male and female impersonators, homosexuals, transvestites and gender switchers encouraged a fad for tuxedo suits for women.

Nouveau society is rife with sexual ambiguity: partygoing ladies with bachelor escorts serving as surrogates for husbands otherwise engaged; male and female designers with magnetic charm for both sexes; and male homosexual couples composed of designers and their business managers.

Yves Saint Laurent, the middle-aged *enfant terrible* of Paris *haute cou-*

ture, emerged from one of his periodic reveries quoting Marcel Proust, thereby prompting a new look at the French writer whose fashion influence had heretofore been confined to the madeleines sold in Bloomingdale's gourmet bakery department. Extolling the splendor of the new rich, Diana Vreeland noted that La Belle Époque was the era of Marcel Proust.

Saint Laurent and his manager, Pierre Berge, bought a house in Normandy and furnished it with overstuffed plush, red patterned walls and carpets, crystal chandeliers and bibelots, a decor like that of the Oscar de la Rentas' Manhattan apartment. "Oscar is a modern Proust, remembering of things past," Hebe Dorsey wrote in *Vogue.*

Saint Laurent used a Proustian theme for the house, naming the bedroom after the characters in *Remembrance of Things Past.* He took the Swann suite for himself and assigned to Berge the rooms commemorating the baron de Charlus, whose homosexuality is revealed by Proust in the fourth volume. A reporter for *W* described the baron as virile and Berge's bathroom as manly. He was probably waiting for the film version to discover the plot.

Saint Laurent's inside jokes were made in the spirit of *épater la bourgeoisie;* in the modern version, the bourgeoisie swallows the joke and enriches the punster. There were as many jokes within jokes connected with the introduction of the Saint Laurent fragrance "Opium" in 1978 as boxes in a Chinese puzzle.

The perfume was marketed by Squibb Corporation, a pharmaceutical company that owned the license through its Charles of the Ritz division, and first introduced in France with an advertising campaign devised by the Mafia agency (an acronym of its partners' names). In the key print advertising, a model dressed in what Saint Laurent called his "opium pajamas," reclined against cushions with her eyes closed and an expression of otherworldliness on her face. The text, *"Opium, pour celles qui s'adonnent à Yves Saint Laurent,"* could be translated as "Opium for those who are addicted to Yves Saint Laurent."

Saint Laurent would entertain no other name for the scent, a heavy Oriental blend, except "Opium." From one perspective, it was a clever choice in that the pronunciation is the same in French and English except for syllabic stress. Practically anyone over the age of six comprehended its meaning in either language without resort to a dictionary to learn that it is a substance from which such addictive drugs as heroin, codeine and morphine are derived.

A mass fragrance manufacturer had already issued a bath oil, "Grass," which hadn't done particularly well—but then, marijuana was the opiate of the Sixties.

Saint Laurent's fragrance was deliberately priced high to assure snob appeal, $100 an ounce, or $400 less than the real stuff.

"Opium is a dignified drug," the designer told a reporter. To another journalist, he said, "Drugs are more than an escape." Citing Cocteau, he added, "They can open new imaginative vistas for the artist."

The campaign was a hard sell of the concept that Saint Laurent's "Opium" connoted the mystery of the entire Orient from mideastern Morocco to far-eastern China, not the puritanical People's Republic but rather the quaintly corrupt Imperial China.

The selection of the name was "really so brilliant," said Geraldine Stutz, president of Henri Bendel, one of the exclusive stores permitted to sell the fragrance in New York. "Opium was part of the lives of elegant, ancient China," she added. She was asked whether she associated it with drug abuse. Not for a moment, Stutz replied. "That's the smarmy, smart-ass way, the way of the outsmarting types." An insider would accept "Opium" on the projection value Saint Laurent offered it, as an association with the Orient.

Initial reactions to the name within Charles of the Ritz in New York were negative, and the chairman of Squibb, Richard M. Furlaud, a Princetonian and Harvard Law School graduate, was concerned. At the time, Squibb needed a winner in its fragrance and cosmetic division to help moderate its lackluster performance in ethical drugs. Saint Laurent was always eager for money to finance his expensive habits. On estimated sales of $100 million at retail for the first year, he was to receive a royalty of about $3 million.

Fragrances run in cycles. After a decade of fresh-smelling and floral woodsy blends, consumers were thought to be ready for a heavy, sensuous perfume like Guerlain's eternally popular "Shalimar." Though Saint Laurent lacked veto power over Squibb in the legal sense, he was the creative spark without which no fashion product can be successfully launched. He would not be budged on the name.

"This was an interface problem to end all interface problems," Furlaud said, but with his French background he was able to communicate with Saint Laurent in his native language. The designer does not like to speak English.

He convinced Furlaud that his "Opium" was not a drug but "something out of Baudelaire and Rimbaud." The chairman failed to note that both dissolute poets of the nineteenth century were well acquainted with ecstasy-inducing substances.

"Saint Laurent is an authentic genius," Furlaud went on to express his confidence to an interviewer. "He thinks of himself as a man who reflects the times. He is more a man of the Sixties than the Seventies, basically a rebel. If he had been an American, he would have been on the streets protesting Vietnam with Shirley MacLaine. He identifies with change. Now he is less excited about the world because it is more conservative. In a decade where things are less strong, he turned to the Orient, to the world of fantasy, creating a kind of dreamworld. The word *opium* symbolizes this and is the one word he feels most represents the mystery of the Orient, the China of Marco Polo, the Japan of Nara and Kyoto."

As it turned out, the most shocking thing about "Opium" was its failure to scandalize. Rumors that "Opium" was to be banned in the U.S. stimulated sales at duty-free shops in the Paris and London airports.

Advertising Age ran an editorial decrying the idea of "linking perfume to habit-forming drugs" and there was a scattering of dismay registered by individuals in the field of drug rehabilitation. "But it's a delightful scent," the director of a clinic added.

Four years after it was introduced, "Opium" was maintaining its rank as one of the ten best-selling fragrances in America. Its price was raised to $160 an ounce.

Encouraged in part by media accounts of celebrity users, illegal drug consumption permeated all reaches of American society. Cocaine was the drug of *nouveau* chic. It had an elegant name, "the lady." In an interview in which she was asked to recall Edie Sedgwick, Diana Vreeland observed, "I've never seen anyone on drugs that didn't have wonderful skin."

The frivolous double entendre apparent in "Opium" and other chic hoaxes of which Saint Laurent was a master perpetrator was characteristic of camp, a sensibility that infected fashion in the Sixties and was a motor for pop art and culture.

As synthesized in 1964 by Susan Sontag in *Partisan Review,* camp was an emphasis on style over content, a third stream of taste in which bad might be considered good, an androgynous, extravagant, antiserious aesthetic.

Though some icons of camp taste, such as Aubrey Beardsley prints and flapper dresses, had a fleeting acceptance, others demonstrated staying power and even proved to be sound investments. The Tiffany lamp, a prop seized by art directors and window-display artists to signal contemporary feeling, had durability. One lamp brought a record $360,000 at auction in the Seventies. Andy Warhol, pop superstar, continued in the Eighties as a guru of camp, although it evolved, for a generation that had been in the playpen when it was first hot, into something called "attitude."

Just as camp had traveled from the homosexual underground to mass culture, so attitude originated in the black ghetto, where it signified an arrogant posture and outlook, and moved on to white dance clubs. Late baby boomers gyrating to the beat of a jeans jingle in their Marilyn Monroe guises and swaggering with Elvis Presley hairdos in used prom tuxedos felt that a Fifties attitude expressed their feelings of powerlessness at being caught in a post-Vietnam, post-Watergate grid.

Decrying the ascendancy of the *nouveau riche*—"All that's left to us is designer jeans" was one way of putting it—they were just as committed to conspicuous consumption. Secondhand clothes were cheaper than new, that was all, and probably better made.

Like camp before it, attitude progressed to Seventh Avenue, where its name was dropped from the lips of rag traders wondering what lay over the horizon from designer labels. "I don't get it. Five hundred dollars for a Prairie attitude," said a buyer, doing a quick calculation on the sum total at retail of three pieces of Ralph Lauren's patchwork.

He might have turned for illumination, once again, to Susan Sontag, this time for an interpretation of Roland Barthes, a French critic, cultural philosopher and contributor to the arcane theory of semiology, a so-called science of signs.

Like many giants on the French intellectual landscape, Barthes, who was killed in a street accident in 1980, regarded fashion as an art worthy of sustained analysis. During the Saint Laurent "Opium" crisis, Xeroxed copies of his writings on myth, in English translation, were passed around among worried marketers of the fragrance.

To explain how a picture or object may signify meaning apart from its content, Barthes had cited a Chinese woman with an opium pipe and "that peculiar mixture of bells, rickshaws and opium dens" as symbols or signs of "sininess." Like Saint Laurent, Barthes harked back to pre-Communist China. Whatever the reality of the individual or the paraphernalia, the mental image they evoked was one of wickedness. Ergo, the perfume seller in New York could draw the conclusion that Yves's selection of a name was just the symbol of generalized naughtiness to promote perfume sales.

In a Sontag essay, Barthes is quoted as observing that "fashion exists only through the discourse on it," another soothing rationale for the present. Given the reduction to absurdity of fashion in the traditional sense of clothing design and workmanship, it was comforting for Seventh Avenue to be able to explain itself in terms of profound meaning.

Only those who could not read signs would be so literal as to look at a badly stitched seam or note that a celebrity designer was either knocking off a deceased couturier season after season or merely switching ruffles, all the while raising his prices.

In *nouveau riche* society, all signs point to money. Conspicuous super-consumers boast of their wealth and also assert that they deserve the best.

Consider the Concorde, the only commercial plane a *nouveau* can take across the Atlantic. A financial disaster for the governments of Britain and France that subsidized it, the SST offers speed to the business traveler for whom it pays to cut the journey in half. Could a *nouveau* admit that a few hours here or there doesn't make much difference? The first-class section of a 747 is more comfortable and, arguably, the food almost as good. If the traveler is compelled to meet a superior class of fellow passenger, he might try the economy section where D. K. Ludwig and his ilk of billionaire usually sit. Nevertheless, the Concorde signifies money and the premium value of the traveler's time.

Consider an advertisement for a Roxanne swimsuit. It shows a chauffeur holding an umbrella over a gaunt woman dressed in a maillot. Her elbows are knobby, her upper arms skeletal, the expression on her face pained. The advertisement presumes a public fed on a media diet of *nouveau riche* images will know how to interpret the signs and take heart from the headline, "You don't have to be *rich* to be sexy." Was it not a woman for whom a king gave up his throne who said (another motto-pillow epigram) that one can never be too rich or too thin?

Consider elegance, about which there is much fashionable discourse of late. "The Eighties are ushering in an age of elegance," a news magazine announced. *WWD* introduced the "Elegant Rich Bi-ch," successor to the "Rich Bi-ch" who wears Oscar de la Renta's dresses.

According to Sontag, Barthes drew a distinction between elegance in the older, exclusivist sense and elegance in the modern, more democratic, inclusive form. Walking an aesthetic tightrope, he could find in the teeming streets of an Asian city—just the sort of places *nouveaux* evade with their tinted-glass limousine windows and the helicopters that keep them aloft—"the transformation of quality by quantity." Barthes greeted this sign as a "source of endless jubilation."

This would seem to be the proper attitude for a society like the *nouveau riche*, which is so surfeited with wealth and overcrowded with candidates for admission. Too many riches are competing for standing, which makes for feelings of unease.

To impose a restrictive code such as elegance in its ancient sign of constant refinement would be a kind of social Darwinism. No one wants to be pronounced unfit to survive. The answer, then, is to apply Barthes's remedy and flip signs. The meaning of *elegance*, like that of *nouveau riche*, can be turned upside down.

BOOK TWO

MONSIEUR MARC: ELEGANCE IN A NEW SOCIETY

1

GOING PLACES

Knowing that it was to be an extraordinary weekend, even by the standards of those who take power and luxury for granted like their morning coffee, I packed carefully.

I slipped my scissors and comb into their kidskin folding case and placed it with some rollers for the hair and a hand dryer in my briefcase. It has a handle and a strong brass lock, the same kind of briefcase in which lawyers and professors carry the tools of their professions. Mine is made of soft black lambskin, absolutely plain on the outside. No monogram, only tiny gold letters on the inner flap—Hermès-Paris.

Into a large brown leather tote bag, also from Hermès, I put my Capilustro electric curling iron and a paper bag filled with croissants. I never go to the White House, or any friend's house, for that matter, without taking a little present.

My Remington 12-gauge automatic shotgun went into its canvas carrying case; my camouflage suit, boots and underwear into a canvas duffel bag. I packed my evening clothes in a Vuitton suitcase. I wish it didn't have Louis Vuitton's initials all over it. Advertising someone else's monogram is rather tasteless, more a sign of insecurity than a status symbol. I prefer my own initials, and then only on my shirts. I make an exception for Vuitton luggage because it is so strong and lasts forever.

As I finished packing, I couldn't help remembering how far I have traveled with my scissors, my gun and my dinner jacket.

The weekend began, actually, on Tuesday when Carolyn Amory telephoned to ask me to escort Bonnie Swearingen to the party at Saks Fifth Avenue. Bonnie's husband, John Swearingen, chairman of the Standard Oil Company of Indiana, had to attend a business meeting in New York that evening. The Swearingens live in Chicago and had invited Carolyn and her husband, Thomas, a management consultant, and me for a week-end of duck shooting at White Lake, Louisiana. Since the original plans were made, the Swearingens had been invited to the White House on Thursday evening to attend a state dinner for President and Mrs. Ferdinand Marcos of the Philippines. Bonnie is a friend of Mrs. Marcos's—"darling Imelda," she calls her.

I am not, as a rule, one of those men who escorts other men's wives to parties. *Women's Wear Daily* coined a name for them—"the walkers." But since the Swearingens have made it clear that they consider me a friend, and this was in the nature of a favor, I agreed.

I would never have thought that I would be friends with the head of the ninth-largest industrial company in America—trade name Amoco—a man who is a brilliant engineer and was rated by other big businessmen the second-best chief executive in the country. My business is rather small in comparison with his, and besides, I really consider myself an artist. Whatever it's called, business or art, hairdressing has brought me in social contact with some of the most powerful men and women in the country, if not the world.

John Swearingen doesn't enjoy going to big parties very much and neither do I. I would much rather jump into my BMW with my dogs, Katia, a Weimaraner, and Tanya, a German shorthair, and go off to my house in upstate New York where I can get up at five in the morning and be with nature. But, to be honest about it, mixing with *le beau monde* is good for my business.

I do enjoy meeting clients outside the salon from time to time. When they are dressed up and in a festive mood, they talk to me woman-to-man, forgetting that I am a hairdresser, and I can discover their tastes and interests, their feminine qualities.

That Tuesday evening, I dashed to my apartment, a block away from the salon, to shower and change into my dinner jacket and black tie. In the lobby of the Waldorf Towers where the Swearingens were staying, I met two clients who were going to the party: Mrs. Edwin Hilson, widow of an investment banker and a beautiful grande dame, and Mrs. Emil Mosbacher, Jr., whose husband is an America's Cup winner and former chief of protocol in the Ford administration. "We'll see you later," they said.

In the Swearingen suite, Bonnie and I decided that she should wear her hair upswept in the style of a Boldini portrait to go with her dress of eighteenth-century lace designed by Pat Kerr, who has studios in Memphis. "Memphis. Don't you love it!" Bonnie said. She was aware that the other women would be wearing dresses by Givenchy, Valentino and American designers like Adolfo and Bill Blass who were being honored that evening.

Bonnie Swearingen pretends at times that she's just a simple girl from Alabama, which she once was—daughter of a poor clergyman. But she's very smart. She was a stockbroker before her marriage to John Swearingen; and since then, an organizer of spectacular charity events. And she has a flair for standing out in any crowd, including New York fashion society, which might intimidate a less confident woman.

The ivory-colored lace set off her blond hair, blue eyes and fair, sun-tanned complexion. The upswept coiffure permitted her to display her diamond pendant earrings and a long double strand of pearls.

Bonnie Swearingen loves jewelry. I did her hair for the first time in Washington for President Reagan's Inaugural Ball. As she was putting on her set of aquamarines and diamonds—necklace, earrings and bracelet—to go with her blue satin dress, I asked her, "What are you wearing in your belly button?" From then on, we became friends.

When she learned how much I love to hunt (and she herself is an excellent shot), she arranged for me to meet her husband and he invited me to go hunting with him and six of his friends in the oil business. I must have proved myself as a sportsman during that stag weekend in winter, because Mr. Swearingen invited me again, this time with his wife and other friends, in early September.

But first she and I were to attend a party at Saks Fifth Avenue.

Europeans try to fool the tax collector by hiding their wealth and having the government pay for health care and the arts. In the United States, the wealthy support those services with the dollars they legitimately withhold from the Internal Revenue Service. As I learned when I came to America, that's the difference between socialism and private enterprise.

Saks charged $125 a ticket for dinner and a showing of the fall collections of five designers, the proceeds to go to the favorite charities of their best customers. Carolyn Amory, for example, wears many Adolfo designs; Adolfo picked the American Cancer Society, of which Mrs. Amory is New York chairman, for his share of the benefit contribution.

As we drew up to the store in the chauffeured limousine, the photographers for *Women's Wear Daily* and the *New York Times* were waiting as though this were a roundup of *le tout New York*, which in fact it was. Nan Kempner was there with Bill Blass, Pat Buckley with Oscar de la Renta. Even Adolfo, a shy, gentle person who rarely goes to parties, came out in black tie. Since Ronald Reagan went to Washington, Adolfo has had to become accustomed to the limelight. As soon as the White House announces that Nancy Reagan will be visiting New York, reporters telephone Adolfo, Monsieur Marc and Le Cirque restaurant, putting us in an awkward position. The press has its job to do and we have all benefited from Mrs. Reagan's patronage, but we don't want to be responsible for robbing her of the little privacy she has left.

I saw several women wearing the same Adolfo evening suit. I wondered if they made mental comparisons when the model strutted out on the runway in the design. It used to be a calamity for two women to be seen in the same outfit, but today it seems to be a point of honor, as long as the designer is a celebrity—like wearing the uniform of an exclusive girls' school.

One of the most outstanding women present that evening was Mrs. Francis Kellogg in a Givenchy dress, her blond hair sleekly combed into a French twist. She is Iranian-born, the stepdaughter of Empress Farah Diba's uncle. I raised my fingers to my lips in a gesture of appreciation for how stunning she looked. In sign language, Mercedes Kellogg signaled me that she had done her hair herself. The fact that this client could manage without my services did not affect the admiration I felt for her innate elegance.

After the fashion show, dinner was served on the fourth floor, where lingerie and shoes are ordinarily sold. Jerome Zipkin came over to our table and announced to Pat Mosbacher, "I'm glad you took off the lampshade." That was his way of paying a double compliment, to Mrs. Mosbacher for the way she looked and to me for changing her hairstyle. When she came to me, this beautiful woman was wearing her hair in the teased, bouffant style with the flip on the bottom that Jacqueline Kennedy made famous. Many society women love it and have to be coaxed to give it up. I suppose it makes them feel safely well groomed because every hair stays in place. But it's passé. Hair should be freer and more natural; it should have movement.

Zipkin's word is law to society women, especially since his close friendship with the Reagans has been publicized. *Women's Wear Daily*, which likes to give catchy titles to the people it writes about, christened him a "walker," the "Social Moth" and, after the inauguration, the "Ambassador to the Court of the Ladies."

John Swearingen arrived when dinner was over to take his wife home. They invited me to go to Washington with them in the Amoco plane early Thursday morning, but I had appointments at my salon and so they offered to take my luggage.

Thursday is always the second-busiest day of the week in a hair salon and my calendar was especially crowded with rescheduled bookings from Friday. At 4:00 P.M. I took a taxi to LaGuardia Airport to catch the shuttle to Washington.

I went directly to 1600 Pennsylvania Avenue. Though I have been to the White House many times since Ronald Reagan was elected president, each time I am overwhelmed at being at the center of power in the most powerful nation in the world.

Nancy Reagan, wearing a peach-colored dressing gown, was waiting in the small white room in the First Family's apartment on the second floor. Exaggerated reports in the press refer to this room as a beauty salon. It contains one beautician's chair, a sink, and a Louis XV–style chair under a hair dryer. Many of my clients have much more elaborate facilities in their homes. The actress Faye Dunaway ran into my salon from the street one day and bought a hair dryer on the spot.

The president was exercising in an adjacent room. He cuts a very trim figure in his shorts, working out on the machines. I was amazed at how good his body was. No flab, no belly, I thought enviously. Most men past the age of twenty-five have a tendency to let go. But not Ronald Reagan. When he was finished, he came in and thanked me, as he always does, for making his wife look so beautiful.

Mrs. Reagan was planning to wear a long white dress by Galanos. I always try to do her hair a little differently each time without departing too much from her basic coiffure, which is very becoming. Would an artist paint a picture the same way twice? Most women are afraid of change once they believe they are in top form, and I have learned to go gradually.

She was used to having a wave and a little flip to the right. I brushed her hair to the center and very close to the head in back. Most women look their best with fullness at the top and less at the bulge of the skull. Too often they appear to be carrying balloons attached to their heads, the leftovers from the 1960s binge of the teased bouffant coiffure.

From the White House I went to the Ritz-Carlton Hotel, formerly the Fairfax, where the Reagan friends stay when they are in Washington. The owner, John B. Coleman, is a member of that circle.

I checked in, took a shower, put on my dinner suit and black tie, and went to the Swearingen suite. Bonnie was wearing an off-the-shoulder dress of hand-embroidered voile, the skirt arranged like a mass of petals. It was a gift from Mrs. Marcos. We agreed she should wear her hair down, to just above the nape of the neck, the right length for a woman of experience.

The party for the Marcoses was held in the Rose Garden, the first time a state dinner was given outdoors. Hundreds of tiny white lights were strung from the bushes, and Japanese lanterns swayed from the trees. The tables were set with white candles and flowers, and the sky was studded with stars. The night was warm for September, with just the slightest breeze, and with the scent of all those roses I felt as though I were on an enchanted island in the ocean.

The Reagans mix their party lists with people from government, industry, fashion and the press. Among the 140 guests were Secretary of State George Shultz and Supreme Court Justice Lewis Powell; Y. K. Pao, the shipping magnate from Hong Kong; Robert Trent Jones, Jr., the golf-course designer; and John H. Johnson, said to be the richest black businessman in the U.S. with his empire of *Ebony* and *Jet* magazines, insurance and cosmetics. The New York contingent included Oscar de la Renta, Arlene Dahl and Marc Rosen (vice-president of Elizabeth Arden); Liz Smith, the gossip columnist of the *New York Daily News;* Andy Warhol, the pop artist; and Bob Colacello, the editor of his

Interview magazine. (Doria Reagan, the President's daughter-in-law, is an editorial assistant for *Interview.*) Jerry Zipkin was escorting Louise Melhado from New York.

We dined on Maryland crab and lobster in aspic, capon with brandy sauce, wild rice, cauliflower and string beans, spinach salad and Port Salut cheese, fruit sorbet and petits fours. The wines were a Chenin Blanc and a Chardonnay from California.

After dinner, the guests moved about on the South Lawn and were served brandy and coffee. Mrs. Swearingen introduced me to President and Mrs. Marcos. "This is Monsieur Marc," she said. Imelda Marcos was wearing a traditional Philippine dress made of embroidered cloth woven from pineapple leaves. The sleeves were shaped like bells. She is a tall, beautiful woman with a firm handshake.

What small talk does one make with a head of state and his wife, who is said to exercise dictatorial influence? "We're neighbors," I said, referring to the mansion on East 66th Street that I pass every morning on the way to Central Park with my dogs. She has furnished the place with valuable antiques. "That belongs to the Philippine government," she said.

President Marcos was very friendly. "Ah, Monsieur Marc, you must be French," he said.

"*Parlez-vous français?*" I asked.

"*Un peu,*" he said, and made a little conversation in French. He is very small and I was surprised to hear some of the women guests saying they found him very sexy. One woman gave a little frisson of pleasure as she told me that. In my business one learns that power turns some women on. Maybe that's why I've never seen as many unattractive men as I have at parties in Washington—but there's never a shortage of women at their sides.

I was up at 5:30 the next morning. Mrs. Reagan was leaving at 7:00 to fly to the funeral of Princess Grace of Monaco, who had died from injuries suffered in the crash of her car on a Riviera corniche. As she drank her breakfast tea, she reminisced about the actress Grace Kelly she had known in Hollywood.

"When movie stars die, it's always by three," she said, biting her lips and with tears in her eyes. In a matter of weeks, Henry Fonda had died, then Ingrid Bergman and now Princess Grace at fifty-two. Doctors said she had been stricken by a cerebral hemorrhage at the wheel of her car.

The Swearingens were waiting when the White House car dropped me at the hotel. We drove to the airport and boarded the Amoco jet for the flight to Chicago. A fourth passenger was John Johnson, who was getting a lift to his office in Chicago. We talked about his Fashion Fair line of cosmetics, which is marketed to high-income blacks but is feeling pressure from big white-owned companies like Avon and Revlon.

Traveling by private jet is like going by magic carpet. You don't have to fight crowds, worry about baggage or seat assignments. The Grumman Gulfstream II didn't sit on the runway very long and the coffee and sandwiches served aboard were as delicious as if I'd prepared them myself.

We spent the morning in Chicago, John Swearingen at his office and Bonnie and I at their apartment overlooking Lake Michigan, where we were joined by Carolyn Amory.

I trimmed Mrs. Amory's hair and gave the Swearingens' maid a haircut, too. One always tries to do something for one's host and hostess and for their staff as well. I usually show gratitude and affection by helping them with their hair or cooking for them.

At 1:00 P.M. we left for Midway Airport, stopping at the Indiana Standard offices to pick up Mr. Swearingen and Mr. Amory and Mr. Swearingen's two daughters and their husbands. We were to be hunting companions for the next two days. The van in which we drove was luxuriously furnished with reclining seats and individual controls for air conditioning and stereo; it was amusing when we pulled up to a McDonald's and ordered hamburgers to eat on the way.

Landing at Crowley, Louisiana, after a two-hour flight, we went by car and then by speedboat to the camp at White Lake, a small boat piled with our luggage and hunting gear following behind. The camp is a one-story brick-and-wood structure fitted out like a deluxe hotel. By the time we reached our rooms, our suitcases were unpacked. John Hill, an oilman from Dallas, and his wife, Jo Beth, were waiting there to complete our party.

It was late afternoon and I was tired, but Bonnie Swearingen insisted we go skeet shooting. Carolyn Amory was a vision in white pants and shirt, a little scarf tied at her neck, every blond hair in place despite the 100-degree heat and the mosquitoes buzzing like the overture to Beethoven's Fifth Symphony. Because she is a crack shot, she could get away with looking so chic. As a rule, one should not be better dressed than one is capable at a sport.

Afterward, we returned to the camp for a hearty dinner of Cajun cuisine: pork and rice, black-eyed peas, corn on the cob, strawberry ice cream and a California Cabernet Sauvignon. We were in bed by 9:30 P.M. because we had to be up early for the shooting.

At 3:30 A.M. there was a knock at the door and a man offered black coffee with chicory flavoring. One sip was enough to wake me up. Breakfast was served in the dining room between 4:30 and 5:00 A.M. and there was no excuse for being absent or late. Everything was organized with military precision to assure we were in the blinds to shoot the teal ducks before daybreak.

We went by speedboat through the swamp, a forty-five-minute ride in humid blackness. We paired off in the blinds. I was with Bonnie Swearingen.

Sport reveals character. When the bird was in the one o'clock position, she would have to aim her gun in front of my face. Rather than do that, she passed up the chance to shoot.

I bagged eight ducks, my quota of four and the guide's as well. Returning to the camp in daylight, we could make out exotic flowers blooming in the swamp. As always in nature, beauty and danger coexist.

During the rest of the morning, we relaxed. Some played cards, others read. I gave haircuts to Mr. Swearingen's daughters and to two maids, then watched the kitchen crew clean our ducks. When I go shooting in the Catskills with my friends, we clean our own game by drawing out the entrails and leaving the feathered birds in the refrigerator. Just before cooking, we soak them in warm water and pluck them. Cleaning and freezing the birds spoils the gamy taste. At a private club, the guest never touches his game between shooting it and receiving a box of ready-to-cook birds at the end of his stay.

We had duck gumbo for lunch and then went back to the swamp to shoot crocodile, a dangerous sport if the speedboat were to tip over. When the guide saw the water moving, he threw the bait and we tried to shoot the crocodile in the back of its head. We got three, each about eight to ten feet long. The guide skinned them and gave us the teeth as prizes. We already had our blue and green teal feathers from the morning's shooting.

Alligator steak was on the menu for dinner, deep-fried and fishy tasting, along with braised duck and rice, vegetables and deep-dish apple pie.

After dinner, Bonnie Swearingen proposed a game of tell the truth. Each man had to answer the question "What could your wife do to improve your marriage?" The wives were asked the same about their husbands.

Bonnie started the ball rolling. "I want John to do things my way, but he always has the last word, and in the end I always realize he is right." That was quite a confession for a woman as strong-willed as she. One husband said he wished his wife were a better cook, and everyone laughed. A wife said she didn't like her husband's bad temper.

I was excluded from the game by virtue of my bachelor status. But at some point during such a weekend, when everyone is feeling sociable and well acquainted, I am called to account for myself. *Question One:* "How come you're not like the rest of them?"—which translates to "I thought all hairdressers were homosexual." *Answer:* "Not the ones who trained me in Europe." *Question Two:* "Then how come you're not married?" *Answer:* "My grandmother used to tell me, 'If you get married or if you don't get married, either way you will regret it.' That being the case, I prefer to be free. My mentor Guillaume said, 'In this profession, you have to give more to your work than you can give to your family,' and I've seen he was right."

At the end of dinner, everyone made a little speech. "I have no family in this country," I said, raising my glass to our host. "In you, Mr. Swearingen, I have more than a friend. I have a family."

"If you call me Mr. Swearingen, I'll throw you to the crocodiles. Call me John," he said.

That's very hard. I respect him too much. I have read newspaper articles that said John Swearingen was the best operator in the oil business, a very demanding boss, and that he was short-tempered when displeased. The John Swearingen I know is an unassuming, down-to-earth, patient and kind man.

On Sunday morning when we returned from duck hunting, he refused my offer to give his hair a little trim. "It's very nice of you," he said, "but I must be faithful to my barber in Chicago."

We flew back to Midway Airport in Chicago in the Amoco plane and then with the Amorys I went by limousine to O'Hare Airport to catch a commercial jet to New York. The first step in coming down to reality was when the airline required me to buy a hard case for my shotgun as required by federal law. The second step was when I rode into Manhattan in a filthy taxi with broken springs.

The third was the next morning at the salon when I stood, two feet on the floor, scissors in hand, saying to myself, "Marc, you're a very lucky man."

2
THE MAKING
OF A HAIRDRESSER

am a sensual man.

I never stop admiring women—their eyes, their smiles, the way they move, the way they put themselves together. I can fall in love just by hearing the sound of a woman's voice on the telephone, and remember forever the scent of her hair, the taste of her skin, the sensations they arouse in the tips of my fingers. For me, the most important sense is touch.

I judge food as though it were a female body, and vice versa. A good lemon or grapefruit should feel like a breast—soft, firm and with a fine skin. A pretty behind reminds me of a peach. I always massage a *gigot d'agneau* with oil and herbs before roasting as I would a woman's neck and shoulders before making love to her. In the kitchen or in bed, preparation is more than half the banquet.

Making love should be like a feast in the time of Louis XV, a meal without beginning or end. At the minimum, one should offer an appetizer, a substantial main dish, a delectable dessert and something to refresh between the courses, a glass of champagne, perhaps, in place of the sorbet.

Food and love are the essential realities of life for me, and this habit of associating one with the other is only natural, I suppose, considering my background.

I was born and raised above my parents' grocery store. My father's family was in the business of importing food; my maternal grandmother had a grocer's shop and after my mother and father married they took it over and made it into a rather fancy emporium, Chez Jeanne, which was her name. It was located on the Chaussée de Boendael in Brussels, where I came into the world, Marcel Henri Louis de Coster, the youngest of their three children, on February 14, 1931, Valentine's Day. I always try to be in a new and interesting place on that day, and have celebrated my birthday in Havana, Santo Domingo, Leningrad, Tokyo, Houston, and on a yacht in Palm Beach, among other places.

My father, Henri Louis de Coster, was tall and very good-looking, with fair hair and blue eyes. I take after him. My mother was dark; I've always been partial to brunettes. She was a woman with a forceful personality and great courage, which she needed during the difficult times in which she raised her children. Her family was of French origin, and very early I got the impression that everything beautiful and fine came from Paris, and that as soon as possible I should take myself there.

The Second World War began in September 1939 when the Nazis invaded Poland. The following May, they staged a blitzkrieg into the Netherlands and Belgium. For a little more than four years, Brussels was occupied by the enemy, which is why my boyhood recollections are rather grim. Cold, hunger, and fear of the dark night preoccupied us. During the first winter of the war, I had only one sweater and, because heating fuel was hard to come by, I was always chilled, indoors as well as outside. I must own a hundred sweaters now, certainly more than I can ever possibly wear. I suppose I'm telling myself I'll never be cold again.

Food was our number one concern, although my family fared better than some others. I recall my father taking me and my older brother, Jean, to the Ardennes to hunt for game. Under the German occupation, civilians were forbidden to own guns, but someone in our party had one with a silencer. We set traps for rabbits. I also learned to fish with a wire and a bit of bait at the end. It was so exciting to catch a fish and show it off. To this day I have that feeling of pride in the catch and then pleasure in cooking it for my friends.

The Germans forcibly recruited civilians in the occupied countries as labor for their factories to replace the men who had been sent to the front. My father worked in a Siemens plant in Berlin that produced airplane parts, and although he did return for a short while, he left again. My mother sent him packages containing jars of jam with money hidden in them, but she never heard whether he received them, not a single word of how or where he was. After the war ended and he did not come back, she concluded that he had died. He might have perished in an Allied bombing raid on the German factories. We never really knew, and as the years went by, my memory of him became very dim.

With my father gone, my mother had to be especially resourceful to feed us. As a grocer, she had an advantage in knowing sources of supply. She made periodic excursions to the countryside. If she was lucky, she came back with a few eggs; the rutabaga the peasants fed to their pigs was a mainstay of our diet. Once she returned with a side of bacon under her clothing. It was wrapped around her chest and secured by a rope around her shoulders.

To earn a few francs after school, I cleaned wine bottles in a café and carried them to the cellar for the owner. I collected bits of charcoal in a sack and sold them for fuel. Barbershops were open on Sunday mornings and a barber named Pierre Jansen let me soap the faces of customers who came to be shaved. Even more than the money, I liked being around grown-up men and listening to their talk. Jansen taught me a lot about hair—its different qualities, how it grows and how to cut it. This was long before the vogue for unisex hairstyling, when it was discovered that the best stylists for women were those who had trained as men's barbers. Jansen has a big shop now in Brussels, run by his son, and he's always happy to see his protégé when I drop by to say hello.

In September 1944, British armored troops liberated Brussels with the help of the Belgian Resistance. I remember a tank with the Union Jack flying as it rolled down the avenues, and my mother serving tea she had hoarded to English soldiers who came to the city on forty-eight-hour passes from the front.

She had worked in England as a secretary at the Austin Motor Company before her marriage and spoke English rather fluently. As I was helping her with the tea things, she tried to teach me a few words—*spoon* was the first—but after that it was a hopeless cause. After more than twenty years in the United States, I still have trouble with the language. When I came to America, I was told that a French accent was an asset, that women found it charming, elegant and sexy. Some people think that I do as the entertainer, Maurice Chevalier, who concealed how well he spoke English lest he lose his terrific appeal to American audiences. But that isn't true. French is my mother tongue, franglais my second.

About the time the war was ending, my sister, Henriette, was already a young woman, very pretty and blond, very fashion-conscious. She was always an authority on *le dernier chic*. Life goes on in countries devastated by war, and young people never stop caring about their looks and having a good time as best they can.

In Paris, which was liberated a week before Brussels, fashion had been a means of expressing defiance to the enemy. The young developed a shabby chic—quite hideous, in retrospect—called the Zazou style. Being undernourished, everyone was fashionably thin. The essential for both male and female Zazous was a mannish tailored jacket with exaggerated shoulders and skinny, tight shirts or pants. For the boys, it was important to show white socks, even when the style evolved into baggy trousers. In America, the look was called zoot suit. Zazou fever spread to Brussels and I caught a mild case, whenever I could borrow my brother Jean's suit. He being older and taller, I had to roll up the pants to make knickers.

The girls wore crucifixes suspended from their necks, and shoes of imitation felt raised on platforms of cork. Long hair was *de rigueur* for both sexes. Men's hair was crossed in back and cut square like a duck's tail, the women's piled above the forehead into pompadours, sometimes decorated with ornaments or funny little hats set on the crowns of their heads as though the ghost of Marie Antoinette's Léonard had come back to haunt the Nazis. The frivolous dress of their conquered subjects irritated the Germans.

Seeing that I knew something about hair from hanging around a barbershop, my sister soon had me in attendance when she and her friends experimented with new coiffures. She would much rather have been a client at Monsieur Roger, the leading coiffeur in Brussels, but that was out of the question. Unless, of course, her brother worked there. I think that idea must have occurred to her in connection with my finishing primary school, and, given the circumstances of our fatherless household, having to begin thinking seriously about going to work.

My mother wanted me to be a doctor, but I couldn't stand the sight of human blood. I didn't have anything special I wanted to do. I just knew I liked to work with my hands and appreciated beautiful things and seemed to have an artistic nature.

"You can be artistic with hair," Henriette said. She had everything figured out. "But it has to be women's hair. If you do men, you will never get anywhere because you will always be doing the same thing. Women like something different and you can be creative." To convince me, she added, "As a hairdresser, you will get to travel. You'll have a chance to see the world."

She took me by the hand to Roger's salon at 88 avenue Louise. It was a beehive of activity with three separate rooms to which clients were assigned according to their social standing or glamour quality. Monsieur Roger himself held forth in the central salon with the most important clients. He had the cream of society and members of the royal family as well.

After cooling our heels for what seemed an eternity without securing an audience with Monsieur Roger, Henriette seized the opportunity when the receptionist turned her back. "Please take him—he will do anything," she said to Monsieur Roger, pointing to me as I blushed furiously. "He'll wash the windows, sweep the floor, do whatever you need done."

I found my voice, miraculously, or maybe it was because she was pinching my arm. "Why don't you let me try while the others are on vacation, Monsieur Roger? I don't need much salary if you will only let me. I will even work for nothing because I have my mother to take care of me while I am learning."

That must have persuaded him—that I was willing to work for nothing in order to learn.

And so I began, literally at the bottom, arriving at eight in the morning to do the most menial tasks. I picked up the towels, cleaned the mirrors, took the receipts of the previous day to the bank and ran into the street to find a taxi for a client. This was the method of the apprentice system that then prevailed in Europe and, regrettably, does not in the United States.

Life continued to be very hard after the war ended in Europe in May 1945, in some respects even harder than it had been under the German occupation. So much had been destroyed, particularly the rail lines over which food and coal were transported to the cities. The weather was abnormally cold and wet. Food was rationed, bread and meat were scarce, and there were queues everywhere. Through 1947 we did without heat and electricity for parts of every day. Guests kept their boots on at dinner, and in the theater, elegant women sat smothered in furs, their jewels and décolleté dresses concealed.

In Paris and Brussels, women walked in the streets with wet hair in pincurls, but in the *salons de coiffure* the apprentices had to make the power to keep the hair dryers running. In the basement of Roger's salon, we mounted three bicycles on pieces of wood to keep them stationary, removed the tires and attached fan belts to the wheels, connecting them to the generators. We pedaled away, pretending we were competing in the Tour de France, a long-distance race that included parts of Belgium.

After a while, I graduated to giving shampoos. How could I have imagined then, a teen-ager in knee pants, that one day I would be shampooing the hair of the First Lady of the United States in the White House?

A perfect shampoo begins with a vigorous brushing. The secret is in keeping an even stroke. Hair brushing has been eliminated from the coiffure process in many salons in the U.S. today, to economize on the employees' time or because they are lazy. The most important thing about the shampoo itself is not to put too much soap on the hair, because this takes away the natural oil, has a drying effect, causes dandruff and static electricity, and generally makes the hair less manageable. The first shampoo should concentrate on the hairline and the neckline, areas that generate the most sweat. The second shampoo should remove general dust and dirt.

We had neither the liquid shampoo nor the conditioning products available today. Instead, we used bars of laundry soap. The best was called Savon Marseille and I always buy some when I am in Europe for my personal use because it is the purest, most natural product. We grated it to make flakes, which we mixed with water and applied to the hair.

The next important step in a shampoo is to massage the scalp, not just to scratch it with the fingernails but to forcefully massage the whole head from the hairline to the base of the neck. Then the hair must be rinsed thoroughly, ending with a cold-water rinse to make the hair shiny. Sometimes we rinsed with chamomile or vinegar. For a conditioner, we applied egg yolk instead of a second soaping, provided the client was able to provide the eggs, which were still a scarce luxury.

As a shampoo boy, I was also allowed to assist one of the coiffeurs, handing him pins and observing how he made the curls. The first step is to learn how to divide the hair. We didn't have rollers in those days, just hairpins and cotton. One had to be very exact. Setting hair was like making a dress. Every mistake showed and the only way to correct one was with a curling iron after the pins were removed. We also had to make finger waves, as the name indicated, with our fingers and hairpins. For setting lotion, we used beer or a combination of sugar and water.

I can't understand hairdressers who say they can't work without their special tools, their own scissors and brushes. Having trained in Europe under such adverse conditions, I can make do with nothing. I once cut a woman's hair with a broken wineglass. We had been drinking champagne and eating oysters, and at four in the morning she said, "What a shame tomorrow is Sunday. I'm going on vacation and need a haircut." I offered to do it then and there. But she didn't have scissors or a razor—her husband was out of the city. So I smashed a goblet and cut her hair with a piece of the crystal.

I cut another woman's hair with nail clippers. I divided the hair in sections, twisted each one and clipped them all to the same length. You have to use your imagination in this profession.

In the evenings, I tried to practice what I had observed on my sister or the woman who worked in the salon. As an apprentice, I followed the same procedure of watching and practicing with the bleaching and dyeing of hair and permanent waving. It was almost two years before I could approach a client, and then only if her regular hairdresser went on vacation and I could persuade her that I knew exactly how he did her hair.

Monsieur Roger took a liking to me, I suppose because I worked hard, never looked at the clock, and showed that I was interested in more than setting hair. I have been blessed in my bosses, men of professional talent and broad cultural tastes, men after whom I patterned myself. As an apprentice, I watched what they did and tried to do the same. Monsieur Roger kissed the client's hand; I practiced that, too. Sometimes he took me with him when he went to the homes of his best clients to comb their hair for big parties. I never said a word unless spoken to, but I took it all in, the fabulous surroundings and the conversation.

Much of it was about art. Many of them had impressive paintings in their homes and they talked about what they had seen elsewhere. Noticing that I seemed attentive, they might say, "We're going to Bruges on Saturday. Would you like to come?" I must have seemed like a mascot to these women. And so starting in the cradle of Flemish art, I was able to acquire knowledge and discriminating taste of my own. Fortunately, I have excellent visual memory; once I have seen a painting or an object, I am unlikely to forget it, and this has been why I can hold my own years later in America when in the company of some of the greatest collectors and patrons in New York.

If you have important clients, you have to know more than just how to comb their hair. You must know something about the things that interest them. You can't say, "Who is Rembrandt?" Or, "I just know Picasso." If they see you really do know, they take you more seriously. Otherwise, you are just a curl maker.

I was especially drawn to carved objects and I began to envision myself as a sculptor. I was already rather talented as a sketcher. "You'll starve," my sister said.

In 1947 I enlisted in the army. It took some doing because I was underage and underweight. My mother gave her permission for me to go, and concealing a weight from one of the scales in her store in my hand solved the second problem.

I had this tremendous desire to see the world and I figured that in the Allied Army of Occupation I would at least get as far as Germany. After basic training, I volunteered for the paratroop corps. I was aware that girls liked the guys with the red berets. If I had it to do over again, I would manage to just buy a beret.

Germany was paradise for a soldier, particularly one like me with a scissors to open his way. I bought a motorcycle for practically nothing by selling my coffee and cigarette rations, and drove out to the villa of our unit commander, a British major. I had gotten to know his maid and I offered to cut her hair. I didn't have any materials, so I rolled her hair into curls with cotton and toothpicks and kept it all together while it dried with the camouflage netting from my helmet. The major's wife noticed how nice her maid looked, and pretty soon I was cutting her hair and the major's as well. Suddenly I found myself excused from guard duty and a lot of other chores. I never peeled potatoes in the army.

We were obligated to one year of military service. When I was discharged, I returned to Brussels and Roger's salon. I had only one thing in mind, and that was to get myself to Paris. Roger had taught me the technique of hair. Now I wanted to learn creativity.

The star of *haute coiffure* at that moment in history was Guillaume. The Napoleon of hairdressing he was called because he was indeed the emperor, and also because, like Bonaparte, he was short, dark and had been born in Corsica. His family name is Guglielmi.

Antoine, the greatest hairdresser of the twentieth century, had spent World War II in New York, a big businessman with a chain of American salons. Guillaume stayed in Paris with the rest of the fashion notables, led by the couturier Lucien Lelong, trying to keep the industry together and staving off deportation to forced labor for their employees.

In the salon he had opened on avenue Matignon in 1936, decorated by Jean-Michel Frank and Louis Sue in the simple but richly surfaced style of *art moderne*, Guillaume had launched the pageboy coiffure. It became the rage of two continents, one of the most enduring coiffures. Even today, some of my aristocratic ladies from Connecticut and the North Shore of Long Island cannot be parted from their pageboys.

Guillaume was a disciple of René Rambaud, of the rue Saint-Honoré, one of two poles of the *haute coiffure* during the Twenties and Thirties. His short, fluffy and free-form hairdos were a countervailing force to the short, lacquered heads turned out by Antoine. With Rambaud, Guillaume was trained to collaborate with the *haute couture* in its twice-yearly presentations that women in Europe and America accepted as gospel.

As soon as Paris was liberated, the *couture* laid plans to reassert its worldwide influence, and Guillaume was to play an important supporting role in this renaissance.

It was vital for Paris to make a severe break with the past seven years of wartime austerity. That was accomplished in one stroke by Christian Dior in his first collection in his own house, which was backed by Marcel Boussac, the cotton tycoon. Dior's New Look for spring 1947 made women on both sides of the Atlantic want to clean out their closets and take what was actually a backward step into a silhouette of voluminous skirts falling below the calf, tight-fitting bodices accentuated by wasp waists, and soft, rounded shoulders. The crinolines and waist cinchers restricted ease of movement and contradicted the notion of independence women had shown during the war. But the New Look caught on, probably for the same reason women started having big families—to defy death by giving life. The hippy, big-breasted woman signified fertility.

Dior asked Guillaume to design a coiffure for his new femininity. He created a small head with hair swept to the side in a cockscomb of curls. It was a reaction to the freakish hairdos and the long manes of the war years.

Guillaume's name was sacred in Brussels, which always looked to Paris for direction. If I were to stay in the profession, he was the master under whom I had to train. A European conference of hairdressers that was to be held in Paris gave me my opportunity. The top coiffeurs give demonstrations at such gatherings and, in addition, Guillaume was generous about inviting hairdressers to his salon to observe him. When I asked him to let me do a "stage" or internship with him, he said, "Roger is my friend. I can't take you away from him."

"Please ask him," I begged. "I'm sure he will agree."

He telephoned Brussels in my presence. "I have a young man here who says he works for you but wants to stay in Paris with me," Guillaume told Roger.

Roger asked to speak to me. "Are you sure you want to do this?"

"With all my heart," I said.

He must have given me a good recommendation, because Guillaume told me I could start right away. It meant stepping down a bit. I would have to go to school at night, and another year or two would pass before I would be allowed to style the hair of his clients.

"Coiffure can be an artist's métier provided you serve a long apprenticeship," he said. For my duties at the salon, I would receive a small salary and would take courses at the École des Arts et Métiers to master basics such as teasing, making braids, and wigs.

I must then attend to my "cultural formation" before I could begin to experience the joy of creation. According to Guillaume, the development of a hairdresser was compounded of "talent, intuition, imagination, culture, artistic sense, sensibility." Finally, one had to know psychology; to seek out the personality of the client could require piercing the unconscious.

I was in Paris, at last. On my own for the first time, I found a room on the Left Bank in the fifteenth arrondissement. The name of the street, avenue Émile Zola, attracted me because I admired the writer. But it was some way by *métro* from the chic eighth arrondissement where Guillaume was situated; after that, I always tried to be within walking distance of my job.

Before long, a girl I had gotten to know steered me to a converted maid's room atop a building in the rue Jean Mermoz, one street removed from avenue Matignon. I had seen this cute brunette walking there almost every day, looking as well dressed as if she had stepped out of the collections of Jacques Fath or Jean Patou.

"I'd like to cut your hair," I said by way of introduction.

"Where do you work? How much will it cost me?" she asked.

"Nothing." I explained that on Thursday evenings after the salon was closed, one of the top hairdressers held class for the apprentices and afterward they could practice the latest line he had demonstrated on their friends.

She came every Thursday after 6 P.M. and I did her hair. She was a *poule de luxe*, of course, as I should have realized if I hadn't been such a naïve kid. The usual story. She came from the provinces without any money and went on the street to make an easy living. She had advanced herself to the number one category of that trade, the prostitutes who worked the Madeleine and the Champs-Elysées districts. They were impeccable. When Chanel came out of retirement in the mid-Fifties, they wore her uniform to perfection, accessorized precisely with the beige and black sling-back pumps and the quilted, chain-handled pocketbooks.

The girls of this rank went after solid citizens, the businessmen from good families who wanted to have a little escapade and were willing to set them up in style. It was not expected that they would quit the street, because most of them rather liked the work. And their pimps wouldn't allow them to stop.

I was fortunate in joining Guillaume just at the unfolding of the fabulous Fifties. For one decade, Paris reestablished itself as the center of fashion and social brilliance. French aristocrats resumed entertaining on the scale of the crazy years—the Twenties. Vicomtesse Marie-Laure de Noailles, Comte Etienne de Beaumont and the couturier Jacques Fath revived the vogue for costume parties. The masked ball to eclipse all others, and to which many of Guillaume's clients scrambled ferociously for invitations, was the eighteenth-century spectacle given by Charles de Bestegui, a nomadic Mexican, at his treasure-filled Palazzo Labia in Venice.

Guests attending these functions were expected to dress with maximum authenticity and their hairdressers to demonstrate skill no less than that of Léonard himself. This required historical research, a trip to the Louvre or to an art library. Years later in New York I was grateful for this experience acquired at Guillaume when Mrs. William S. Paley asked me to turn her into a Greek goddess for a party she was giving. What do you tell such a client if all you learned is how to cut and blow dry? You must know that a Greek coiffure demands ribbon, and you must know where to cross it and where to put the little wave and the curl. Costume parties seem to be gaining popularity again and recently I rose to the task of creating a coiffure for a lady of the Japanese Imperial Court and for a woman who might have been painted by Boldini.

During the Fifties, wealthy foreigners reopened their houses in Paris and joined Guillaume's clientele. Among them were a number of elegant Latin Americans such as the wives of Antenor Patiño, Arturo Lopez Willshaw and Rodman de Heeren.

Two women of elegance combined with intellect were especially kind to me. Both were Slavic by birth and married to Americans. Vera Lounsbery's husband, Richard, a banker, was an heir to a gold-mining fortune. She held a salon for artists, writers and members of the Académie Française at their apartment at the Ritz. Ray Schuster was the wife of M. Lincoln Schuster, founder of the Simon and Schuster book-publishing company in New York. She was in charge of its European office and made frequent visits to Paris to order clothes from Dior and, later, exclusively from Balenciaga. Then she set forth to see her friends and authors like Sir Max Beerbohm, the Aga Khan and Bernard Berenson at his Villa I Tatti in Florence.

Mrs. Schuster was a dynamic, worldly woman and a sensitive one as well. Guillaume himself did her hair, but once he was called away and handed her over to me. When he was out of sight, she whispered, "Do you think you can do it?" I assured her I could, and was devoted to her ever after. She used to tell me that I had the face of an artist and that she was particularly drawn to artists.

The notion that hairdressing might be considered one of the arts made it a more appealing choice of career for me than any other. Guillaume was an artist to the core. Sculpture was his hobby. He was a friend and associate of leading figures in the arts such as Marie Laurencin, the painter; Jean

Cocteau, the versatile genius of the avant-garde; and Christian Bérard, the costume and set designer for Cocteau's productions. Bérard made paintings of Guillaume's coiffures.

Another friend, Louise de Vilmorin, the poet and novelist, wrote this tribute to him: "Guillaume has the feeling of an artist who would see in beauty a means of expression, but of a vivid expression from which we would all benefit: men in looking at women . . . and women in attracting the attention of men. All his efforts tell us that in order to attract, it is necessary to please for no one is attracted to one who is displeasing."

She went on: "If I cannot speak of Guillaume as *a* hairdresser, it is because he is *my* hairdresser. He knows the temper of my face, its sadnesses and its brighter moments and I have always found him able to subdue in me that which might be displeasing and bring out what still might be able to charm. He is my adviser and I have never made a mistake in obeying him. To do as Guillaume says is what I would wish for all my friends."

Through exposure to women like Madame de Vilmorin, I came to realize how powerfully seductive great intelligence can be—and, on the contrary, how boring a woman who has only a beautiful face.

Twice married, Louise de Vilmorin was the close friend of André Malraux, the scholar and Resistance hero who served as Charles de Gaulle's minister of information, later minister of cultural affairs in the Fifth Republic. Malraux was also married, and by the chance that is common in the coiffeur's world, later on I did the hair of his wife, Marie-Madeleine, the pianist, in my salon in New York.

Madame de Vilmorin had a rare ability to use vulgar slang elegantly. As a writer, she could not resist a play on words and peppered her conversation with puns and double meanings. "Ah, I see you have long pants," she said the first time I did her hair in New York. This was a reference to having known me as a young shampoo boy. "I hope everything else has grown, too," she added.

She cast her eyes around the salon and remarked about some of the other clients that they looked *mal baisées*, literally badly kissed, but translated to mean in need of a good lover.

When Guillaume sent me to her château at Verrières-le-Buisson on the outskirts of Paris, where she and Malraux are now buried, I saw her as mistress of the manor. She had been riding her horse and was wearing a long, sidesaddle skirt, impeccable boots and tweed jacket.

She pointed out the silver-fox coverlet on her bed. "See, it has thirty-one tails," she said with a smile. "I have one for making love each day of the month. Why don't you count them?"

On another occasion, she instructed me how to comb her hair. "*Bouffes-moi le devant et remontes-moi derrière.*" I understood her to want her hair teased in front and combed into a French twist in back, but her instructions could have served as well for lovemaking.

Still another devoted friend of Guillaume's was the artist Léonor Fini, a dark, fierce woman born under the sign of Leo and passionately fond of the cat family, from the pets in her apartment to the beasts of the jungle. He designed a coiffure for her that he christened *La Lionne*—Lady Lion. The hair was cut short and deceptively tousled so that it appeared long and full. A timeless coiffure, it is the forerunner of the style Nancy Reagan has worn during her White House years.

Guillaume created a radical coiffure for Yvette Chauviré, premiere ballerina of the Paris Opera, who was rehearsing the role of Helen of Troy in a new production, *La Belle Hélène*. He did away with the traditional dancer's chignon. The hair was smooth and gently waved over the ears in a helmetlike effect. In the love scene with Paris, it was released to cascade about her shoulders. The secret was in the cut.

When Chauviré danced Gisèle, Guillaume extended the concept to coiffures for the entire corps de ballet. He then made a film about it, *La Ligne Danse*, depicting the entwined histories of coiffure and dance. He assigned me to work on the film, preparing the dancers for the camera. He also cut Zizi Jeanmaire's hair in a razor-sharp gamine coiffure for Roland Petit's ballet *Carmen*. The hairdo became the ballerina's trademark and was copied by countless midinettes and secretaries.

Through his friend, Marcel Achard, the playwright, Guillaume gained Edith Piaf as a client. Standing alone on a darkened stage in a simple black dress, La Môme Piaf poured heartbreak into every note. She was then at the height of her form. One of her protégés during the war, Yves Montand, was already a star of the music halls and was beginning a career in film. We liked to think that Montand had gotten his start in our profession. As a kid, he had worked in his sister's beauty shop. When I met Montand in Washington in December 1982 after his whirlwind one-man-show tour in the U.S. and Japan, he reminisced about the permanent-wave machines in use at that time. "And I did coloring and styling, too," he said.

Guillaume was deeply involved in the theater and in films. He coiffed the stars of the Comédie Française such as Madeleine Renaud and Marie Bell. Jeanne Moreau, even now in her fifties an incredibly sexy woman, was a client, as was Anouk Aimée, a wistful-looking actress for whom he suggested a simple, smooth style with a casual wave. Aimée epitomizes sensual, classic French beauty, my favorite type of woman. I confess I still have a crush on her.

Jean Marais, an idol of stage and screen, used to come to the salon to have his hair tinted by Guillaume's brother, Otello, a gifted colorist. Jean Cocteau had ordered the chestnut-haired actor to become a blond for his wartime film *L'Éternel Retour—The Eternal Return*—and also for *La Belle et La Bête—Beauty and the Beast*—after Liberation. Marais had gotten used to the change. At seventy, he has been rediscovered by French youth. In the grip of a passion for the Fifties, young men are combing their hair in the same pompadour style he wore in those years.

There was always a stream of international movie actresses at Guillaume's: Anna Magnani, Greto Garbo, Paulette Goddard, and Ingrid Bergman. When Guillaume was away, I got to do Bergman's hair. Such a natural person she was, and she spoke excellent French. The short haircut she wore in *For Whom the Bell Tolls* had tremendous repercussions. The film was made in America during the war and shown in Europe afterward. I think it did as much to popularize short hair as the Italian cut taken also from movies made during the war and shown in France and the U.S. during the Fifties.

The fact is that Hollywood was the single biggest influence upon *haute coiffure*. French couturiers may have created the fashions in clothing, but California dictated hairstyles. "La Coiffure Américaine" was what Paris called them, particularly the languid manes with sinuous waves or ruffles of curls such as the sex goddesses Veronica Lake and Rita Hayworth wore in films like *I Wanted Wings* and *Gilda*.

The stylist who inspired awe among European coiffeurs was Sydney Guilaroff of the M-G-M studios in Culver City. His scope was formidable. Guilaroff was a genius both at historical interpretation and in solving such modern problems as keeping Esther Williams's hair in place underwater (the secret, as I learned later on a tour of the studios, was to apply paraffin just before the shapely swimmer dived into the pool).

No modern hairdresser has attended to as many film stars as Guilaroff, now in his seventies and a free-lance in Beverly Hills: Greta Garbo, Claudette Colbert, Joan Crawford, Judy Garland, Marilyn Monroe (a close personal friend), Natalie Wood, Elizabeth Taylor, Jane Fonda and Garland's daughter, Liza Minnelli.

Although it was exciting to gaze at movie stars and occasionally be able to run my fingers through their hair, the contact with fashion mannequins was more frequent and enjoyable. Guillaume collaborated with many couturiers on the collections they presented twice a year to what was assumed to be an audience of the world's women holding their breath for word of changes in silhouette and hemline. First among these great designers was Christian Dior, but also Jacques Fath; Madame Grès; Cristobal Balenciaga, the monkish Basque, and his disciple, Hubert de Givenchy, who opened his own house in 1952 and, with the promotional assistance of the actress Audrey Hepburn, created the "little-nothing" look that Jacqueline Kennedy would disseminate from the White House in the early Sixties.

The first time Guillaume tapped me to accompany him to Dior, I felt as though I were entering a magical kingdom. The House of Dior was decorated in a Louis XVI style as filtered through the consciousness of La Belle Époque. In his *maison de couture*, Dior attempted to re-create his family's apartment in the Passy section of Paris in 1910: pale gray walls and white woodwork, white enameled furniture, crystal chandeliers, doors sparkling with panes of beveled glass, a profusion of flowers. The slightly suffocating scent of the latest Dior fragrance wafted through the crowd of spectators wedged elbow-to-elbow on frail chairs and on the steps of the curving staircase where vendeuses in black dresses were positioned at intervals like a papal guard.

The coiffeur and his team could only peek at this public spectacle from behind the gray curtain of the models' *cabine* on the second floor. Here the white-smocked mannequins edgily awaited our ministrations, which would enable them to go forth and earn stardom for themselves while selling the designer's line of the season. Dior personally pinned a spray of lily of the valley on each model before she left the *cabine*. From 1950 until his death in 1957 from overindulgence in food and wine, the couturier gradually retracted his New Look and, with his wandering waistlines defining successively his Princess line, H-line, A-line and Y-line, at last endorsed the chemise. The sack—as it was called, not always flatteringly, in the U.S.— undermined the structure of dressmaking and ultimately the authority of *haute couture*. With so much ease and comfort, the discipline of being well dressed was relaxed.

As soon as the war ended, the most beautiful girls in Europe flocked to Paris to become mannequins. How much luckier could a young man be than to find himself in their midst as an assistant in the most important *salon de coiffure*. The work in itself was challenging because we would transform a model with the clip of our scissors and the turn of our curling irons into someone even she could not recognize. We could make her a star, if only briefly.

There was Victoire, by previous standards too small to be a model. She had long dark hair and looked like a poor student from Le Quartier Latin. Guillaume cut her hair, the makeup man took over and, *voilà*, she was Dior's *petite duchesse*. After that, every house wanted one small mannequin, at least.

The most fantastic model I ever saw was the tallest, a blonde whom Dior nicknamed "France" because she was synonymous with the best. Before her, models carried furs on their arms. France was assigned a white fur coat that she just let drop to the runway and dragged behind her like a train. "Pick it up," we called from the *cabine*. "It's heavy," she muttered. France started a minirevolution and, from then on, the more expensive the fur, the more carelessly was it presented. That was throwaway chic.

France met the destiny to which all models aspired. A wealthy South American fell in love with her and carried her across the ocean to be his wife. Blondes are very popular in Latin countries. France was a French girl, but most of the blondes who captivated Paris were Swedish. They had such silky hair, skin like porcelain and bodies sculptured to perfection.

Being exposed to sensational women at an early age made me skeptical about beauty. If that's all there is, a man soon tires of it. I prefer a woman who is a type rather than a great beauty—one who is intelligent, has a sense of humor, one to whom I can talk. I like to be impressed by a woman because she's not only good-looking; she knows something.

They say *"le voyage forme la jeunesse"*—"travel is broadening." Guillaume used to send his stylists to the resorts where his clients were to be found during the season, and with the hope of attracting new ones. I went with Paul—another of Guillaume's boys, who is now a success in London—to Deauville and Biarritz during the summer, and to St. Moritz in the winter. The owner of the beauty shop at the Palace Hotel in St. Moritz paid our fare, put us up at the hotel and gave us a small salary. The tips were huge. The clients came to the salon after 4:00 P.M., leaving us free to ski from 9:00 to 2:00. We weren't supposed to ski, because if we had broken our legs, he would have been out the money advanced us. We said we were taking the sun on the roof.

At St. Moritz I became really proficient, practicing on the Corviglia-Piz Nair, that vast area of slopes encircling the village. It was glorious—the snow and sunshine and the sexy-looking women. Stretch pants came into style in the Fifties and they made such a difference. I'd be skiing down a slope seeing only trees and snow and suddenly there was the shapely silhouette of a woman ahead of me. I'd ski close to her and she'd be so pretty with that rosy face and white teeth. It was very stimulating. I met the most incredible women at St. Moritz, mostly English and Italian in those days. It was very chic for Paul and me, who didn't have any money, to return to Paris with our tans. The clients were impressed. Where had we been? Oh, skiing at St. Moritz. I would definitely recommend that anyone who wants to meet people and get ahead take up skiing.

A few years ago, I was at St. Moritz on a real vacation. By then I didn't have to work my way to the Alps. I met a client, Mrs. George Livanos of London, on the slopes, and after I helped her a bit with her turns, she invited me to the Corviglia Club on top of the mountain. Supposedly it is one of the most exclusive clubs in the world, its membership limited to 150. Giovanni Agnelli of Fiat belongs and so does Alfred Heineken, the beer baron, and many titled types. It is said that the list of those who cannot get into the Corviglia Club is just as important as those who can.

Mrs. Livanos, who is Christina Onassis's aunt, asked me to her chalet for lunch the next day. It sat in a compound of houses belonging to Greek shipowners in an area behind the Suvretta House Hotel, past the big gray monstrosity with a copper dome then occupied by the shah of Iran. The Livanos chalet was named Bambi. As I arrived in her chauffeur-driven car, a fawn and a doe were nibbling at the shrubbery by the front door. The villa was furnished in Swiss style, every object an antique. A child's sled was filled with flowers, creating a poetic image of nature blooming in snow. The house was so warm and cozy, so lacking in chichi, it made me feel right at home.

I did Mrs. Livanos's hair, and her mother's and her daughter's. Afterward, we had lunch together. Once again, my scissors and my sportsmanship had taken me where most people could never go.

3
AMERICA, HERE I COME

In 1952 I accompanied Guillaume to New York to assist Christian Dior in putting on a show at the Waldorf-Astoria. Guillaume is a generous human being. Like a great teacher proud of his pupils, he liked to send them forth to make their own reputations and at the same time to spread his gospel. He had already sent one apostle to New York. Marcel Eichi, a Swiss, became famous as the man who brought the Italian cut—actually, Guillaume's version of the short, easy hairdo—to America, and also the color technique known as frosting. Marcel died in February 1956, wiped out by cancer in his late thirties. His wife and business partner sent a distress signal to Guillaume. He sent me to bring the French twist—the coiffure he had created for Dior's A-line—to New York.

I arrived in America with $50 in my pocket and checked in at the Hotel Pierre because it had a French name. When I got the bill a week later, I had to borrow money from Madame Marcel to settle my account and moved to a furnished room on the West Side.

I also changed my name a bit. Clients were calling and asking for Marcel, only to be told he had died a few months ago. So I dropped the last two letters and became Marc. Now only my sister still calls me Marcel.

I hadn't been at Marcel very long when a client of Guillaume's whose hair I had done at Biarritz appeared at the salon. Laura Tarafa Caracci de Vilapol was the wife of a Cuban industrialist, a stunning woman. She asked me to go to Havana to do her hair for a party she was giving in honor of her husband's birthday.

"I'd love to, but I can't afford it," I said.

"*Chéri*, don't worry. I will take care of everything. I just want you there to do my hair," she said.

What a party that was. I was the same size as her husband, so Madame Laura gave me one of his white tuxedoes to wear. Two orchestras played, one for the tango and the cha-cha, the other for the merengue and the rhumba.

I was a pretty good dancer, very good at the tango, which was the rage in France, and because I had rhythm I could pick up the other steps quickly. It is important to be a good dancer, because then, no matter who you are, women want to meet you and dance with you. Those brunette Cuban women were fantastic. I was a rare bird to them with my blond hair and skin as white as aspirin. They all came up to me and pinched my cheek and with their black eyes gazed into my blue eyes. As they say in Europe, you don't take beer to Munich. What would I have done if I had been married?

The party lasted one night, but I stayed six weeks. I telephoned New York and told Madame Marcel I had some trouble with my passport and was cabling France for resolution. I didn't know when I could leave and I didn't tell her where she could reach me.

I stayed with the Vilapols. Madame Laura was very hospitable. Every morning, her chauffeur drove me to work at a beauty salon on La Reforma where I did the hair of the wealthiest women in Havana, sent to me by Madame Laura, of course. I shared the receipts fifty-fifty with the owner. Madame Laura went to the beach in the morning and I waited until she came to the shop to comb her hair. At two, the chauffeur picked me up to take me wherever I wanted to go for the rest of the day.

Anything under the sun I wanted, I could have. Madame Laura picked up the tab. I went to the yacht club, and to Varadero Beach. Madame Laura arranged for me to go dove shooting. She loaned me a Purdey shotgun, the best. The others in the party were lawyers and industrialists. The Cubans were very fond of France. Because I came from Paris, was a guest of the Vilapols and—this was the key—was a good shot, they accepted me.

In the evenings I went to the restaurants with a beautiful girl I had met. To the Sans Souci and to the Monseigneur, which was Maxim's with palms. We drank daiquiris and listened to the violins. Everywhere the red carpet was rolled out for me because of Madame Laura. Why was she so kind to me? I guess she thought I was cute—*precioso*, she said.

I have never spent such a month and a half. I could have stayed forever and lived like a king in Havana—at least until Fidel Castro took power and my friends departed with their money. But I returned to New York, and shortly afterward received word that my mother had cancer.

If I were on the other side of the Atlantic, I could be near her when she needed me. Guillaume took me back as a stylist, and when my mother's condition appeared stable, he sent me to London for a *stage*—an internship—to learn English. His friend René Moulard, a disciple of Antonio, had opened a salon at 66 South Audley Street in Mayfair, where it was a rare day not to find at least a Guinness and a duchess or two under the dryers. Princess Margaret was received in a private room to the left of the entrance.

Tall, blond and blue-eyed, René was another in the category of manly hairdresser. His clients adored him. His wife, Huguette, officiated at the desk, discouraging the ladies from getting too romantic.

René had savoir faire. If you want to be more than just a curl maker, observe the great hairdressers—Roger, Guillaume, René—study their work and actually steal some of their savoir faire.

A few months later, my mother died. I couldn't bear the thought that she was gone forever. Guillaume and my sister suggested I return to New York.

I took a studio apartment in a brownstone on West 88th Street owned by a French couple. The rent was $20 a week including laundry service. Madame Angèle also gave me breakfast and dinner in exchange for combing her hair every morning. To this day, she says she got the better of the deal.

Because my landlady and most of my friends in the beauty and restaurant trades were French-speaking, I didn't make much progress with the English language. About all I could say was "You look beautiful," "Thank you very much," "You want it short?" and "You like it on the left?" A sufficient vocabulary for the salon, but once I stepped outside, I had to use my hands or draw sketches. There were some embarrassing gaffes, as when I said to a client who complained that her set didn't hold in back, "When you take a douche, your hair gets wet." Liliane DuBane, a manicurist, pinched me and hissed, "You don't say that in America." In French, douche means shower.

I have a terrible memory for names, but that may be because as soon as I learned a client's name, she divorced and took another through remarriage. I decided that must be why Americans called each other honey and darling; it was easier than remembering names.

One client buried five husbands. She always had her hair done for the funeral and after a brief interval she'd say, "Guess what, Marc. I've met a marvelous man and we're going to be married." I'll never understand how a widow could go to the hairdresser before the burial service.

Marcel's salon occupied five floors at 12 East 56th Street. The business was a mass-production machine turning out between 200 and 300 coiffures a day. The clientele ranged from international elégantes to women from Park Avenue and the suburbs with more money than taste. In a beauty salon, celebrities are bellwethers for the doctors' and accountants' wives, but celebrities are fickle or are gone six months of the year, while the others, who may not bring prestige, do pay the overhead.

At first I was stationed on the second floor, but soon I developed a following and moved to the fifth with my own receptionist, two assistants and two manicurists. At that time, there were perhaps twenty or thirty good hairdressers in New York, no more than that. Today there must be a thousand. I had that Paris cachet—and my training with the masters. I could please any type of woman. In those days, most hairdressers were doing the Italian haircut, but if a sophisticated woman asked for a chignon, they were stumped. One woman told another about "this new stylist from Paris" who could do chignons and anything else they might name, and soon everybody was coming to me. I was lucky.

Clients who had known me at Guillaume, like Mrs. Lounsbery and Mrs. Schuster, sought me out at Marcel. Mrs. Schuster had three daughters, who became loyal friends and clients: Sylvia, now married to Dr. Roland Mindlin, a Chicago physician; Pearl, married to Ephraim London, a distinguished New York lawyer; and Beatrice, who became the wife of Walter Eytan, Israeli ambassador to France for eleven years. Mrs. Eytan divided her affection between Alexandre, her primary coiffeur in Paris, and me in New York.

Today, when the Monsieur Marc salon is considered the New York haven for le tout Paris, it is because of a reciprocal relationship between me and Alexandre, and with Maurice Franck, another star of haute coiffure. They entrust their clients to me and vice versa. Nothing could be more disconcerting to an elegant woman than to find herself in a foreign city without a hairdresser in whom she has confidence.

Mrs. Schuster's daughters are different types who lead very different lives, and it has always been a challenge to satisfy them all. Guillaume taught me that the coiffeur's task is like that of the portrait painter: to bring out the personality of the subject.

It was never my intention to make my permanent home in America. I planned to work hard, make as much money as I could, meanwhile traveling and seeing the Western Hemisphere, and then return to buy a little business in the south of France and live peacefully ever after.

Marcel paid the lowest salaries among the top-notch salons. I earned $75 a week, but the tips were good. The cash flowed. I worked like a dog at the salon and then I'd go home and give permanents in my studio. After two years, I took a working vacation in Brazil. Renno, who had been at Guillaume in my time, invited me to the salon he had opened in the Copacabana section of Rio de Janeiro.

Walking on the street in Rio was like attending a tennis match—my neck kept turning. The women were incredible. Swedish women are beautiful but very cold. Italian and Spanish women are beautiful but very temperamental. English women are passionate, even though they live in a cold climate. Brazilian women are very warm but they aren't possessive or jealous. Sex is simply part of their lives, like the weather. I spent three months in Rio and loved every minute. But I went back to New York. That was in the prejet era and Rio just seemed too far away from Paris, my spiritual home.

Several women offered to back me in my own salon, but I didn't take them up on it. I thought they had more in mind than a strictly business relationship and I didn't want to get involved.

One day in the early spring of 1961, I was strolling along Madison Avenue and saw a FOR RENT sign on the second floor of a building at the corner of 65th Street. Remembering that the space had recently been occupied by John Bernard, who had been hired away by Charles Revson to run his Fifth Avenue beauty salon, my curiosity was piqued. I think what sold me was the building—five stories high with a staircase leading to the second floor, which had floor-to-ceiling windows behind low railings of grillwork. I could have been in Paris.

Friends had been urging me to go into business for myself, but I was afraid of the responsibility and of not going back to France. I had had offers to work for other salons, but I felt I couldn't do that to Madame Marcel. If I left her, it would be only to go on my own.

I had saved what seemed to me a lot of money, but I soon found out it wasn't nearly enough. At that time, it took about $70,000 to equip a salon of modest size. I went to Citibank wearing a navy blue cashmere coat, my Hermès briefcase in hand. The vice-president who welcomed me thought from my appearance that I was coming to deposit a million. When I asked to borrow $45,000, he inquired about my credit standing. I had none. As a European émigré, I always bought everything, even my car, for cash. "Didn't you ever buy a refrigerator on time just to show that you paid the money back?" he pleaded with me. Never.

In the end, several clients advanced security for the loan. One was Ann Cone, wife of Benjamin Cone, chairman of the board of Cone Mills of Greensboro, North Carolina. Another was Vera Lounsbery, who was to come to my assistance whenever I needed it during the next twenty years. She was then in her late fifties and slightly eccentric. She always wore white gloves and what seemed to be the same black dress and cape by Dior. Actually, she kept reordering new ones. She accessorized that costume, for which she paid several thousand dollars, with a white scarf she bought at Alexander's for 75 cents.

Vera Lounsbery liked her fine, chestnut-colored hair styled with a center part and two little combs on the side. It was no use whatsoever suggesting a change to her. She was also what the French call *maniac* about cleanliness. She kept her comb wrapped in Kleenex, had the maid change her bed linen every day and never handled money that didn't look as though it had just rolled off the printing press. She distributed hundred-dollar bills and airplane tickets to Paris to employees in the salon who told her hard-luck stories and to whom she had taken a liking. After her husband died, she carried his ashes back and forth across the Atlantic between their apartment on Park Avenue and their rooms at the Ritz in Paris. It must have taken some doing to get around French government regulations forbidding the import of incinerated remains.

I believe Vera Lounsbery's interest in me was maternal, certainly not romantic. She gave me a 12-gauge Purdey shotgun; now I could hunt pheasant and deer with the Rolls-Royce of weapons. Twenty thousand dollars was nothing to her to help a struggling young businessman. When she died in 1980, she left an estate valued at $20 million to charity.

Another client from the suburbs advanced $10,000 on condition of absolute secrecy. A French woman was very helpful, not only with money— she gave me several thousand dollars in cash and a $2 bill for good luck— but by recommending steady clients. She sent me the most elegant women of European background who wore the most exquisite jewelry and needed to have their hair done constantly. I have never been curious about the occupations of my clients or their husbands. If someone tells me, "Her husband is chairman of the XYZ Corporation," or "He is a partner in J. P. Morgan," I say, "That's nice," and forget it.

I assumed this French woman was in business; what kind I did not bother to inquire. Later, after she returned to France, one of the women she recommended told me she was a madam, conducting her business entirely on the telephone. She should have known, being one of her call girls.

I deliberated about what to call my salon. De Coster is a name people seem to have trouble with. I figured that everyone in America could pronounce *Monsieur*, and Marc was short and simple. MONSIEUR MARC COIFFURES—the sign went up beneath the windows on the Madison Avenue side of the building.

I opened for business on May 1, 1961. The expenses of installing air conditioning and new plumbing left me in a financial squeeze. I brought two chairs from my apartment for the clients to sit on until I could afford furniture. Lacking money for stands on which to mount the hair dryers I had bought, I placed them on their packing boxes and hoped the clients wouldn't mind holding them steady as they sat under them. I did my first shampoo in the ladies' room with cold water, the hot water not having been connected.

"The place is unfinished so I really don't know what to charge you," I said. In those days, $7 to $10 would have been a fair price for a shampoo and set. One client gave me $20, another $1,000.

No one can ever tell me that America is not a land of great opportunity if you are willing to work. The day before Christmas that year, I did sixty-one sets between 8:00 A.M. and midnight. The receptionist, an assistant and two manicurists left Marcel to join me. After a while I engaged a few hairdressers with followings. It took me five years to repay the loans.

4

PATRONS

When I signed the lease for my salon, never anticipating that it would be renewed many times during the next twenty years, I discovered that the building was owned by Mrs. Charles Shipman Payson, the most charming landlady anyone could wish for.

Joan Whitney Payson was one of the wealthiest women in America, sister of John Hay Whitney, who had just returned from serving as ambassador to Britain in the Eisenhower administration, and the truest American gentleman it was ever my privilege to meet. His wife was to become my client, and in the most fateful way for me, her sister, Mrs. William S. Paley, as well.

It was only after these two ladies began coming to Monsieur Marc that Mrs. Payson did, too, and then only for manicures. "I must be faithful to my hairdresser in Manhasset. I don't want to hurt his feelings," she said. I loved her all the more for her loyalty. The Paysons, the Whitneys and the Paleys had neighboring estates on Long Island. That was typical of Mrs. Payson, a very sympathetic though private person who became a popular celebrity after she bought the New York Mets baseball team.

Though her passion for baseball was a public one, she tried to be discreet about her fondness for the wines of France. She always brought a bottle of Coca-Cola to have with the lunch we ordered for her. One afternoon I poured a drink for her and observed a lack of fizz. "Your Coca-Cola is flat," I said. "Shh," she replied, raising her fingers to her lips. "*C'est du Beaujolais.*"

The woman who made my reputation in New York was Barbara Paley. She was the youngest of a famous trio of sisters, the daughters of Harvey Cushing, a Boston surgeon. All made brilliant marriages: Betsey to Jock Whitney after her divorce from President Franklin D. Roosevelt's son

James; Mary to Vincent Astor, whom she divorced, then marrying James Fosburgh, an artist; and "Babe," to William Paley, founder of CBS, after she was divorced from Stanley Mortimer.

In an edition of *Vogue*, for which she worked briefly as a fashion editor, published just before her marriage to Mr. Paley in 1947, she was described by Erwin Blumenfeld, the photographer: "[She] makes me remember the ancient Greek myth of the Golden Apple which Paris finally awards to the goddess who was for him the most feminine beauty on earth."

Blumenfeld would have awarded it to Babe. "The shape of her face is as attenuated as an El Greco," he wrote. "She has the most luminous skin imaginable and only Velázquez could paint her coloring on canvas. Her mouth is like that of the fascinating Madame Arnoux in Flaubert's novel *Education Sentimentale.* She has the gentleness, poise and the dignity of one of those grandes dames whom Balzac described in his *Comédie Humaine.* As for her clothes, instead of merely wearing them, she carries them."

The first time she came to my salon, she requested an appointment with a hairdresser on my staff, and observed me out of the corner of her eye. She did the same in restaurants, going unobtrusively at first so that she could judge the service without anyone making a fuss over her. As she was leaving my salon, she said to me, "Next time I come, I would like you to do my hair." I replied, "You will make the dream of my life come true because I have always wanted to run my fingers through your hair." She laughed. Mrs. Paley had a good sense of humor.

She was the essence of elegance. Only God can give a woman a face as beautiful as hers, but her elegance permeated her whole being, her clothes, the homes she made for her husband and family, her conversation.

She died in 1978 at the age of sixty-three, and I do believe her husband will never stop mourning her. When I go to their apartment on Fifth Avenue to cut his hair, Mr. Paley's English butler, Mr. John, never fails to say, "Monsieur Marc, no one yet has passed through that door like Madame did."

Before she drew her last breath, she planned to the minutest detail the luncheon that was held after her funeral at Kiluna Farm. It was a Saturday in July; she also had prepared instructions for a winter luncheon.

Waiters stood at the entrance with trays of champagne and Ladoucette Pouilly-fumé, her favorite white wine. The cutlery was wrapped in napkins folded to look like flowers in wicker baskets. The centerpieces at the tables, which seated ten, were Chinese porcelain bowls filled with the black cherries she preferred to flowers at meals. The main course was Chicken à l'Estragon. Unconsciously, everyone was looking for her. "The only one missing is Babe," they said.

Mrs. Paley had been named fourteen times to the best-dressed list and to its Hall of Fame. She was the darling of the fashion press although she almost never granted interviews. After she came to me, Monsieur Marc was mentioned in *Women's Wear Daily*, the bible of the fashion trade and of people who want to be in fashion, and in the *New York Times*.

Then it seemed as though everyone came to me—her sister, Mrs. Whitney; her stepdaughter, Hilary Byers, now Mrs. Joseph Califano; the Old Guard of New York and Long Island society. And countless other women who wanted to emulate her. When she entered a room, those who didn't recognize her asked, "Who is that woman?" Those who did wanted to know, "Where did she get those glasses? That sweater?" It never occurred to them that those things would never look the same on them as on her.

Alexandre sent the duchess of Windsor to me. She had discovered him when he was working for Antoine in Cannes and was known as the king of the egg shampoo.

Her patronage impressed a certain older, American clientele who still cared that a king of England had given up his throne for her. I never considered her a real duchess, although she expected to be treated like one. Wallis Windsor had a way of letting you know she expected flowers in the room when she was having her hair done.

I would send my assistant, Lili Lupatelli, to greet her as she stepped out of her chauffeured limousine and to escort her upstairs to the private room in the back of the salon. Lili carried the two Vuitton bags with DUCHESS OF WINDSOR stamped on them, containing her own rollers and spray. She always tipped Lili before the shampoo and inquired about her little daughter in fluent, English-accented French.

She kept her hair pretty much the same over the years, as Antoine had coiffed her in 1937 for her marriage, with a center part and a wave over the ears. That was her look of classic elegance and she didn't allow me to vary it.

Contrary to the reputation the Windsors had for freeloading, she paid me for my services. Usually the duke signed the check. He was very pleasant and had a wry sense of humor.

His Royal Highness used to watch while I combed her hair in their suite at the Waldorf Towers. He had that Englishman's flair for dressing, an audacious eye for combining patterns one expected to clash, such as a checked tweed jacket and a plaid shirt. As an admirer of Savile Row tailoring, I was surprised at the advice he gave me. "Have your pants made in New York—they don't know how to do them in England," he said. He always ordered extra fabric for that purpose. English tailors make pants high over the waistline so that they can cut the vests shorter to achieve a neater look when the wearer is seated. They also add pleats so that the pants are as comfortable as a skirt. American men like to feel their pants tight against their bodies.

Mrs. Alfred Bloomingdale made an appointment at the salon after seeing a photograph of one of my coiffures in a magazine. She lived in Beverly Hills and stayed at the Mayfair Regent Hotel, a block away from the salon, when she visited New York.

"What would you like me to do?" I asked her.

"What would you suggest?" she replied.

"We have just met," I said. "After we are engaged, I will tell you what I want to do. For now, only your feeling can tell me. Your eyes are below the hairdo and can see much better than mine." Her hair was short and layered in curls, a style derived from the artichoke coiffure by Alexandre in Paris. I loosened it, made it more natural, and did away with the bangs.

She sent me a note from California: "I think it will be a short engagement—and we shall be married very soon! I'm so happy to be one of the wives. Gratefully, Betsy Bloomingdale. P.S. When we get married, I shall have to fly to New York every two weeks for my haircut . . . with pleasure!!"

Mrs. Bloomingdale sent me her friends from Los Angeles—Mrs. Armand Deutsch, Mrs. Ray Stark, Mrs. Jules Stein. One day in the early Seventies, she telephoned and said, "I'm bringing you the wife of the governor of California."

Nancy Reagan said to me, "I give you carte blanche." I told her she looked very well but perhaps I could add a little flair. She had a short cut like Mrs. Bloomingdale's, but it was too well coiffed, a bit stiff-looking, like that of a little doll in a shop window. I like *chic negligé*. I ran my hands through her hair and made it look more natural.

Sometimes, if I was very busy, I would let other hairdressers at my salon take care of important clients like Mrs. Paley and the duchess of Windsor so they wouldn't be inconvenienced by having to wait. For some reason, I always did Mrs. Reagan myself. She sent me a note saying she wished she could wrap me up and take me home.

She usually came to the salon whenever she was in New York, but occasionally she asked me to comb her hair at the apartment of friends where she and the governor stayed. He sat in the room, watching me work or looking at television, and was very friendly and casual. It was obvious that they were very much in love even after so many years of being married. On her birthday, he sent flowers to her mother. She looked at him as though he were a god—as the American public is now aware from photographs and TV shots of their president and his First Lady.

When Mr. Reagan was running for president, friends and clients asked me to confirm that he dyed his hair. As if that had anything to do with his qualifications to be president of the United States. I said then and say now, having seen him many times in his private quarters at the White House, that, yes, I have looked at his hair and if it is tinted, then it's an exceptionally good job. As far as I can see, his hair looks natural, with a few gray hairs showing around the ears.

Mrs. Reagan is a gracious woman, very considerate of those who serve her. She always thanks the staff when she leaves, always remembers something about them, such as the health of their husbands and children or the fact that Lili was impressed with Governor Reagan's navy blue pajamas.

During the campaign for the presidency Mrs. Reagan asked me, "If it doesn't go through, will you still do my hair?" I replied, "You will always remain my client."

The day after the election, I sent her a bottle of pink champagne tucked into a tricolor bouquet of flowers, with a note: "This is a little water from France. You should have some of it at the White House."

When I saw her a week later, she threw her arms around me and said, "Marc, I'm so happy for my husband. I'm so happy for our country. I'm sure we're going to do whatever is in our power to do right."

When she knew she was going to be in New York to do some shopping, she called me herself for an appointment. She still does that from the White House, always phrasing her request "If you're not too busy . . ." She didn't change after she became First Lady–elect, although her life did. She was no longer a private person. Forty-five minutes before she came to the salon, the Secret Service arrived to check every drawer, look behind every mirror, verify the back door for escape if necessary, and then station themselves by the checkroom.

On that first visit after the election, she was accompanied by Mrs. Bloomingdale, whom the papers had started calling First Friend, and by Jerry Zipkin. He had been with the Reagans on election night.

I first met Jerry in the summer of 1971 on Charles Revson's yacht, to which I had been invited, all expenses paid, to comb Lyn Revson's hair for the Red and White Gala Ball at Cap d'Antibes that was organized by Celebrity Service's Earl Blackwell.

In America, Jerry is a guru for what the media, after the Reagan inauguration, started calling "bicoastal society." The Bloomingdales and their friends, who were influential in getting Mr. Reagan elected president, were the West Coast leaders. On the East Coast, the stars were the Buckleys; Nan Kempner, whose husband Thomas is an investment banker; and the Oscar de la Rentas. The dinners these people give are notable, not so much for the excellent food and wine as for the power rating of the guests. When they aren't giving parties, they are attending them, and since the husbands of these socialites don't have the same stamina as their wives (Oscar de la Renta excepted), Jerry Zipkin serves as the women's escort.

He does this on an international scale; bicoastal society makes its seasonal excursions to London, Paris and the Riviera, and their European friends reverse the migration. In late November and May, the French branch descends on New York by Air France Concorde, to be joined by the West Coast contingent for a round of parties. The Texans fly in, usually in private planes. On a typical afternoon, Betsy Bloomingdale, Fran Stark, Pat Mosbacher, Princess Edouard de Lobkowicz, Mme. Edmond Bory, and Mme. Jacques Rouet may be found at Monsieur Marc exchanging gossip and information: who will be wearing her Givenchy; which one offers not to wear her Adolfo if the other one wants to wear hers. Lynn Wyatt and the Baroness Sandra di Portanova—whose husband, Enrico, is a grandson of the late Hugh Roy Cullen, so-called king of the wildcatters—telephone for appointments.

I rush to the Waldorf Towers to comb the First Lady, who is in New York to receive an award from the Salvation Army for her work with children, to dine with the C. V. Whitneys and to see her son, Ron, and his wife, Doria.

Jerry Zipkin will be at all the parties. He met Betsy Bloomingdale in Paris and Brussels in the fall of 1982, her first trip abroad since she was widowed.

It's no mystery to me why Zipkin is so beloved by these women. He does for them what few husbands or lovers can do: He tells them the truth in detail about how they look. Most women, no matter how rich, are hesitant about their clothes. Is this the right color? The right length? Is this the right dress for a particular party? Jerry knows the answers. He goes to all the fashion shows, all the openings; he knows what the new color is, what's the new trend; and when he advises them, they feel confident. "You look so pretty," he'll say. "Now this is the shoe you should have, with this heel."

Zipkin introduced the ladies from the West to New York taste. New York is the city of fashion, after all, and when they come here, instead of asking other women, they ask Jerry where to go and what to do.

I call him the Yellow Pages because he's a directory of information. He arranged for shoes to be brought to the salon so that Mrs. Reagan could make her selections while she was having her hair done. "Cinderella," he said as she opened the shoe boxes, and she laughed. Nancy Reagan needed to buy suitcases but didn't want the Gucci double G's on her luggage. "T. Anthony has the best suitcase in New York," Jerry declared.

After she was finished at the salon, he escorted her and Mrs. Bloomingdale to Le Cirque for lunch. The next time Mrs. Reagan and Jerry were at Monsieur Marc, he ordered lunch sent over from the restaurant: chicken salad, a tomato cut in the shape of a rose, assorted pastries and Sanka.

Zipkin instructs his friends on where to eat and what to eat. At the inauguration, he was informing them that they had to try the soft-shell crabs at the Jockey Club in the Fairfax Hotel. Mrs. Reagan enjoys his company,

I believe, because he makes her laugh. His humor is clean if a bit childish. "I know a four-letter word in every language," he says. "Taxi." Actually, he speaks fluent French. The Secret Service squad that came to the salon on one visit included a pretty woman in a blue suit. "Are you the one who's carrying the big number?" Jerry whispered to her, playfully alluding to the black bag that could begin World War III and is usually carried by a man in the president's entourage.

There's no denying what the election of Ronald Reagan has meant to me. It has brought a new clientele from California, Texas and Washington, and even Chicago and Birmingham, Alabama. I'm a nonpolitical man and some of my best clients are Democrats, but it must be said that Reagan Republican women love to dress up and go places, and they do what is necessary to look their best.

Mrs. Reagan sent me an invitation to the inauguration. I stayed at the Fairfax (now the Ritz-Carlton), where Betsy Bloomingdale and most of the Reagan friends were lodged, and commuted between the hotel and the salon of Robin Weir a block away. The pace of activity was wild.

I still had heads to comb when the time arrived to go to the Inaugural Ball at the Kennedy Center. I dressed in white tie and tails and knocked at the door of the Buckleys' room. William Buckley, whom I recognized from TV, opened the door. "I have come to see your wife," I said. "Pat, I think the French ambassador is here to see you," he called out.

Sirio Maccioni of Le Cirque and I drove to the Ball and descended into the spotlighted circle of reporters and TV cameras. "Who are you?" voices shouted. It must have been my black evening cape, white silk scarf and black homburg that made them think I was somebody. "Monsieur Marc," I said. "I did some of the ladies' hair for the inauguration."

Perhaps it was the evocative line of Mrs. Reagan's costume at the swearing in that brought back memories of another inauguration twenty years ago. Jacqueline Kennedy at thirty-one became a world symbol of fashion, taste and elegance. Nancy Reagan, almost twice the age Mrs. Kennedy was when she entered the White House, has done the same in a slightly different way.

For a country that has always overemphasized youth, she and the president have shown that it is possible to be healthy, happy and handsome in maturity. Mrs. Jane Pickens Hoving put it very well when she was presenting the award to the First Lady at the Salvation Army benefit: "It's like seeing a drama, *United States of America,* starring Ronald Reagan and Nancy Reagan."

It certainly seems that way when television shows them kissing goodbye before a separation of a few days—such as Mrs. Reagan's departure for London to attend the wedding of Prince Charles and Lady Diana; there were four passionate embraces on the White House lawn and the president said, "Be careful. I love you."

Ronald Reagan is in unbelievably good shape for seventy-two. Except for the lines in his face, which give character, he could be taken for a man in his fifties. Mrs. Reagan has the slight figure and the laugh of a *jeune fille*. Her hazel eyes are her most expressive feature. They smile with happiness when she greets a friend, with joy when she looks at her husband and her son, Ron. Once when I was doing her hair at the White House in the presence of the president and Ron, her son got up to leave for New York. As she embraced him, I saw sadness mixed with the joy in her eyes. "Mrs. Reagan," I said, "you look as though he were going to the army."

I believe she has been unfairly criticized for her interest in fashion, for being what an editorial commentator on a TV program referred to as "a walking advertisement for Galanos, Blass and Adolfo." It had just been revealed that the designers had made gifts to her of some of the clothes, and that some of the jewels she had worn were on loan. Her image as a woman of expensive tastes was said to be an affront at a time of economic recession. Some of the critics seemed to equate the number of dresses in her wardrobe with the rate of unemployment.

That's politics, I know. The wife of the president has always been a target for deflecting some of the criticism aimed at his policies. Yet, is it not desirable for the American fashion industry to rival the French as had happened in recent years? But where the French recognize the value of having public figures promote the fashion product, Americans treat this as something unethical. Having a woman in the White House who takes pleasure in American fashion and wears her clothes well must contribute to creating jobs in that industry.

As for the brouhaha of the jewelry, it seems to me there ought to be American state jewels that all presidents' wives would wear during their husbands' terms of office. My friends tell me, however, that this would be un-American, "inconsistent with democratic standards."

Since moving to the White House, Mrs. Reagan has used three hairdressers, always concerned about keeping our feelings unruffled. Robin Weir in Washington sees her most often, being right there on the spot. Julius Bengtsson, a free-lance with a Hollywood clientele, whom she used when she lived in California, comes to the White House once a month to do her coloring. He applies a mixture of Miss Clairol "Moon Gold" and "Chestnut Brown" to the roots and adds highlights to achieve a honey-tone effect. Julius is a consultant to Clairol.

I take care of Mrs. Reagan when she is in New York, either at the salon or at the Presidential Suite in the Waldorf Towers, and at the White House for special occasions and whenever I can tear myself away from my responsibilities at the salon to take care of other clients in Washington.

On the one hand, famous clients like the First Lady attract new patrons to a hairdresser and shed a little glow on his faithful customers. But only up to a point. If I am unavailable to my regular clients too often, they are annoyed and don't hesitate to show it. Some get the impression that I have time only for celebrities, which is totally false. Mrs. Reagan is aware of this and has said to me, "I wish you could do my hair more often, but I can't take you away from your business."

Some of the press seem to regard Mrs. Reagan's chic as a second Watergate story and try to discover whether she pays to have her hair done and, if so, how much. I can answer only for myself. I have a fixed schedule of rates for my services, but I am an artist as much as I am a businessman and I put my heart into my work. With clients of long standing who have been exceptionally kind to me and for whom I have developed feelings of friendship, I try to find means of reciprocating. It may be with trout or game, or with a scarf or necktie I found in a boutique in Paris. Every now and then, it may be with my services. Just as the owner of a famous restaurant will send a bottle of wine to the table of his steadiest customer to celebrate a special occasion, so will I show my appreciation.

Nancy Reagan is the wife of the president of the United States, but she was my client before, and will, I hope, be my client afterward. To that degree, she is no different from my other very best clients.

The first time I went to the White House, I felt as though I had reached the culmination of my life's work. A car sent from the White House was waiting for me at the airport. It was a navy blue Dodge with a driver in a plain gray business suit. Since then, I have been picked up by such official cars many times and although they are always unmarked, nondescript vehicles and the men at the wheel in civilian dress, I can always pick one out from twenty limousines. It may be the clean-cut, expressionless faces and the erect bearing of the drivers, like that of Secret Service men and other security guards.

That first time, as the car drove up to 1600 Pennsylvania Avenue, the driver reporting our whereabouts by radio several times, I could hear my heart thumping. At the side entrance to the White House, my identity was checked by two security men who were expecting me but nevertheless scrutinized my American Express card and driver's license and examined the contents of my briefcase. I was escorted to the elevator leading to the private apartment by a Mr. Chesterfield dressed in a dark suit and a white bow tie. I felt as though I were playing a bit part in an Agent 007 movie. On subsequent visits, he told me that he has worked at the White House for twenty-two years. "I served a lot of presidents," he said, "but this is the nicest couple of all."

I shampooed and cut Mrs. Reagan's hair—which, incidentally, has wonderful texture, a hairdresser's joy to work with. I set it in rollers to dry under the machine for thirty-five minutes. Then I brushed it very thoroughly in every direction to create the shape of the line I desired and ran my fingers lightly through the hair to give it a final touch of *chic negligé*.

We usually have a lighthearted conversation as I do her hair, much as I would have with other good clients. I might tell her about fashion shows and art exhibitions I have seen, or report the reactions I have heard to her television appearances in behalf of combating teen-age drug and alcohol abuse, her major project as First Lady. Sometimes she asks me when am I going to get married. "I'll come to your wedding," she'll say.

"Would you like to have a look around?" Mrs. Reagan asked me on that first visit. She gave me a tour of the family quarters herself. What struck me was how much like a home it is, just as it says on the white match folders printed *The President's House*, not at all like the kings' palaces in Europe. With the help of her friend Ted Graber, an interior designer from Los Angeles, Nancy Reagan has made a warm and comfortable environment for a typically American couple whose children are grown and living elsewhere, who entertain a lot and like to be surrounded by mementos of their friends and their previous home. There wasn't one room in which I felt ill at ease about where to sit as in some houses I've visited where the decorator imposed his taste and drowned the personalities of the residents.

In the president's study, my eye was caught by the mass of photographs of his wife, starting with her at the age of eight or nine in a cloche hat, looking very much as she does today. In contrast to the Oval Office, this room, which is decorated in red and white, is furnished with the president's personal belongings, such as a massive mahogany partners' desk and a lamp base made from a silver fire chief's horn. On the side tables are crystal jars filled with jelly beans.

Next to the study is the Reagans' bedroom, in predominantly white and salmon tones. The king-size bed seems nestled in the outdoors because of Chinese wallpaper handpainted with tiny birds in flight. Adjoining the bedroom is Mrs. Reagan's dressing room, also in salmon color, with an impressionistic portrait of herself and her daughter, Patricia, as a child. The First Lady was a brunette then. How wise of her not to cling to a dark shade when her hair started changing color, but to have gone to the lighter, softer tones.

The dressing room and her office, which is done in green and white, are filled with photographs of her family and friends. If the living room looks homey it's because the Reagans had furniture from their house in Pacific Palisades moved in on Inauguration Day. The large twin sofas upholstered in a quilted red floral print with a needlepoint pillow marked R. R. look inviting enough to stretch out on and take a nap.

Mrs. Reagan took me to the Oval Office to present me to the president. I would have been overcome by the aura of power if he hadn't seized on my tie tack, a pair of tiny scissors, and exclaimed, "Why, this is charming!" "Yours is very nice, too," I replied. He was wearing a tack in the shape of a boot.

"May I see the kitchen?" I asked afterward.

"Everybody wants to see the Lincoln Room," Mrs. Reagan said. It was disappointing—solid but not very beautiful, and I had a feeling there were mice in the walls. Muffie Brandon, her social secretary, took me to the kitchen, where the Swiss chef Henry Haller let me taste a mousse of asparagus. Mrs. Reagan is not a cook herself, but she understands and appreciates good food. She only picks at her plate, however, which may be why she has kept a girlish figure. I have told her she is too thin and ought to put on a few pounds.

Then on to the floral room, a flower shop, really, with shelves of vases, containers, and ribbons, presided over by a floral director who confers with Mrs. Reagan, Mrs. Brandon and the chief of staff, Peter McCoy, on arrangements.

There are those like Mrs. Paley who don't like flowers with food, believing the scent conflicts with the taste. Mrs. Reagan favors fragrant flowers like tuberoses and sweetpeas, and, in season, lilacs and lily of the valley.

I had lunch in the White House mess that day, then went to see my other clients. As I was crossing Pennsylvania Avenue, a blue Mercedes honked urgently. "Monsieur Marc, hello!" a client called to me from behind the wheel. "I'm so glad I had my car washed today. I've already seen Bill Blass, and now you."

That evening I was back at the White House for a cocktail party and buffet for 300 Republican Eagles, an elite group of contributors who give $10,000 or more to the Party. Then it was off to a Bill Blass fashion show to benefit the Phillips Collection. The black-tie party was held at the museum, a sellout at $250 a ticket. The *Washington Post* described it as "a flashlit melting pot of cave-dwelling Washington, New York fashion society and Ronald Reagan's White House."

No one could remember the last time a president left the White House to go to a fashion show. Actually, he and Mrs. Reagan only dropped by on the way to another charity ball, but they chatted with their friends and Mrs. Reagan gave her hugs to Bill Blass and Jerry Zipkin. Jerry noticed something amiss in her green silk Blass dress and set about rebuttoning it as the Washington socialites watched unbelieving.

What kept running through my mind that night, as I prepared for bed at the Fairfax, was how grateful I feel to the United States of America for all it has given to me. The chance step I took of going into business for myself kept me in this country although I fully intended then to return to Europe. I became an American citizen in 1961 when I realized I could never make my home in Europe again. Fractured English and all, I was an

American at heart. After living in the only real democracy, after breathing the air of freedom, I could not be happy elsewhere.

In America all things are possible if you work hard and stick to your ambition. Even this social activity, which I find silly and boring except in small doses, is proof of how democratic America is. It doesn't matter where you were born or how humble the circumstances, as long as you achieve.

A European woman of high position in a United Nations embassy remarked once about me, "Why, he has more social mobility than I—and he is only a hairdresser." I can appreciate how she felt, a woman with several university degrees and a job at the center of the diplomatic universe, moving in a defined and rather dull circle of acquaintances, only able to read about some of the places I went and the company I kept. On the few occasions our paths crossed at U.N. receptions, she asked, "And what are you doing here?" knowing full well that I had been invited by one of the ambassadors' wives who was my client. It was even funnier when someone would address me as "Mr. Ambassador," attributing rank to me on the basis of my gray hair and moustache and, I suppose, those de Coster genes.

5

TRAVELOGUE

M y sister must have been clairvoyant when she predicted that as a hairdresser I would travel. The profession has literally taken me around the world, from Europe to Japan and back again via Sydney and New Delhi, to South America and to the Caribbean, and to numerous cities and society playgrounds in the U.S., Canada and Mexico. I have been invited to give demonstrations of my work to professional groups, have gone on location for magazine and advertising photography, and have traveled to accommodate clients who desired my services in their homes.

These excursions away from the salon have been educational, to say the least, exposing me to the life-style and idiosyncrasies of the super-rich, and to their joys and miseries.

I made several visits to Greenville, Delaware, a suburb of Wilmington, a city associated with the Du Ponts, a family of French émigrés that got its start in America nearly 200 years ago making better gunpowder. In the twentieth century, with more peaceful designs, Du Pont revolutionized fashion and home life with the manufacture of synthetic fibers. No matter how practical nylon and dacron may be, I find them disagreeable to the touch because they are not living materials.

Mrs. Edmund N. Carpenter II asked me and my assistant, Lili, to Greenville to cheer her mother, Mrs. Gordon Rust, who was in the terminal stages of cancer. Frances Rust was born a Du Pont and as a teen-ager in the 1920s sowed so many wild oats that her father, Philip du Pont, practically disowned her. He left the Black Banana, as she was known in society, a mere $2 million. One of her daughters by her first marriage, F. Carroll Morgan, married the son of Walter S. Carpenter, the first president of E. I. du Pont de Nemours, Inc., not born a Du Pont. Mrs. Carpenter put us up in a guesthouse near her swimming pool. I did what I could for Mrs. Rust, who, despite her hopeless outlook, showed sparks of her youthful vivacity. Finally, I made her two wigs so that she could pass her dying days under the impression she was still beautiful.

Mrs. Carpenter presented me with a Lucite tray encasing a needlepoint mat she had made after consulting the French consul about the citation for the Legion of Honor. On it was inscribed MARC OF DISTINCTION.

She was more than kind to Lili. For years, she gave her clothes for her little girl, dresses her daughter had worn once or twice. When she learned that Lili's mother had cancer, she telephoned from Greenville to say, "I'm here, Lili. Just tell me what I can do."

On one of our visits, we were sitting in her kitchen drinking coffee with Mrs. Carpenter and Mrs. A. du Pont Dent when Mrs. Dent said, "Come with me. I must show you Nemours."

Her husband's grandfather, Alfred Irenée du Pont, had built Nemours early in the century as a copy of Versailles. On bad terms with many of his Du Pont relatives, he had a nine-foot wall constructed around the property with pieces of broken glass and iron spikes embedded at the top.

We drove past gates that had been originally made for Catherine the Great in St. Petersburg, and swept through immense gardens with espaliered shrubbery and small lakes fed by the Brandywine Creek. Had Marie Antoinette appeared in her dairymaid costume, we would not have been surprised. A structure of pink stone modeled after Le Petit Trianon was pointed out to be a family mausoleum with vaults for their pets as well.

The door of the seventy-seven room château was opened by an elderly butler, the sole occupant for many years. Forty years after the owner's death, the property was to be converted into a children's hospital. As we had another cup of coffee in a pantry filled with Limoges china, we heard more stories of the family history. Although you can never convince people who have too little that this is true, too much money is not conducive to happiness.

Unlike the Du Ponts, who lived off wealth made by their ancestors and increased by their professional managers, Charles Revson acquired every cent of his cosmetics fortune by himself. As far as I could tell when I was with him on his yacht or at his triplex apartment in Manhattan, which had belonged to his rival, Helena Rubinstein, Revson was devoted to his young wife, Lyn.

He was very demanding, however, and she dressed as he instructed her. When women of all ages had adopted the mini, she had to cover her kneecaps. Yet counteracting that conservative, slightly dowdy look was her exceptionally beautiful light brown hair, which she let grow below her shoulders and wore loose or clasped back into a luxurious ponytail. The effect was both schoolgirlish and sensuous.

One day after Lyn Revson had her usual lemon shampoo (a Revlon product, of course), her hair seemed impossible to comb. She telephoned her husband and he sent two men to the salon to investigate at once. A half-hour later, Revson himself appeared and proceeded to question the Haitian maid who was in charge of the room in which the products were stored. "Don't be nervous," he said, "but tell me exactly what you did with this bottle." The poor woman was terrified. Unable to read English, she had ignored the instructions on the label for diluting the shampoo.

The chairman of a company with sales at that time in the hundreds of millions of dollars had gotten to the bottom of the mystery involving a single bottle of shampoo. That he would bother said it all. His products were Number One to Charles Revson. The business was his whole life.

He had a reputation for being an ogre to work for. When he wanted to hire someone, he couldn't do enough to woo him. Then one day he would fire him, just like that.

"You know, Marc," he said one evening when I was cutting his hair at the apartment, "it doesn't matter what kind of company it is. If you have somebody good, you have to throw him out after ten years because he becomes your competitor."

His executives would have been interested to hear that. If they were too capable, they posed a threat to him. I was glad I had turned down his offer, when I was at Marcel, to head up the Revlon beauty salon.

In the spring of 1974, Antenor Patiño, the Bolivian tin king and his wife, Beatriz, a client of Guillaume's who came to me in New York, staged a summit meeting of the jet set to promote the opening of Las Hadas, his $30-million resort in Manzanillo, Mexico.

Air France jets were chartered to transport the guests. Le tout-Paris came: Prince and Princess Edouard de Lobkowicz; Helène Rochas, the widow of the couturier Marcel Rochas, and her companion of that moment, Kim d'Estainville; Gerald van der Kemp, the curator of Versailles, and his American wife, Florence; Jacqueline de Ribes and Countess Cristiana Brandolini, the Fiat heiress; Pierre Cardin's associate, André Oliver; and Baron Alexis de Redé, financial consultant and formidable Paris partygiver.

New York was represented by Nan Kempner, Mary Lasker, Estée and Joseph Lauder, Arlene Dahl and the Levitts, William and Simone. Unlike Charles Revson, who named his yacht Ultima II after a Revlon product line, Levitt, the real-estate tycoon, christened his yacht La Belle Simone after his wife.

The Los Angeles group included the Alfred Bloomingdales, the Prentiss Cobb Hales and Mrs. Jules Stein. Oscar Wyatt, the Texas oilman, was there with his wife, Lynn.

Then there were those hard to identify with one city, state or country because they circulate so much: Emilio Pucci, the Florentine marchese whose printed silk jersey dresses were status symbols in the Sixties; Cornelius Vanderbilt Whitney and his wife, Mary Lou; and Count Vittorio de Nora and his wife, Chantal, both of them pilots of their respective jet planes.

Since there would be no point in having such a rendezvous of the Beautiful People without press to record it, there were, among others, Eugenia Sheppard and her inseparable companion, Earl Blackwell.

Beatriz Patiño invited me and Laurent of Paris, each of us to bring a hairdresser from our salons. Since the ladies spent the days at the beach and showered afterward, there wasn't much we could do with their hair except mend the damage with Carmen curlers and curling irons. The resort, intended to be the most luxurious in the world, with marble floors in all the suites and custom tiles in the swimming pools, lacked hair dryers. The clients were told to give us what they felt like. Most thought $50 was appropriate for a comb-out. One woman gave me $200 each time I did her hairdo for the evening.

There was an amusing sidelight to that weekend. For all his high-priced planning, Patiño overlooked the mosquitoes, which drove everyone crazy, particularly at night.

I wanted to take in the spring skiing at Sun Valley, Idaho, and was able to hitch a ride with the Bloomingdales and Baron de Redé to Mexico City in a private plane sent by one of his friends—and then I continued by commercial jet to Los Angeles.

Palm Beach has been called the dowager of *nouveau riche* resorts. Certainly, money is what counts on that glittering island off Florida's Gold Coast and there is very little hesitancy about showing it. I have seen more Rolls-Royces and Mercedes parked along Worth Avenue, one of the world's most expensive shopping streets, than in all of Deauville. At lunch in the restaurants and in the beauty salons, women wear engagement rings that look like hailstones captured in platinum settings.

I've observed two distinct groups in Palm Beach—the new rich and the old; they rarely mix except at charity balls. Palm Beachers are very philanthropic. They raise enormous amounts at parties, usually to benefit research for curing diseases. I suppose that's natural considering that the majority of the population is of retirement age.

On my most recent visit to Palm Beach, I was invited by Mrs. F. Warrington Gillet, Jr., chairman of the benefit for St. Mary's Hospital. Elesabeth Gillet, a steel heiress from Birmingham, Alabama, guaranteed the hospital $50,000 from the party, which was held at the Henry Morrison Flagler Museum, the former palace of a railroad tycoon. Guests paid $100 a ticket to see the spring made-to-order collection of Arnold Scaasi. I was at Mrs. Gillet's house when she learned the benefit was oversubscribed. She called her cook. "Madeleine, we'll drink champagne."

I did the hair of the models and of Mrs. Gillet and her friends, one of whom was Mary Sanford, the queen of Palm Beach. The blond and exuberant widow of Stephen ("Laddie") Sanford, a renowned polo player, is rightfully proud of her legs. She displayed them elegantly with one of Scaasi's short, covered-up black lace dresses.

The Sisters of St. Francis of Allegheny, who run the hospital, attended the party and clapped enthusiastically at the cocktail dresses and ball gowns. I wonder if the nuns realized Scaasi's dresses cost from $3,500 to $6,500. No prices were mentioned at the show. That would have seemed crassly commercial and, as one woman said, "It might have scared the husbands." I doubt that very much.

Mrs. Gillet had asked me to stay at her house, but I was afraid of inconveniencing her since I knew so many clients would be telephoning me for appointments or to extend invitations. So I accepted an offer to live aboard the sailing yacht *Whitehawk*, which is owned by a client from New York and her husband, Thomas E. Zetkov, a retired insurance executive. The Zetkovs have a house on the ocean in Palm Beach.

To keep from being bored, Olga Zetkov opened a boutique on Worth Avenue, the Needlepoint Gazebo, which sells sweaters and those pillows with messages about the satisfactions of being rich.

She picked me up at the airport with the captain of the *Whitehawk*. "It's yours. Invite your friends," she said. I felt like a millionaire on the 109-foot racing ketch, which is currently the fastest and most luxurious boat of its kind afloat. The hull is made of mahogany and cedar veneer. The main saloon has a wood-burning fireplace faced with old Dutch tiles; the rug is an antique Persian. I slept in a queen-size bed and bathed in a tub carved of Maine cedar. The basin fixtures in the head were gold-plated. The bar was stocked with champagne.

Every morning a member of the crew brought me freshly squeezed orange juice and warm croissants from a French bakery. The laundry service was as good as at the Ritz in Paris.

Some people with a great deal of money put distance between themselves and those not so well endowed. But the Zetkovs, like the Gillets, were warm, friendly and unaffected. They took me sailing twice and Mr. Zetkov gave me a short course on navigation at the wheel.

I had one of the best working vacations in years. A few afternoons I took care of clients, making my base at Margrit's salon on Worth Avenue. Most of them were patrons of my New York salon who vacation in Palm Beach, but a few of my Long Island ladies—like Mrs. Thomas H. Choate of Brookville and Mrs. Robert Montgomery, the widow of the actor—came from Hobe Sound, an Old Guard resort forty-five minutes to the north by car.

I had lunch at Café l'Europe on Worth Avenue, which has earned the title "Le Cirque of Palm Beach." Lydia, the wife of Norbert Goldner, the owner, is a beautiful young Brazilian, a former Pan Am stewardess and one of the most elegant women on the island.

It was mid-February, the height of the social season, when it seems that every hour of the calendar from noon to midnight is booked with parties and every hotel and guest-room bed is occupied by a socialite or a fashion designer. I ran into Jimmy Galanos, who was making his yearly appearance at Martha's on Worth Avenue.

Like New York, Palm Beach has acquired a pronounced foreign accent, brought on by the flight of capital from Europe and South America. There was titles galore, such as Princess Maria Gabriella, daughter of former King Umberto II of Italy, now the wife of Robert de Balkany, a French businessman and polo player; and Baron Arndt Krupp von Bohlen und Halbach, who is easily recognized by his makeup.

Roger Dean, the largest Chevrolet dealer in the area, put a Camaro at my disposal. The Deans have their own jet and their house looks like a country club with a swimming pool and tennis courts. "Do you remember how we met?" Mrs. Dean reminisced one day at lunch. She reminded me that she had been having lunch at La Caravelle in New York some years ago and had noticed two beautiful blond women at a nearby table. She asked the maître d' if he could find out for her who did their hair.

"Why that's Hilary Byers and Sydney Gould and the man with them is their hairdresser, Monsieur Marc," he said. I had taken them to lunch to celebrate Mrs. Byers's birthday.

By coincidence, I was scheduled to fly from Palm Beach to Washington to do Mrs. Byers's hair for her wedding—to Joseph Califano, the former secretary of health, education and welfare in the Carter administration.

She wore a pink suit by Adolfo with a little chignon of silk flowers at the back of her head that Givenchy had made for her. She had also invited Carlos from my salon, who does her hair when I am away, and after the ceremony she posed for a photograph with both of us. "See, I have two hairdressers, too," she said laughing.

I saw Houston for the first time when I was called there on a fascinating assignment. Mrs. Douglas Marshall, Jr., whose husband is a grandson of the late Hugh Roy Cullen, was to have her portrait painted. My job was to arrange her hair for a series of preliminary poses to be photographed by the painter Aaron Shikler, whose portrait of Jacqueline Kennedy hangs in the White House. He also did a portrait of Ronald Reagan in blue denim looking like a cowboy for a cover of *Time.*

Alexandra Marshall chose to be portrayed in evening dress and was deliberating among a Givenchy, a Saint Laurent and a Mary McFadden. For two days we worked hard, starting at seven, because Shikler wanted the morning light. Mrs. Marshall would put on a dress, I would style her hair, and Shikler would begin photographing. Then we would repeat the process with a different dress and coiffure. My work ended when Shikler selected a pose and was ready to begin painting.

Having always believed that coiffure and portraiture are alike in the challenge to express the subject's personality in the most flattering way, I was excited to be involved in an actual painting.

The first coiffure I tried was a complicated one. Mrs. Marshall's blond hair was brushed away from her face and braided into a chignon studded with jewels. It was a proper hairdo for a magazine editorial or an advertisement for diamonds, but too artificial for a portrait of a beautiful young woman that was to hang in her home for her family and friends to enjoy. After I took her hair down and brushed it into a simple, natural line, she and the artist agreed I had proved my point.

Mrs. Marshall arranged for me to attend several parties, including a black-tie dinner in her home at which she announced that it was in honor of my birthday. The guests were an interesting mix of Houstonians, including several Europeans. "How come you aren't gay?" they asked.

The next day, she entertained at luncheon and served lobsters flown in from Maine. The maid was at a loss what to do with them, so I went into my favorite room in any house and dissected twenty shellfish. Mr. Marshall was astonished. "I can do anything, sir. Just ask me," I said. Later I fixed a broken radio. I like to feel useful when I am a guest in someone's home.

Houston left me with an impression of enormous space and isolation, an ultramodern city growing out of a desert. I felt as though I were in an air-conditioned box. In San Francisco, in Chicago, in New York, you see people on the streets. On Madison Avenue, I meet someone and say, "Let's have a drink." That could never happen in Houston. To go shopping, to see people, you go by car.

I have never seen as many beautiful, blond, Anglo-Saxon-type women as I did in Houston. Or heard so much talk about money. At one point, I had to make a joke about it. "I don't have any money," I said, "but I have a good heart."

Conversations were mostly about modern art, music and rodeo. There was a lot of laughter, but they didn't talk about themselves as persons or reveal what they were like inside.

Houston seemed very competitive, a perpetual race to see who has the most jewelry, the biggest car, who travels the most. In New York the game is name-dropping; in Houston it's place-dropping. Everyone was showing off where he or she had just been. The cars parked at a restaurant I visited for a ballet benefit were Mercedes, Maseratis, Lamborghinis. Distance is nothing; private helicopters and planes were like station wagons in New York, to be used for visiting one's second home in the area. After lunch one day, Mr. Marshall took me for a two-hour spin over Texas in his jet to show me a ranch his grandmother had built for raising Arabian horses.

After I combed one woman's hair, she insisted on taking me shopping and offered to buy me a pair of gray and white ostrich cowboy boots— price tag $1,500. I thanked her and said they hurt my instep. When I refused to accept the boots, she tried to press upon me some $65 cowboy shirts. I had heard that Texans are very generous.

When it comes to gifts, there's no doubt that hairdressers, particularly males, are among the most indulged members of society. I suppose this is a reflection of how deeply women feel about their hair and the emotional intimacy that can develop between them and those who get to know their innermost selves in the course of styling their hair.

As the owner of the salon, I do not accept tips, and this may be part of the explanation for some clients' largess. But there are hairdressers who are regularly tipped and still receive Tiffany watches for Christmas.

I neither expect nor encourage presents. I believe that I am well paid for the service I render. Yet I shall always treasure the jar of jelly beans with the presidential seal embossed on the crystal that was the Reagans' memento of their first Christmas in the White House, the ceramic rose paperweight the following year, and the package she gave me in Paris in June 1982 saying, "for all the good hours we spent together." Inside was the gift distributed to those who accompanied them on the president's first trip to Western Europe, a quartz watch and alarm clock etched with the seal, his signature and a map of the countries visited.

I am touched when a client shows appreciation for my efforts to please her with something that indicates she gave thought to my personal taste as though I were a good friend.

Some have given me tickets to concerts and plays they have subscribed to as members of benefit committees; wine; and cakes they have baked themselves. After I bought my house in the country, my gardening clients showered me with bulbs and seedlings. Learning that my beloved Purdey was lost in the theft of my Mercedes convertible, someone replaced it with a Luger shotgun. One of my hunter clients presented me with two brace of pheasant and quail she had shot.

A client took me in her Rolls-Royce to an atelier in Greenwich Village to be measured for an American Indian jacket of white ponyskin with fringe and bead embroidery. I had admired a fringed coat she was wearing that Givenchy had copied for her from a similar jacket. "Now I know what to get you for Christmas," she said.

What she wanted from Santa Claus only her husband could provide. On Christmas morning, she looked out of her window and there on the lawn was an airplane, wrapped in blue ribbon, for commuting among their various homes.

I wore the jacket she gave me skiing in Austria; I felt like a bird slaloming down the slopes. Another client saw me and wanted a jacket like mine for herself. The next time she was in New York, we went in her Rolls-Royce to the shop in the Village. "Where do you get all these women with big cars?" the owner asked me.

As I have indicated, my passion for sports has opened many doors. For many years, I skied in the Austrian Tyrol. At the Gasthof Post in Lech, Queen Juliana of Holland remarked on the haircut I had given the owner, just out of camaraderie for another skier and hunter, and that resulted in my coiffing my first crowned head of Europe.

I met several clients skiing at nearby Zurs. Allyn Urbahn introduced me to her husband, Maximilian, a noted architect. After he and I got to talking about hunting and fishing, he invited me to the Dutchess Valley Rod and Gun Club in Pawling, New York.

Casting for trout is my favorite kind of fishing and it was a thrill to be at the club when Charles César Ritz, the hotelier and one of the world's leading fly-fishermen, was a guest. He was then eighty years old, small and gray-haired with a pencil moustache and a handshake like a truck driver's. Charles Ritz had presence. He carried a name that the *New York Times* described as "probably the most elegant four-letter word in the English language," had been a friend of Ernest Hemingway's and had himself written books on fly fishing. Once a year he gave a dinner at the Paris Ritz for a group of top fishermen whom he had organized as the International Fario Club (named after a species of trout).

Naturally, everyone was in awe of him that afternoon in Pawling. After lunch, we moved from the clubhouse to the trout stream that flowed behind the houses of Max Urbahn and another architect, Robert Jacobs, to watch Charles Ritz demonstrate his high-speed, high-line casting technique. Questions and Cognac followed. "Here's a little bit of water from France," he said, offering me a drink from his bottle.

That's what I love about sports. You talk about your rod or your gun, you share your knowledge and show what you can do. The sport is the common denominator, the equalizing agent. If you're good, it doesn't matter what you do or what your background is.

True, the first time I was with John Swearingen and the heads of five oil companies at White Lake, Louisiana, I felt like a little boy. I could tell by the way they looked at me, especially the ones from Texas, that they were thinking, Who is this guy? What's he doing here? When it came out that I was a hairdresser, I sensed there was a little fence between them and me.

It was lowered a bit after I got my first quota of ducks very quickly. Then the gun of one of the Texans jammed and he panicked. "Give me the gun, I know what to do," I said, taking responsibility for a potentially dangerous situation. He thanked me profusely and I knew I had his confidence.

When I tied for the highest score with Mr. Swearingen in shooting clay pigeons, I became a good old boy. They were intrigued that I held my gun at the waist until ready to fire, when I lifted it, which is more difficult than keeping it at shoulder position. Where did I learn to shoot? they asked. Where had I hunted?

In Austria, for chamois and fox and wild rooster; in England and Cuba for pigeon, I told them. In Alaska, I got a bear on my second shot, and also a wolf and wolverine. A client had asked me to keep her husband company because he couldn't find anyone to go hunting with him in Alaska.

With Mr. Swearingen's friends, the talk was mostly about hunting and very little about business. Of course, they asked me the inevitable question, "How come you're not gay?" So I asked them, "How is it that you are supposed to be competitors in the oil business, Amoco, Exxon, Conoco and so on, and here you are all together, good buddies?" They laughed and said, "Business is something else. We may fight, but we love to see each other."

The only question they had about my business concerned Frank Sinatra. Was it true that his hair transplant was so painful that he decided to wear wigs instead? These big industrialists were interested in the same small things as everyone else.

No matter how close I have become with prominent people in a social context, I always remember to keep my place. I know who I am and who they are, where I came from and where I wanted to go—to the top of my profession. To maintain that position, I must be accepted by the rich, the famous and the powerful, just as it's essential for me to display power once in a while, such as the ability to get a good table at Le Cirque and La Grenouille.

I confess to having goose pimples when I met some of the great ones, especially great artists like Isaac Stern, the violinist, whose wife, Vera, is a client. But I never let any of it go to my head. Even when I was with the duke and duchess of Windsor, I said to myself, When you get right down to certain natural functions, everyone is the same, even a king.

I enjoy a taste of the high life now and then, but I don't make the mistake of some in the fashion and beauty world who think they can live like their customers and be one of them. When the party's over, I'm happy to go back where I belong, to polish my own gun, clean the fish I caught and experience the joy of making women happy.

6

HAIRDRESSER

In a chest of drawers in my apartment is a collection of envelopes filled with locks of hair. It began with a cutting of my mother's hair, to which I added snips from clients I particularly liked. I told myself these bits of tresses might come in handy for chignons, but down deep I know I wanted to possess something uniquely their own.

"A woman's hair is her most precious possession and you must remember that she is entrusting it to you," Guillaume used to tell me. In exchange for this trust, the hairdresser is obliged to make the woman feel prettier, more desirable, to bring out her individuality. And to do this, he must give something from his heart. "If you can't give your love to the work, don't become a hairdresser," Guillaume said.

It's the same as a musician. The feeling in his fingers has to originate in his heart.

I really hate the word *hairdresser*. It sounds to me like a butcher, which some hairdressers indeed may be. A good hairdresser is a sculptor who works with living material and a vision of what he wants to accomplish.

The greater hairdressers were designers like the *hauts couturiers*. The evidence is in the lasting quality of their creations: Antoine's La Garçonne and Coup de Vent (windblown) hairdos; Guillaume's pageboy, his short and curly L'Aiglon (after Napoleon's son who never ruled) and La Lionne; Alexandre's artichoke; and the geometric cut of Vidal Sassoon.

Between a hairdresser and a client there can develop over a long period of time a closeness like that of a couple who can read each other's thoughts. The creation of the hairdo becomes a mutual endeavor, a joyful experience.

I shall never forget the time Mrs. Rodman de Heeren asked me to her Manhattan town house to comb her hair for an official dinner sponsored by the Brazilian government. Aimée de Heeren was one of the leading Parisian hostesses I had known at Guillaume's, a belle from Rio de Janeiro married to a descendant of the Wanamakers of Philadelphia.

Before going to her home, I went to a reception where I was introduced to Princess Margaret of Britain by René Moulard, in whose London salon I had once worked. René was part of the princess's entourage on a visit to the U.S. When I told him of my appointment, he said, "Let's go together. Madame de Heeren is my client, too."

She was delighted to see René and rang for the butler to bring champagne. On the way upstairs to her bedroom, we paused to admire the extensive collection of paintings by Paul Helleu, the portraitist of French society early in the century, that were hung throughout the mansion.

We reminisced as René and I started to set her hair together; he placed the rollers on one side, I on the other. After we had finished, she reminded him of another coiffure he had done for her to wear to a ball in London, whereupon he undid our work and re-created it. "Ah, but, Marc, remember how you did my hair for that party in Paris?" she said. So it was my turn. René and I stayed past midnight, setting and resetting her hair, drinking champagne and nibbling on smoked salmon and pâté. Madame de Heeren never did get to that dinner.

"The coiffeur is the second most important man in a woman's life," Kitty Carlisle Hart, New York City chairman of the New York State Council on the Arts, once wrote in my autograph book. It was a very thoughtful tribute coming from this TV personality and public citizen, considering how gifted she is at doing her own hair. She comes to Monsieur Marc just to have it trimmed.

But what she wrote points up the advantage—an unfair edge, I sometimes think—that men have had in the hairdressing profession since the time of the great Léonard. Before Léonard of Versailles, women's hair was mostly dressed by other women.

There are many talented female hairdressers: Francine and Catherine at Monsieur Marc, to name but two. My clients who winter in Palm Beach swear by Margrit on Worth Avenue. But few women have carved an important niche in the history of coiffure. In the Fifties and early Sixties in Rome, Alba and Francesca were brilliant with long hair, which they worked into fanciful braids. The two who left an imprint on that period were Maria and Rosy Carita of the Faubourg Saint Honoré. These sisters from Toulouse brought back the fashion for wigs, and with their use of oversize rollers and the revived technique of back-combing or teasing, they were responsible more than anyone else, I say with mixed feelings, for the bouffant hairdo.

Many women leave the business to marry and have families, and it may be that those who stay lack the talent for self-promotion. Certainly, some women feel that a hairdresser of their own sex is more understanding, more sensitive to their feelings and needs, less intimidating than a man.

But many women prefer male hairdressers, possibly because they are used to taking orders and receiving the authoritative word on any subject from men. Some, it seems obvious, like to feel a certain sexual current between themselves and those to whom they entrust their hair.

I got a lot of laughs out of the 1975 Warren Beatty movie *Shampoo*, even though its depiction of the hairdresser as stud was grossly exaggerated. I think even less of the recent image of an unkempt individual in leather and chains acting like a rock star with his hairbrush and blow dryer.

But it is true that a woman who is feeling miserable about her love life or who just likes to keep in practice as a flirt at all times may get ideas about a male hairdresser. From time to time, the manicurists are asked, "Does Monsieur Marc go out with clients?" Answer: Once in a while he goes to lunch with clients who are old friends, or to dinner with clients and their husbands.

I find that husbands sometimes need assurance. Once when I went to comb a client at her apartment, her husband scolded her for letting me see her in a filmy peignoir. I told him I had just come from a fashion show where, as is the hairdresser's lot, I not only had to do the models' hair but help some of them in and out of the clothes. "In my business, I'm sorry to say, we get so accustomed to half-naked women that we don't even notice," I said. I hoped he believed me.

There have been some awkward situations, such as the time a jet setter with a home on every continent received me in her Manhattan apartment in late afternoon wearing a see-through nightgown, a bottle of Dom Perignon cooling in a silver bucket on her dressing table. I combed her hair, then we drank champagne and talked. I managed to keep the conversation going until the telephone rang. It was her husband calling. I whispered *au revoir* and left.

More than one client has said to me, "I prefer to come to you than go to a psychiatrist. You at least have a sense of humor and I always leave here feeling better." Maybe it's the physical contact that makes some women unburden themselves with their hairdressers as they would never dare to do with their friends. Or perhaps they feel vulnerable when their hair is wet and uncombed, almost as though they were stripped for a doctor's examination and feel that the person who sees them regularly in such condition is the one to whom they can confide their innermost thoughts. They know that whatever they tell me will go no further.

"I'm due for another lift," an aging beauty used to admit to me once a year, gazing at her reflection in the mirror with coldly critical eyes. After so many visits to the surgeon, her face became a mask.

I hear a lot of harmless gossip, much of it picked up from newspaper and magazine columns I don't read even when they have something nice to say about me. I figure sooner or later someone will bring me the news. Women tell me funny stories, and tragic ones that make me marvel at the human tolerance for pain. It's only when I'm asked for advice that I feel uncomfortable. Should she call her old boyfriend who's in town? She's really crazy about a guy, but since he's involved with her best friend, would it be wrong for her to go after him? When I figure I'm only being used as a sounding board, I try to make light of the matter. "Why not? You only live once," I might say. Or, quoting Oscar Wilde, "The only way to get rid of a temptation is to yield to it."

To the ones who persist in treating me as though I were Ann Landers (an attractive woman from Chicago whose hair I have combed when she visited New York), I say, "I can't help you. I've never been married." I could add that some of the tales I've heard over the years may have discouraged me from going to the altar. What I usually say, though, is "Why don't you give him another chance? After a rainy day, sunshine always follows."

Lately, successful businesswomen have been asking me, "Where am I going to meet a real man, a man as strong and successful as I am?"

A woman like that may not face up to the fact that she puts men off. She meets a guy, invites him to her apartment for a drink. She lets him know she paid for every stick of furniture, every objet d'art. It's all hers, just like her mink coats, her house in the country, her trips on the Concorde. She doesn't realize she's advertising, "I don't need a man."

That may be true, and there's a positive side to it. As Hebe Dorsey wrote in her column in French *Vogue*, "Marriage is démodé. After years, the woman who works has acquired a status, a place in society she never had." Hebe ought to know. She's made a place for herself in international society as a single woman with a fascinating career, and she's also had many amours.

What often happens with a self-made businesswoman is that she becomes so powerful that she won't listen to a man unless he has more money than she has, and then she runs after him.

Most men don't want to compete with a woman who acts like another man. They want someone warm, delicate, lovable. This doesn't mean a woman shouldn't be successful. It's just that after business hours, she should forget the office and go back to being a woman. And not talk business. Maybe it's the novelty of making good in a man's world, but some women are so engrossed in their work that they have no other subject of conversation. No man wants to feel that the most important thing in a woman's life is her business, even if that's the case. Women resent it when that shoe is on the other foot.

Despite the tales of woe a hairdresser hears, it's fair to say that many women talk only of their concern for pleasing the men in their lives. If there's one thing I have become convinced of after a lifetime in a feminine environment, it's that every woman longs for a *grand amour*. She never gives up hope of finding a great lover who will put her in seventh heaven. Some are lucky. But others want money and power, too, thinking they can have it all. Unfortunately, very rich, very powerful men can get in the habit of only offering material things to women. But it's not just by buying gifts that a man proves his love. It's by constantly making a woman feel desired, and that means being attentive, noticing when she has a new dress or coiffure.

Most hairdressers find that after a client is divorced, her husband's next wife also becomes a client. Strangely enough, she turns out to be the same type as the first. Whether this means she also has the same taste in coiffure or whether by coincidence, Monsieur Marc has had the patronage of more than one wife of such noted men as Winthrop Rockefeller, onetime governor of Arkansas, and Prince Stanislas Radziwill, brother-in-law of President John F. Kennedy through his marriage to Lee Bouvier.

Prince Radziwill's first wife, the elegant Grace, was already Lady Dudley of London when I had the pleasure of doing her hair at Guillaume's, a pleasure that continues when she visits New York.

Something of a record may have been set when Ruth, Rita and Jaquine Lachman, the first, second and third wives of Charles Lachman, cofounder with Charles Revson of Revlon, Inc., simultaneously had their hair done at Monsieur Marc.

Beauty salons are like stage sets on which dramas and comedies are performed nonstop six days a week. The backdrops are important in communicating an ambience to the clientele. A certain Belle Époque bordello look that was *le dernier cri* in the Sixties has given way to a high-tech or scientific-laboratory decor. The personality of the owner is less a factor than that of the staff these days as salons have been bought up by large cosmetic companies or chain operators. One trend of which I disapprove is for hairdressers to wear blue jeans. When a woman comes to be made stylish, she doesn't expect a truck driver to do her hair. My working uniform is a pair of dark trousers; a custom-made dress shirt in a solid pastel, check or stripe; and a dark sleeveless, collarless jacket, one of a collection I had made by Kilgour, French & Stanbury in London.

After more than twenty years at the same address and under the same proprietorship, Monsieur Marc is something of a rarity in New York. The salon has gone through several transformations, always keeping to a tone of *chic negligé* that is expressed in my hairdos and my attitude about fashion. For a long while it was country French, at one point like a hunting lodge when I hung the stuffed head of a caribou I had shot in Alaska over my work station. My hunting clients were enraptured; those who deplore the killing of animals for sport were dismayed. At present, the mood is serene simplicity with pale apricot walls covered with Léonor Fini watercolors.

Ici on parle français, but not exclusively. Spanish—both Castilian and Latin-American—Russian, Finnish, Hungarian and various American dialects are spoken, too, at Monsieur Marc.

Some new clients accustomed to arrogance in salons that have celebrities among their patrons express surprise at the warmth and friendliness. As one client of many years described it, Monsieur Marc is like a neighborhood café on the Left Bank of Paris where everyone knows *le patron* and his family of employees, where the regulars rule the roost but strangers are made welcome.

Madame Marcelle, the doyenne of the checkroom, is *mon petit coin de Paris,* or little corner of Paris, as I call her, a maternal woman with an optimistic philosophy of life. Madame Simone, her alternate, has a place on my list of the most elegant women I have known. The widow of a Tour de France bicycle-racing champion, she once owned a nightclub in Paris. Edna Nielson has a real New Yorker's view of life.

Like customers in a café or club, some come to sit quietly and anonymously, others to see and to be seen. One woman who feels it necessary to impress anyone within earshot announces distinctly, "I just got off the Concorde." In the early Seventies, a client from London used to call out as she crossed the threshold of the salon, "I just came on the jumbo."

Alicia and Marianne at the reception desk are accustomed to being asked rather bluntly, "Who do you have that's famous right now?" or "When is [a certain noted client] booked for her next appointment?"

Although some women are utterly faithful to one hairdresser, others are quite fickle. They wander from salon to salon, not so much because they are dissatisfied with the service they receive but because they want to be identified with celebrities even if in such a remote degree as patronizing the same hairdresser—or restaurant, or wearing the same designer clothes. If this fills some psychological need, well and good, but they should observe the rules of salon etiquette. Despite the open spacing of the modern beauty salon, most women regard it as a place of refuge where they go to have personal services performed. It is unfair to a woman who happens to be famous to have her hour of privacy disrupted by a celebrity-hunter.

It is a simple rule of courtesy not to barge into the checkroom when the door is closed, indicating that a woman is inside undressing. I recall a woman doing just that and after a few minutes emerging to announce as though she had won first prize in a lottery, "I just talked to *her.*" She had trapped one of the B.P.'s whose photograph she had just seen in W.

It's amazing how long it takes for hair to dry when celebrities are at the salon. One hunter used to stake out a position under a dryer facing the manicure table at which Charlotte Ford was having her nails done. When

Mrs. Reagan visits the salon, some women cannot be budged from under the dryers lining the path to the private room in back.

The command center of the beauty salon is the reception desk. Here requests for appointments are taken on the telephone, clients are welcomed as they arrive and directed to the shampoo room or to the colorists. The reception desk monitors the flow of activity and presents the clients with their bills.

It is the receptionist's responsibility to guard against overbooking. Clients get angry if they have to wait, particularly between the shampoo and the styling, or between the dryer and the combing, because they feel helpless to do anything about their plight. But there are clients who bypass the reception desk and demand to speak directly to the hairdresser, pleading to be accommodated. "I don't mind waiting if you'll just do my hair for this very important party," they wheedle. But once they arrive at the salon, their patience evaporates and they want to be taken immediately. Unavoidable delays are caused by clients coming late, or when I have three in a row who were booked for styling and suddenly decide they want their hair cut as well. A salon is no more able to achieve a clockwork rhythm than a doctor or dentist's office.

Another matter of salon conduct. A woman will warn the hairdresser repeatedly not to cut too much. Two weeks later, she upbraids him for cutting too little and objects to being charged for a second trim.

Another woman washes her hair at home before going to the salon for a set and complains when she is charged for a shampoo. Would she take her own steak to a restaurant? I wonder.

How much should one tip at a hairdresser? This is a worrisome subject for many women, particularly when visiting a salon in a strange city for the first time. Customs vary from city to city and country to country. In some European countries, service and value-added tax are now incorporated in the bill without being listed in detail. When in doubt, ask the receptionist what is expected.

As in a restaurant, you should tip according to how pleased you are with the service. I realize that this is a subjective matter. Some people are more accustomed to demonstrating satisfaction than others. I had clients who were sisters, married to two of the wealthiest men in America. One was stingy, the other generous.

From the standpoint of the person who performs a service, there is no such thing as too big a tip, but, objectively speaking, women who are not in the business world are notorious undertippers or overtippers in comparison with men. Whether this is a matter of insecurity or ignorance, I have never figured out.

A reliable formula is to tip in a beauty salon as you would in a restaurant: 15 to 20 percent of the total bill, dividing it among those who served you according to the quality of the service. In New York, these would be considered fair tips in a topflight salon: $1 for the shampoo, $1.50 for a manicure, $3 to $5 to the hairdresser for a set, $15 for a permanent and set, $5 to $10 for color depending on the length of time involved, 50 cents to $1 for the checkroom and for the hairdresser's assistant.

At Christmas, regular clients usually remember those who served them during the year with a small personal gift or with money.

Owners of salons are usually not tipped. If you are not sure of the status of the hairdresser, ask the receptionist.

STANDING UP TO THE HAIRDRESSER CAN TAKE A KIND OF COURAGE. That was the headline above a story in the *New York Times* reporting tales of arrogance and cruelty, including one about a stylist who told a client, "If it wasn't for me you'd still look like Brooklyn." A French hairdresser put down a social leader with the comment "You look like Louis XV." Being an educated woman, she knew enough to take offense.

Hairdressers who take out their frustrations on clients are either neurotic or badly trained, or both. The message driven home in my apprenticeship was this: The hairdresser exists to please the client, no matter who she is.

The word *plaire*—to please—is ingrained in French sensibility. A Frenchwoman is born knowing her mission is to please men, something no amount of feminist consciousness will erase. A Frenchman is aware that his success as a lover depends on his pleasing women. In my profession, the objective is the same. When interviewers ask me if I consider myself the number one hairdresser, I answer, "The number one hairdresser is the one who pleases the client." If she isn't satisfied, then no matter how artistic he may be, he has failed.

Some women are afraid to assert themselves with hairdressers, doctors, lawyers and haughty maître d's. They cringe, seeking their approval, when it should be the other way around.

Too many hairdressers forget they are working on human beings. They put their creations first. Anyone who tries to impose his coiffure on a client—regardless of whether it is becoming to her—is not a hairdresser by my definition. The greatest compliment I can be paid is for my client to be asked, "Who did your hair? You look beautiful."

More than any hairdresser of the postwar generation, Vidal Sassoon called attention to the importance of cut in coiffure. He brought the profession into the modern era with his blunt cut and his straight, very definite geometric style. Sassoon is an artist. But his design has suffered from mass production, and a generation of hairdressers who came after him know one thing—cut and blow dry. That's not hairdressing. That's wash and wear and let it all hang out.

It still takes an artist to create a style with his scissors and blower to suit an individual. He must remember he's working on a woman and that he should bring out her femininity. He has to consider her features and the quality of her hair. A geometric cut isn't becoming to someone with thick lips and a prominent nose. Gray hair cut in points is hardly flattering to a softening chinline. Straight hair and bangs don't suit everyone.

Not all hairdressers know how to use a hand dryer. Some of them just blow it against the hair instead of creating a coiffure with the dryer and a brush. Watch a hairdresser's eyes as he works. He should not be looking at the hair. He should be studying the woman's face to see where she needs width, whether he should make the hair a little looser. The brush can't be used the same way all around the head.

A blower only works well with certain types of hair. It's great for loosening up hair that has a strong wave; it keeps curly hair straighter a little longer. But it shouldn't be used on fine hair, because it doesn't give body, or on very coarse hair, which may look good when the client walks out of the salon, but the next day—pftt.

The blower is just one of those tools of the trade that go in and out of fashion. Like the scissors. Alexandre's were gold. Sassoon used small scissors and that's still the rage. I prefer medium scissors that feel well balanced in my hand. Mine are by Tondeon, a German manufacturer of surgical instruments. The crucial thing about the cutting tool is not its size but its sharpness.

One of the stars of Paris in the Fifties was Katia of the rue du Cirque. His salon was indeed a circus. He had more than a dozen pairs of scissors and he handled them like a juggler. He would strike a pair against the counter, throw it in the air with one hand, catch it in the other and start cutting. That was showmanship, but he was also an artist. You could spot a woman in the street who had been to Katia.

After World War II, Georges Hardy came up with the technique of cutting the hair after the shampoo while it was damp, and then drying it with an electric comb or a hand dryer to keep it straight and fluffy. Then followed the big rollers and the teasing and the spray. That was the worst period in modern coiffure. I'm opposed to teasing except in one situation—a woman with long straight hair wants a hairdo for that evening. Then you tease to give body and to help you work the hair.

Sassoon's geometric cut was a much-needed revolution against teasing and spray. Afterward, the blow-dry technique was revived in combination with the sculptured haircut. Nothing is new and nothing is applicable to every head of hair. What counts is the desire of the hairdresser to do his best for the client.

I insist on being introduced to a new client before she has her hair shampooed. I want to know who recommended her and what she has in mind. Right away, I try to imagine how I would like her to look if I were going out with her. This little game helps me to make her look more desirable. Most of the time I like to cut her hair dry so that I can see how it reacts in a natural state. Certain textures, however, are better cut wet.

I would rather the person who recommended her not be too enthusiastic. When a client tells her friend, "Monsieur Marc is a magician," it raises unrealistic expectations. I know I'm usually disappointed in a movie that had rave reviews.

Sometimes the woman who recommended her friend is a different type or has better hair. I can't say that to the new client when she looks at herself after the final combing and says, "It's nice but not exactly what I wanted." She was carrying the picture of her friend in her mind. It's wrong to try to look like someone else. You should try to find the best look for you.

I often get requests from new clients for "Nancy Reagan's hairdo." When I first opened the salon, women were asking for "Jackie's hairdo." Essentially, Mrs. Kennedy had a pageboy, which is a simple, set coiffure and much easier to do than the freer, very natural hairdos of today. Every styling is different from the one before and the one I shall do next.

A Washington socialite announced one day, "I don't want to look like Mrs. Paley anymore. I want to look like Mrs. Harriman." I controlled the urge to burst into laughter. She was a lusty southern woman in her thirties and it amazed me that she could believe for a moment she resembled Barbara Paley—that cool, refined great lady—or that she could come close to that storybook English beauty, Pamela Churchill Hayward Harriman, with her rose-petal skin and auburn windblown hair. I had coiffed Winston Churchill's former daughter-in-law for her sudden and very quiet wedding in 1971 to Averell Harriman, the multimillionaire and grand old man of the Democratic party.

Clearly, the Washingtonian was trying to tell me something, but as often happens in a dialogue between a woman and a hairdresser, the message was delivered in subconscious code. I decided she wanted a new man in her life and she thought a change of personality might help, with a change of hairdo as a means to that end.

Usually women are more straightforward. They'll say, "I'm bored with my hair. I want something different." It's healthy to want to change your look to something more up-to-date and I'll never understand why so many women resist change. A new hairdo isn't like a marriage. You can always go back to what you had or go on to something else if it doesn't satisfy you.

Of course, mistakes can be made. Farrah Fawcett, for example, completely destroyed her image when she cut her hair. I must admit this was an exception to my belief that cutting long hair usually improves a woman's looks.

It's frustrating for me when I know a woman will look better with a cut or a modification of color, such as adding highlights, and she rejects my choice. Then she goes on vacation to Paris or Rome and comes back with what I had suggested. Maybe she feels more relaxed or has met a new man. "Look what they did to me over there," she'll say. And I answer, "I'm so happy. I've been after you to do that for three years."

"You were right, Monsieur Marc," she'll answer.

When an elegant woman feels she has reached her top form with her hair, however, she usually stays with it. Mrs. Paley wore hers essentially with the same line all the years I knew her—short all around but a little longer on top to give height and fullness. She just switched the direction from one side to the other. Beatriz Patiño likes her hair smoothed back with a comb on each side. That's her style and she knows she would look ordinary if she changed it.

The line is what's important, like the silhouette of a dress. If it's most flattering, keep it. It can be varied, as I have done for my clients who are partial to La Lionne. With the blower or with my brush and fingers, I can loosen it up.

A new client may say to me, "Do whatever you want," but I sense she's fearful. I must win her confidence, establish contact before doing anything too radical, and so I go slowly the first time.

Sometimes a woman will show me a magazine photograph of a hairdo she likes. If I think it might be becoming to her, I go ahead. But if not, I try to tell her so, tactfully. "Do you mind accepting the truth from a stranger?" I might begin. "You look very intelligent to me. If I were to do that, then you would look like . . ." And I explain that her hair is too fine, her neck is too short, her face too full, or whatever reason the hairdo idealized on a model is not for her. I put my heart into my coiffures and I can feel when I'm doing beautiful work. So when a new client gives me orders, "This is the way I wear my hair. Do this and this and this," she kills 50 percent of my enthusiasm immediately. I'm not a superstar, but if I feel I can do better and she won't let me try, its discouraging. I do exactly as she tells me and when I finish combing her, I say, "Now let me tell you why you would have looked better if you had let me do it my way." Invariably, she'll say, "You should have insisted."

I had to teach her a lesson.

I see a woman in her early thirties sitting in the chair. She looks depressed. Her hair is dark, long and straight with bangs to the eyes. All the lines are pointing down. She tells me she is a journalist. I might have guessed. The women correspondents on the public-TV programs discussing world affairs wear such curtains of hair, like Juliette Greco made famous twenty years ago with a black turtleneck. I suppose they imagine that this Left Bank student look stamps them as being very smart. They want to be taken seriously, but meanwhile they would like us to remember that they are women. After they say something meaningful, they push the curtains away from their face.

"Let's just talk about what you want me to do today," I say. I don't pick up the scissors. I feel her scalp, and her hair, and I already know what I would like to do, but I wait to hear what she will give me.

"Don't you think bangs are good for me, to hide the lines in my fore-head?" she asks. "Why not?" I reply. "But in that case, you need some softness." All those straight lines are depressing. Her face is long and thin and so is her hair. I must create an optical illusion by giving her some width.

"You have a smile in your eyes but not in your face," I say. "I should like to cut your hair, not much. I'd like to leave hair around your neck, but if I give you some movement around your face, you will be much happier."

"I trust you," she says.

I cut her bangs, thinning them out and tapering the ends to get rid of that straight look of the Chinese doll. I cut the hair on the sides in little layers so that everything around the face is tapered, and cut the back only a little. She will still have enough hair to tie back in a ponytail if she wishes, or to make a chignon, or to wear loose, but the effect is of short hair in the front.

When I finish, the woman sitting in the next chair says, "I can't believe how different you look." All I have done was to remove that straight, hanging look that made her appear so sad. Because she feels happy, she is automatically going to smile.

A woman of twenty-seven tells me she has been working for four years in the foreign-exchange department of a bank in Wall Street. She sits in a large room with lots of people who keep their eyes on the computer termi-nals in front of them or on the display board on the wall. No one looks at her. She has asked for reassignment to a branch office of the bank, where she will be meeting the public.

"I feel plain and unattractive. I want to feel different," she says. She hopes a new hairdo will do it and she gives me carte blanche, but with one stipulation: The hairdo must be one she can keep up herself, one that will survive her going into the shower every morning.

She has a long, thin face, and ash-blond hair that is flat on top and hangs down the sides. A sad madonna.

"Your hair is straight and very fine. You need a permanent," I tell her. "We'll keep your hair about four inches all around but slightly tapered in back, full on top, full on the sides, a little longer toward the neckline." I cut her hair and then we give her a miniwave over the whole head. After the hair is rinsed, we put her under the Infra Rouge Lamp so that it dries almost as though she were sitting in the sun. It's a wonderful technique for someone with straight hair who wants to feel as though she has a natural curl. In the old days, she would have a permanent and it would come out tight and kinky. With a very light permanent like a miniwave and the natural drying under the lamp, her fine hair appears full and fluffy.

I then tell her to shake her head vigorously from left to right, as a woman does when she is saying no to a man. Everything should fall into place. I show her how to run her fingers through the hair, starting at the base of the neck and proceeding outward to fluff it after she washes it in the shower and dries it with a towel. It's a fun hairdo, good for a young working woman, for a woman who travels a lot. I give her a tip: If the hairdo looks a bit wilted, spray it lightly with water and shake the head as indicated before. *Voilà*, the new woman. She gives a gasp of delight and kisses me.

A society woman comes to me, recommended by an old client from Greenwich, Connecticut. "Do what you think best," she says, but I can tell by the flip hairdo she is wearing that she is used to having every hair in place. *Doucement*, I say to myself. The most I can do the first time is modify.

Her gray hair is thick and healthy, a bit wiry. "You should make the most of it," I say. The top is flat as a pancake. "Let's soften the front and loosen it a bit. We'll begin by reshaping the top a little and giving it a little body wave to get some fullness." She bites her lips. Do I see a tear in her eye? "I assure you I won't make the back short," I say. She relaxes a little. As long as a woman like that can have the feeling of long hair, she will take a chance. When she realizes how flattering it is, maybe next time I can cut the back a little, but I will always leave it longer than the sides. At a time in life when a woman's chin gets a bit soft, *ça meuble la nuque*—the added length in back decorates the nape of the neck.

The next week she returns and tells me her husband approves. I know I have scored a victory. She adds happily, "My friends asked me, 'What have you done to yourself? Have you had a lift?'

"I told them, 'I've been to Monsieur Marc.' "

7

HAIRDOS

If indeed fashion makes statements about individuals and the times they live in, as scholars say, then hairdos speak volumes. I often wonder, though, how many women realize what garbled messages they are sending.

Take, for example, the movie 10, which I felt had an important lesson for men. We see a beautiful woman and we'll do anything to go to bed with her. When we get her there, we discover there's nothing. It's like seeing a beautiful dish of strawberries, taking a bite and finding they have no taste.

But the message that got through to the short, heavyset women of America was "Braid your hair like Bo."

Here was a hairstyle originated in Egypt in the time of the Pharaohs, centuries later adopted by slaves in the American South. It was translated (offensively, some thought) for Anglo-Saxons in a film about a sexy young woman with perfect features against a background of sun and swimming.

To save my reputation, and the dignity of most of the women who asked for the Bo braid, I played stupid. "Sorry," I said, "I don't know how to do it." I didn't want them out in the world advertising that they got the hairdo at Monsieur Marc.

There's nothing wrong with wanting to look like someone else. Whether in the choice of career, style of life or image we wish for ourselves, we are all influenced by others. In matters of style, very few are capable of originality. Every era is stamped with the coiffures of a few popular idols: Marilyn Monroe in the Fifties, Jackie Kennedy in the Sixties, Farrah Fawcett-Majors in the Seventies, and, so far into the Eighties, Princess Diana.

Certain hairdos are artistic creations that reflect credit on the hairdresser or on the model or actress for whom they were designed. It can be fun to experiment with such coiffures, assuming you have a reasonable resemblance to the goddess who introduced it, but you should take care not to stay with it too long. Nothing dates a woman more than a hairdo that has lost its *raison d'être*. It constantly amazes me how women who are the first in their circle to wear a new fashion will cling to the coiffure of another generation.

Certain hairdos become perverted by usage, like any fashion over a period of time. Take Guillaume's pageboy, a classic, elegant coiffure inspired by the medieval youth in training for knighthood, with the hair turned under at the nape of the neck.

The page was undermined starting in the mid-Fifties by the oversize roller used in conjunction with back-combing or teasing and hair spray.

Women tend to become attached to the hairdos of their youth, as they do to the memory of the men they loved, and they refuse to let go. To be fair about it, some hairdressers won't let go, either. The teasing technique and the spray can are their mechanical security aids, the easiest way to appease the client who wants her coiffure to hold its set—in a windstorm, in bed, in the shower.

So it is that many women of all social and economic levels look as though they belonged in one of those time capsules buried at the opening of world's fairs to mark a particular era for posterity. Some of the leaders of fashion, high society and, above all, political life are not immune to this failing. How I should love to confiscate Prime Minister Margaret Thatcher's spray supply and then run my fingers through the Iron Lady's typically conservative hairdo to give it a less set appearance.

Here are some instances of *déja vu* or outdated coiffures that have a particularly tenacious hold on women's affections.

THE RAM OR MOUNTAIN GOAT

This is a perverted pageboy, swollen at the back of the head by teasing, swept under the earlobes like the horns of a male sheep and sprayed for eternity. Beware of running into it in the dark—you could break your fingers. Very popular with fashion-industry women of a certain age and with ladies from Florida and big cities west of the Hudson.

THE FLIP

Cousin to the ram except that the hair is flipped up instead of under. In its extreme versions, it reminds me of Salvador Dali's waxed handlebar moustache, so I also call it "the moustache." Upper-crust London turns the flip into a row of curls, a look that dates back to the Thirties.

The flip is a favorite of old New York society and the ladies from the North Shore of Long Island and Connecticut. I'm told that if I simply referred to them as WASPs, everyone would know what I mean, but it's almost impossible for a French-speaking person to pronounce the word.

Many of Mrs. Paley's friends, knowing they couldn't look like her, asked for the flip so they could look like Jackie Kennedy. From the moment she entered the White House, the Jackie look was mass-produced. The Paley look is very hard to duplicate.

These women are so devoted to the flip because it gives them a false sense of security, lets them feel well groomed at all times. With a good dose of spray, they need never worry about a hair out of place. Those who still do worry add those invisible hairnets that so impressed me on my first visit to America when I attended the Horse Show at Madison Square Garden. The women riders all wore pageboys under their black velvet hunting caps with those hairnets for extra precaution.

What have I got against the flip? Its rigidity. Today, hair should look freer and easier. And the wearers appear frozen in the mood of twenty years ago when their idol was a young woman of thirty. Jackie is now past fifty and she has developed another widely imitated habit—hooking one or both flips behind her ears for formal occasions when she wears jeweled earrings.

Another widely photographed devotée of the flip is Gloria Vanderbilt, the socialite fashion designer, who is now close to sixty. As she goes around the country promoting the jeans manufactured by Murjani under the Gloria Vanderbilt label, she gets across to the masses the impression that a coal-black flip, rice-white complexion, and rounded manner of speaking English spell class.

Since memories are seldom reliable, it is worthwhile to study old photographs to determine the validity and elegance of a style. In the early Sixties, the Jackie flip was a pretty hairdo most appropriate for the young wife of the president of the United States. The shape was moderate and the length of the hair was just below the earlobes.

As time went by, Jackie and her brunette followers let their hair grow. For her marriage to Aristotle Onassis in 1968, it was down to her shoulders, where it has more or less remained. From constant teasing, straightening and tinting, it has become a lank curtain.

Fine, curly hair like Mrs. Onassis's is very difficult to control. It kinks at the slightest humidity and resists the comb and brush. She looked charming as a senator's wife with short, curly hair, and it would become her now. She has chosen otherwise. Because of the stubborn curl, she has to let her hair grow fairly long and have it straightened so that it can look decent without having to go to the hairdresser every day.

I should like to see her give up the flip. A most attractive look for her would be to have her hair the same length all over, four to five inches at the most, set with big rollers and brushed back in a soft smooth line to give the illusion of long hair she seems to like.

BABY JANE'S LION MANE

My term for a style that has captivated the would-be blondes still rooted in the Sixties.

I did Jane Holzer's hair for her wedding in 1962, and what a lovely twenty-two-year-old bride she was. Later, Diana Vreeland, then editor of *Vogue*, spotted her in the audience at a fashion show in Paris and was captivated by her mass of blond hair, which reminded her of the mane of a young lion. If Guillaume's *La Lionne* was tousled with restraint, Baby Jane Holzer's was *sauvage*—wild. With Mrs. Vreeland's endorsement and the inspiration she provided the fashion press, Baby Jane Holzer became a celebrity. Tom Wolfe christened her the Girl of the Year 1964.

Today she lives quietly out of the publicity spotlight. It is doubtful that anyone younger than thirty-five, unless a student of the Sixties pop culture, remembers who she was. Only her trademark of wild golden hair lives on among women now twice twenty and more. It can still be sexy and elegant when the hair is natural-looking and clean, bouncy on the shoulders and not too *sauvage*. But a teased, shapeless mane, with coatings of gold atop layers of muddy beige or gray falling to the shoulder blades, is ludicrous.

Still more leftovers from the same era are the Brigitte Bardot ponytail and the George Washington, its New York society counterpart. Both are intended to accomplish the benefits of long hair and the neatness of short, and both lose their effectiveness when the wearer's chinline is no longer sharply defined. At that time, wearing the pulled-back style should be restricted to cleaning the house and digging in the garden.

THE SAUERKRAUT

An aberration of the Seventies. The loose, curly look of an unfinished permanent wave was adorable on a pert face like Diane Keaton's, an actress who in her film roles and off-screen life projected an image of a disconnected free spirit, a sweet neurotic. Most women who adopt the unkempt hairdo succeed only in looking as though they've lost their wits.

Naturally kinky hair, genuine Afro or otherwise, can be charming if carefully trimmed. Sonya Rykiel, the French designer of elegantly unstructured clothes, looks as though an electric current has just passed through her red frizzy hair, but this is an expression of a distinctive personality by a woman of proven taste.

THE NO HAIR LOOK

This look has, for some puzzling reason, been taken up by buyers and other women in the fashion industry who ought to know better. Neither young nor great beauties, they conceal their hair completely in turbans or children's berets. It takes a sensational face to be presentable without a frame. The impression these women leave is that they are recovering from a grave illness or would rather be practical than look attractive.

After John Z. DeLorean, the maverick automobile manufacturer, was arrested in Los Angeles on charges of drug conspiracy, his wife, the model Cristina Ferrare, flew to New York to have her luxuriant hair cut, and to buy a new wardrobe. The frustration in her life, the fear that her husband might go to jail, showed in the sharp, boyish hairdo. She felt herself a different woman.

I've never seen it fail. Women take their emotional crises out on their hair. When a client says, "Cut my hair," I know that something has happened. She has lost her husband, is angry with her lover, is looking for a new job. For whatever reason, she wants to signal a new beginning. The same may be true when she decides to let her hair grow, but because the process is slower, there is less urgency behind the decision. Boredom makes hair grow; shock prompts a haircut.

Because my preference is for shorter hair, I think it's a shame that cutting is still so often associated with sacrifice and punishment. That attitude is embedded in Western culture, which glorifies woman's hair as her crowning glory. In art and literature, the glory is in having lots of it. Eve in the Garden of Eden covered her nudity with hers. Rapunzel in the Grimm fairy tale unplaited her "beautiful long hair" for the prince to climb to her room.

Orthodox Jewish women hid their hair under wigs after marriage because it had erotic connotations. In painting and in film, a woman's hair, freed of its ribbons and pins, was let down in the boudoir for the pleasure of her lover.

During the nineteenth and early twentieth centuries, hard-pressed women sold their hair for money. In the O. Henry story "The Gift of the Magi," the young wife sells hers to buy her husband a Christmas gift. After Liberation in France, women who had consorted with German soldiers were shorn of their hair.

The pain associated with short hair may be meaningless in contemporary terms, but many women today are still convinced that only long hair can be sexy and feminine.

This belief shows up peculiarly among the women who are supposed to reject such attributes for themselves, the so-called liberated women of the 1980s. The business or professional woman who "dresses for success" in a pinstriped man-tailored suit and leaves her hair loose and flowing to her shoulder blades, or in a lacquered flip at the shoulders, is sending a mixed signal. Is she saying, "I want it both ways—to be treated equally in a man's world, but I don't want anyone to forget I'm a seductive woman"? Or is she saying, "I'm confused about who I am"?

This confusion is particularly noticeable among television newswomen, who are supposed to be among the most articulate and knowledgeable of their sex. They tend to have the most trouble controlling their hair. Barbara Walters seems to flounder as to style and color. In contrast, male correspondents and anchor men seem to know exactly what image they wish to project—mellow, investigative, wise, dashing—and which skilled hair stylist to patronize.

Teen-age girls let their hair grow to announce that they consider themselves women. Snip an inch off and they dissolve in tears. Long past adolescence, women who are not terribly sure of themselves take refuge in long hair. They say it's easier to arrange, that it assures them of their femininity. Long hair alone will not make a woman feminine.

What most women don't realize is that long hair is harder to maintain. You can run your hand through short hair, brush and fluff it, and it looks presentable. Long hair must be shiny (Rapunzel's "shone like gold") or else it can look like witch's locks. Long hair must be very clean, fluffy, voluptuous; it must have vitality and bounce.

I was asked to create "a million-dollar hairdo" for Brooke Shields for a Wella promotion using Harry Winston jewels. Her hair is long and thick and therefore requires an hour and a half to dry. Time was running short; when she came out from under the dryer at the Monsieur Marc salon, I brushed her hair but decided to do the braiding and insert the jewels after we arrived at Regine's, where the press conference was to be held. Since the distance between the salon and the nightclub is only six blocks, we went on foot. She went ahead with the Wella representative and I walked behind, with her mother, mesmerized by the bouncy movement of her hair. With each step Brooke took, her hair went boom, boom, boom, boom. Down Madison and over to Park; boom, boom, boom.

Brooke Shields was a healthy sixteen-year-old girl. It is very unusual for hair to retain its lively qualities past the age of thirty-five. The years take their toll in air pollution; the chemical wear and tear of permanent waving and straightening; drying from sun, chlorine and too frequent use of the blower; and individual physical deterioration. Lyn Revson was an exception to the rule; her hair was almost a miracle of nature. But she gave it scrupulous care with brushing, conditioning and a process called "brûlage"; strands of hair are twisted from the crown like a rope so the split ends emerge, and they are burned off with a candle. It's a technique best left to professionals if you don't want to set your hair on fire.

A man sees a lovely creature ahead of him on the street. He is attracted by her long bouncing hair, by her gait, her figure, the movement of her hips in her snug pants, her fine silk shirt and the little leather bag swinging from her shoulders.

He quickens his step, he draws even with her and steals a look at her face. Not twenty, not thirty, but a woman of experience. He feels disappointed.

Many women won't accept the facts of aging, that their faces and bodies change, that what was appropriate in a hairstyle or a clothing fashion when they were in their teens or twenties is less attractive when they are mature. Long hair exerts a downward pull that is unflattering to a face already feeling the gravity of years. Even mannerisms should synchronize with chronological age. Pushing aside a curtain of hair as she talks is cute in a wide-eyed youngster, annoying in an adult of forty.

By my definition, hair is long when it touches the shoulders; beyond that is out-of-bounds for a woman of experience. A good length for the woman who wants the feeling and versatility of long hair is from four to five inches all around, covering the ears and the nape of the neck. With that amount of hair, she can wear it brushed back with fullness framing the face, straight with bangs, or piled up with curls on top, a French twist or a chignon.

This length serves Hebe Dorsey's need for a hairdo that looks good eighteen hours a day, seven days a week. As correspondent of the *International Herald-Tribune* and columnist for French *Vogue*, Tunisian-born Hebe commutes between her home in Paris and her home-away-from-home, New York. She is an active journalist, partygiver and guest in both cities. Her copper-colored hair is thick and stubbornly curly; to keep it manageable, she really has no choice but to go for length. Hebe's trademark is a long version of La Lionne, not the least *sauvage* but elegantly controlled so that the top layers camouflage the wiry curls underneath.

Hebe's mentor, Eugenia Sheppard, keeps her pale blond hair short, in proper proportion to her doll-size figure. A short woman with flowing locks looks unbalanced. Eugenia likes the feeling of naturally curly hair she can have with a miniwave. After her shampoo, she sits under the Infra Rouge Lamp while Carlos shapes the line with his fingers.

Another petite woman who looks elegant and impeccably groomed at all times with short hair is Joan Raines, associated with her mother in the Seventh Avenue firm Adele Simpson, Inc. Mrs. Raines travels a great deal, taking the pulse of fashion in the U.S. and Europe and presenting the Simpson design image to the public. To play up her arresting feature, slanting blue-green eyes in a tiny face, I keep her hair one to one and a half inches long on the sides, two inches on the crown to give a little height and proportionate volume.

On balance, I prefer short hair because it's easy to care for—and young-looking at any age. When a woman cuts her hair, she feels younger. Antoine more or less invented the short coiffure in 1909 when he was faced with the task of transforming a forty-five-year-old actress, Eva Lavallière, into an eighteen-year-old girl for a stage role. He did it by bobbing her hair, explaining that he was inspired by Joan of Arc, who went to the stake at nineteen, and that moreover a small head looks younger than a massive one. That's as true now as ever.

One can vary short hair in an amazing number of ways—with bangs, with a postiche and with skillful brushing.

By increasing the volume of curls on her usual La Lionne hairdo, I was able to give Betsy Bloomingdale a properly romantic look to go with the bustled Dior dress she wore to the La Belle Époque party at the Metropolitan Museum of Art.

For a cocktail party and a ball that Paige Rense, editor in chief of *Architectural Digest, Bon Apétit* and *Geo,* was attending in New York, I set her short blond hair in rollers with pincurls on the sides, and, in the brushing, twisted a few sections on both sides to give an illusion of long hair swept up à la Gibson Girl.

Layered cutting gives Nancy Reagan's short hair an illusion of length, height and waviness. For very formal occasions, she can add a chignon or a braid framing the back of her neck.

In the summer of 1982, the French fashion houses went crazy about the *hérisson* or porcupine hairdo, which spread like wildfire to the New York models and the young hip crowd. It was a punk-and-leather look with the hair cut very short on the sides and standing up like quills on top. I interpreted it with a dignified look for Mrs. Reagan to wear one evening a few weeks later; I brushed her hair back smoothly on the sides and on top to the center of the crown to look full but not spiky. Absolutely no teasing, just my fingers, brush and comb. I felt as though I were making a flower arrangement.

In the fall, London took up the Lulu hairdo that Louise Brooks had worn in the 1928 German film *Pandora's Box.* The publication of her autobiography, *Lulu in Hollywood,* made Miss Brooks a cult figure and revived interest in the short, symmetrical hairdo with bangs.

One Lulu can yield three hairdos.

For the basic Lulu, the hair is parted in the center, combed from the crown straight down on the sides and cut just below the earlobes and in bangs to cover the forehead, leaving the eyebrows visible.

Variation One: With the part moved to the side to give a diagonal slant to the bangs, the hair is brushed back in a windblown effect, à la Princess Di.

Variation Two: With small rollers or a curling iron, set the hair in curls.

A word about bangs: Heavy bangs are more effective on brunettes than blonds, and should be avoided entirely by women with strong features. Bangs that hide the eyebrows are the sexiest, but only if the face below is delicate.

Despite what I've said about the youthful effect of short hair, an extremely short coiffure can be aging in its way. Just as it takes youth to carry off lots of hair successfully, a woman has to be young and sexy-looking to get away with a boy's haircut.

What then is the correct length? The answer is a matter of proportion, of hairdo in relation to body height and width, and of compatibility with facial characteristics and quality of the hair. To help you decide what is best for you:

• Study yourself in a full-length mirror. A short woman cannot wear long hair unless she doesn't mind looking like an inverted mop on top of a broom handle.

• Study yourself in profile. The hair in back should not be cut higher than the line of the chin. With a short hairdo, the neck needs a little fringe. The most becoming length in back is one to one and a half inches of cover for the neck.

• Never let a hairdresser shave your neck. Remember that the neck is one of the most sensuous parts of the body. The nape should always look kissable. Who would want to plant his lips on sandpaper?

• A face that is less than perfect needs some hair for a frame all around. Unless you have delicate features and the neck of a ballerina, avoid chignons and other styles in which the hair is pulled back tightly from the brow.

• Height is flattering to a mature face. A flat top adds years just as much as a curtain of hair hanging on the sides.

• Brush hair away from the face to give prominence to small features; brush forward to make a large face appear smaller.

• A good haircut shows the shape of the head and is flattering from all angles.

• Another test of a good haircut: Shake your head vigorously, leaning forward and then back. The hair should fall back into place.

• Go easy on spray. Hair should move as the body moves.

• To cut down on static electricity in winter or in very dry climates, spray hair lightly, then comb or brush. Use a tortoiseshell or wooden comb, never plastic.

For healthier, livelier hair:

• Shampoo as often as necessary to keep hair looking clean and smelling fresh. Daily shampoos are not harmful if one soaping is used.

• If your hair is very fine, shampoo two days before a big event. On the day of the party, have it set after simply wetting.

• A conditioner to apply at home: Apply three to four beaten egg yolks to the hair, rubbing with a circular motion, cover with a hot towel for twenty minutes, then rinse with lukewarm water. Warning: A hot shower will produce scrambled eggs.

• Prolonged exposure to sunlight can be damaging to the hair. At the beach, tie a scarf around your head. If you must go bareheaded, apply a little baby oil or sunscreen lotion or cream to the hair as well as to the skin. Shampoo afterward.

• Salt water and chlorine are also harmful. Shampoo after swimming. Test by rubbing fingers against the hair from the crown down to the sides. If it feels as though the hair is putting up resistance, it's clean. A smooth, slippery sensation means another soaping is in order.

• Brush your hair every morning to stimulate the circulation of blood to the scalp and again before bedtime to remove the dust and dirt accumulated during the day. Don't be afraid to loosen the set with brushing. You won't, but brushing will make the hair shinier.

• Use a blow dryer sparingly, and not at all on fine, dry or permanent-waved hair. If you do use one, remove moisture first with a towel and hold the dryer at least two inches away from the head. Use only brushes with pure boar bristles; Mason and Pearson and Kent are good brand names.

• Overzealous straightening can rob hair of its life. A two-step straightening, a week apart, is preferable to one concentrated treatment.

At one point or another in their lives, most women probably feel dissatisfied with the color of their hair. Brunettes think they might rather be blondes because gentlemen prefer them or because blondes are supposed to have more fun. Both points are debatable.

The myth of the dumb blonde has been debunked by such hardheaded businesswomen as Mary Wells Lawrence, founder of the Wells Rich Greene advertising agency, and Mary Cunningham of Seagram's, who figured in the take-over battles of Bendix Corporation, her husband, William Agee's, company.

At times blondes long to be brunettes, for dark-haired women have captured men's attention and enjoyed enduring adoration from the public—Cleopatra, Elizabeth Taylor and Jacqueline Kennedy Onassis, to mention a few.

Rarest of all are the redheads, supposedly hot-tempered and mercurial. You can tell the genuine ones by their freckles.

Why shouldn't a woman change her hair color? It's a free country. She can change her name if she doesn't like it. Yet despite all the openness about personal lives today, there's a certain reluctance among American women, which I fail to understand, to admit using artificial means to beauty and a youthful look. Some women will do anything to conceal it. Whether out of perfectionism or a desire to delude their lovers, some go so far as to match their private parts to their heads, a procedure that requires utmost care since body hair is more porous than the rest.

Never, never say dye, I tell my staff. The word has a fatal connotation. Madeleine, Irene and Maya are the colorists at Monsieur Marc and what they do should not be referred to as dyeing hair but as adding color, improving color or changing color. A woman doesn't go gray; her hair loses color.

Tremendous advances have been made in products and techniques for hair coloring, and the work of the consumer movement in the U.S. and the Federal Food and Drug Administration has greatly lessened the danger to health. Still, in changing the color of her hair, a woman runs a psychological risk of being disappointed in her appearance after a do-it-herself attempt or at the hands of an inept professional.

Fewer women hope to alter their personalities through a drastic change of hair color than want to enliven dull-looking hair or to cover the first signs of graying, which throw them into a panic.

Whatever the reason, unless she moves cautiously and gives consideration to what she is doing, a woman may end up looking vulgar rather than alluring. The best way to start is by buying or borrowing a wig and wearing it for a few days to test the reactions of herself and her friends.

"Nature needs artifice, but art should imitate nature." That was Guillaume's philosophy about coloring. I say, Help nature along if you must, but be natural about it. You can never go wrong by sticking close to what God gave you.

Rule Number One: Go by your eyes and eyebrows. A woman with dark eyes and eyebrows should not try to be blond. She will only look ordinary. Many Oriental women, particularly Japanese, yearn to be curly blonds. The strong, stiff texture of their hair resists the bleach and the permanent-wave lotion, resulting in reddish-brown sauerkraut not half as attractive as their naturally straight black hair.

Rule Number Two: A natural head of hair has *nuance*, subtle shades within the same tone. So should hair that is artificially colored. Monotone is uninteresting. Avoid one unrelieved color unless you are striving for a painted look.

Rule Number Three: Lighter colors around the face are softer. A brunette should go for light brown highlights, a fading redhead for a richer tone. Blondes whose hair has lost luster must accept a darker base tone with paler highlights.

Blondes are like daffodils that bloom in the spring for a short period. Few blondes maintain their natural glory past their twenties. By thirty-five, either their hair is mousy or silver threads have appeared among the gold.

The biggest mistake a mature blonde can make is to bleach her hair to platinum. Nothing can tarnish good looks faster or do more to harden a face. The bleached-blond Hollywood sex symbols in their white foxes and diamonds belong to the fantasy world of the screen. If you long to be one for a night, go to your next costume party as Jean Harlow or Marilyn Monroe.

With the technique of streaking introduced in the Fifties and perfected since then, the faded blonde can imitate nature by taking one shade deeper than her God-given color for the roots and background, and adding highlights to brighten the top layers and the area around the face. The hair will look as though it were lightened by sun and salt air at the beach.

Judgment about depth of tone and how long to apply the highlights is critical to a soft, flattering effect and depends on the quality and texture of the hair. That's what spells the difference between a skilled professional colorist and an amateur.

Perfection rarely comes at bargain rates, but some women think they can economize in their quest for eternal blondness. They have a coloring of gold applied to the whole head and then after a few weeks let the dark roots show. They are kidding themselves if they think this is streaking. It can be amusing as a punk look, but it's not flattering and certainly not elegant.

The rarest of Mother Nature's colors is red hair. Henna, a natural coloring derived from a shrub and known to the ancient Egyptians, brightens faded red or chestnut hair. Applied excessively, or to blond or white hair, it produces the carrot shade of a Raggedy Ann doll's mop, which is just as cheapening as platinum.

Dark brown or black hair loses color in a variety of ways, but it is impossible to predict whether it will turn blotchy, acquire a fine shading of silver fox or the pure white of cotton. The dark head may begin to sprout wiry threads of silver, which the woman takes as a depressing sign of advancing age.

The process is more alarming for a brunette than for her blond sister in whom white hair blends to a drab tone rather than conspicuously standing out. Many try a desperate cover-up.

The brunette is advised to go to a chestnut tone, to a warm brown or to deep honey. Anything is better than looking as though she's polished her hair with boot blacking. Very dark tones accentuate the aging lines in the face and defeat the purpose of the concealment. Nature must have had a purpose in causing the hair to lose color, to make it compatible with the changes in skin tone. Even more disastrous is the look of sparse dark hair against a white scalp, as after menopause, when some women's hair thins noticeably.

There is an exception to what I believe is the error of dark hair coloring, and that is when a woman consciously sets out to develop a striking style without regard for looking feminine and pretty.

Cordelia Biddle Robertson, a jolly *grande dame* of the Philadelphia aristocracy, looks like a debutante of fifty years ago when she wears a long, raven-colored fall. I was her dinner partner at a party given by her friend Kay Chaqueneau, another perpetual brunette.

"What do you like best about sex?" Mrs. Robertson, who was wearing a Saint Laurent blazer, asked me.

"Do you mean love?" I said.

"Whatever you want to call it, what's the best part?"

"To me," I said, "the greatest satisfaction a man can have is to open his eyes the morning after and to see the face of the woman he made love to on the pillow beside him."

"Honey, if you'd see me in the morning, you'd drop dead," Mrs. Robertson said.

Diana Vreeland, former editor of *Vogue* and consultant to the Costume Institute of the Metropolitan Museum of Art, personifies the woman of style who has made character triumph over her natural looks. Her black-lacquer ram's hairdo accentuates her strong features. She could have a softer appearance with a looser coiffure in a lighter tone, but then she wouldn't be Diana Vreeland.

A woman who is uncertain about hair color can experiment with one of the rinses on the market that last for five or six weeks. The trick is in interpreting the instructions on the package, which are addressed to generalities rather than variations in quality and porousness of hair. If, in your anxiety to hide your white hairs, you leave the preparation on too long, the hair that has retained its natural color will appear much too dark.

Go warily at first. If the directions suggest leaving the color on for twenty-five minutes, apply for fifteen or twenty minutes. It's easier to increase strength and length of time than to subtract once applied. If you really want to fool your friends, wrap a few strands of white hair in tinfoil so that, after rinsing, the whole head won't be one flat color.

Rinses are effective when the natural color is predominant. Once the balance tips and the white takes over, you are forced to go to professional tinting.

Points to remember:

• Lighter tones around the face are more flattering than dark.

• Don't concentrate on the hair color alone. Take in the whole picture, including the color of your eyes and skin.

• If you were brunette, do not pencil the eyebrows to your former tone. Lighten up around the eyes as well.

Considering the vehement feelings Americans have about aging and the association they make between gray hair and growing old, it takes a certain courage for a woman to make the decision not to conceal that her hair has lost color. For some the process begins as early as the teens, when it is hardly a sign of decrepitude.

I have known women who asked their husbands' permission to stay gray, and widows who made appointments with a colorist the week after the funeral. Clients have told me of being sharply criticized by their family and friends. "If you are gray, how old will people think I am?" a thirty-five-year-old woman was asked by her sixty-year-old mother. Another woman says she is intrigued by the pointed remarks of friends, both female and male, who have chosen to color their own gray hairs. " 'So-and-so looks so old and *gray*,' they'll say. I don't know why but my gray hair is threatening to them," she says.

A woman may forgo coloring for reasons of health or economy (good coloring is expensive), or because she is self-assured enough to accept what nature has dealt her. But some experience anguish, believing that with gray hair they will no longer be attractive to men. "Have you ever heard a truck driver whistle at a gray-haired woman?" I'm often asked.

Perhaps not, but I question the significance of whistles and wolf calls from passing strangers. What counts is the effect a woman has on a specific man in whom she is interested. I can guarantee that a woman who acts confident about feeling attractive will always be appealing to men. The color or absence of color in her hair is not enough in itself to guarantee results.

If in doubt, have your photograph taken. It will tell you much more than an hour of study in front of the mirror. Better still, have a reel of Super-8 movie film taken to show you how you look at all angles and in action.

Gray hair may be more flattering to a woman of experience than any color she might apply. A lot depends, of course, on the health and lustrousness of the hair, the manner in which it is losing color, her complexion and her features.

I have known more than a few gray-haired beauties. Barbara Paley headed the list. I doubt that she ever walked down a street or into a room without men and women turning to look at her. Her dark brown hair began to lose color before she was forty. When I met her, it was steel-gray. Appreciating the flattery of light around the face, she had a White Mink rinse applied to the back of her head only. The result was a darker tone to the back, a lighter tone to the face.

Pat Mosbacher's prematurely gray hair points up the brilliance of her hazel eyes and her radiant smile. Her hair is naturally darker in back and a rinse also brings out the contrast of shades in the same tone.

In the 1930s, Antoine introduced pastel rinses for pure white hair, using Lady Mendl—the former interior designer Elsie De Wolfe—as his guinea pig. It may have seemed chic at the time for great hostesses to sport mauve and pink heads against their *art moderne* and Louis XVI settings, but by the time the vogue hit American suburbia in the Fifties, something had been lost in translation. Occasionally, an elderly client from west of the Hudson appears at Monsieur Marc with a rosy mop and I shudder.

The designer Zandra Rhodes and her hairdresser, Leonard of London, have seized on candy-colored hair as an attention getter for young women

Nancy Reagan and Monsieur Marc at the White House, 1982.
WHITE HOUSE PHOTO

Anouk Aimée is by Monsieur Marc's definition a sexy elegant woman. CHRISTIEN SIMONPIETRI/SYGMA

Brooke Shields having hair done by Monsieur M for a Wella promotion. DOR

Mr. and Mrs. William S. Paley at a Museum of Modern Art gala. BILL CUNNINGHAM

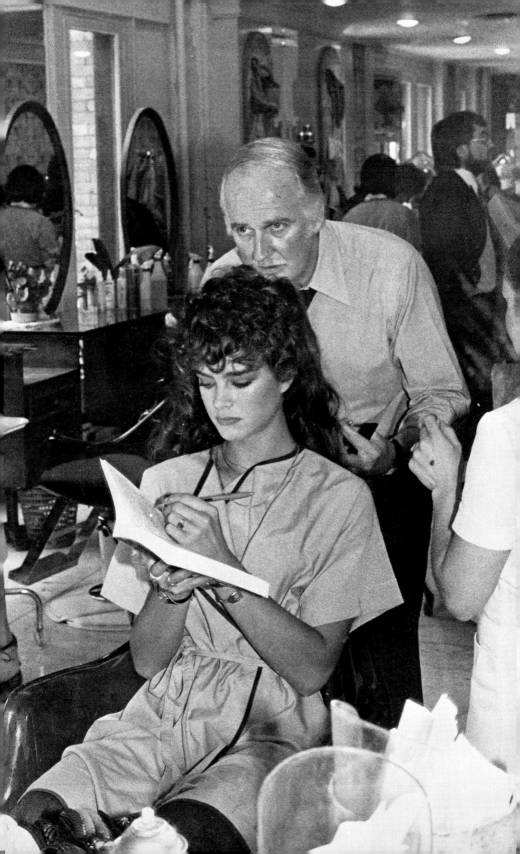

Eugenia Sheppard, doyenne of fashion society columnists, in her Shirley Temple costume. BILL CUNNINGHAM

Hebe Dorsey, correspondent for the *International Herald Tribune* and columnist for French *Vogue*. JOE DORSEY

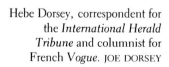

Reva Ostrow, fashion entrepreneur and self-made woman of
elegance. ALBERTO RIZZO

Baroness Sandra di Portanova of Houston. Her dress is by
Valentino; makeup by Garcia. NORMAN PARKINSON

Mrs. Douglas Marshall, Jr., of Houston in a portrait by Aaron Shikler.

Two of Monsieur Marc's gray-haired beauties: Mrs. Emil Mosbacher, Jr., of Greenwich, Connecticut *(left)*, and Mrs. Edwin Hilson of New York. LAWRENCE MARX, JR.

At the Monsieur Marc salon, Mrs. Emil Mosbacher, Jr., in an Adolfo suit. At left, Raphael and Mrs. Robert Johnson Arnold, formerly Mrs. Charles Lachman and before that, Countess de Rochambeau. MARYLIN BENDER

Betsy Bloomingdale with Monsieur
Marc at the salon. JOE DORSEY

Mexico City, April 1974. Left to
right, Baron Alexis de Redé of
Paris, Mr. and Mrs. Alfred
Bloomingdale, Monsieur Marc.

Monsieur Marc with Georgianna and Armando Orsini at their
home in upstate New York. MARYLIN BENDER

Sirio Maccioni, owner of Le Cirque restaurant. ALICIA STEWART

Gisèle Masson, owner of La Grenouille restaurant. MARYLIN BENDER

Portrait of Simone Letourneur (then Simone Colombert) in 1941 when she was the owner of the cabaret La Sirène in Paris.

Louise Rouet at a Christian Dior fashion show in Paris. Her husband, Jacques Rouet, is director of the Dior empire.

SEXY ELEGANT

Betsy Kaiser, named to the International Best Dressed List's Hall of Fame and Monsieur Marc's list of sexy elegant women.

Terry Allen Kramer, investment banker and theatrical producer, is also on the sexy elegant list.

Paige Rense of Los Angeles, editor-in-chief of *Architectural Digest*, *Geo* and *Bon Appétit*: in an ad done for Rolex. Her hair is by Monsieur Marc. © LEON KUZMANOFF

Princess Edouard de Lobkowicz with Maurice Franck, her Paris coiffeur and Marc's friend. CAROLA LIETEN

Guillaume with two of
his clients and friends,
Yvette Chauviré, the
ballerina *(left)*, and
Louise de Vilmorin,
the novelist.

In the 1950s, Marc,
then an assistant at
Guillaume's in Paris,
worked on a film
about ballet and
coiffure, *La Ligne
Danse*.

Virginia Regan and hotelman John Coleman at their wedding in New York in
1983. (Monsieur Marc is coming through the door to congratulate them.)
Her dress is by Mary McFadden. HELAINE MESSER

Marc and Mrs. John Nicholas Regan at the wedding of her daughter,
Virginia, to John Coleman. Her hat is by Adolfo. TED COWELL

(a bleaching process is necessary before the color is applied). As a fleeting joke, it's appropriate. But if nature had wanted women to look like rainbows, I'm sure it would have arranged it long ago.

Gisèle Masson's hair is one of nature's miracles, the color of sterling silver. The proprietor of La Grenouille (with her son, Charles, since the death of her husband in 1975), Mme. Masson has developed her own particular elegance based on a hairdo that suits any age. I cut her hair short all around, reaching just below the tips of the earlobes on the sides and with bangs to the eyebrows. The hairdo emphasizes her expressive blue eyes and dazzling smile.

To counteract the tendency of pure white hair to take on a yellow cast, we give Mildred Hilson a White Mink rinse. One never thinks of age in connection with Mrs. Hilson, who has guarded the beauty with which she was blessed in the cradle. What a pretty woman, one thinks upon seeing her, and, after talking to her, How much fun and how stimulating it is to be with her. She raises millions of dollars for the Hospital for Special Surgery and keeps up with legions of friends. Significantly, most of them are younger than she.

Dorothy Schiff, the former publisher of the *New York Post*, disproves the theory that a woman can't be sexy with silver hair. Slender, aristocratic and coquettish, Mrs. Schiff has that certain gleam in her blue eyes, and although politics was her life for many years, she is always eager to talk about the equally fascinating subject of love. She once asked me to translate one of Edith Piaf's favorite songs, "À Quoi Ça Sert L'Amour?" We concluded that the message was valid: That life without love is empty, and that even if a love affair turns out badly, you have the memory to console you forever.

8

IN SEARCH
OF ELEGANCE

It is hard for someone like me, who came of age in an era of elegance, the Fifties, and in the capital of elegance, Paris, to reflect on what has happened to that singular attribute that is associated with fashion but, in fact, is more comprehensive and more enduring than fashion.

Strange as it sounds to say, elegance has been out of fashion for almost a generation. It came under attack during the youth explosion of the Sixties, and throughout the Seventies it carried the stigma of being *démodé*—old hat.

Supposedly, it has returned to favor in the Eighties. "People are more into looking elegant," said Ralph Lauren, a taste shaper through his multimillion-dollar empire of franchised fashion. He was putting it most inelegantly, which is a big part of the problem.

Fashion today is lights, prancing models, sound effects on a runway; everything hangs on the beat of the music, not the creativity of the designer, and certainly not the elegance of his collection. Or it is "a look," such as Lauren reconstructs from the classic taste of certain upper-class Americans and English aristocrats, to which he adds his emblem of a polo player. It's clever imitation, but it isn't elegance.

These days, I am often asked about elegance: How does one acquire it, and, by the way, exactly what is it? I ask myself, How can one acquire something if one can't recognize it?

Defining elegance has always been difficult. The late Gloria Guinness, who was Barbara Paley's rival for the title of the most elegant woman during the early Sixties, named Jesus Christ as a unique example of supreme elegance. She was trying to convey the thought that elegance was three-dimensional, involving body, soul and mind, but she looked rather foolish doing so.

Jacqueline de Ribes, who appears on everyone's list of elegant women, has said, "There is no elegance without grace, no grace without ease. There is no ease without naturalness. Nothing is false or overdrawn in elegance, but it sometimes takes study."

There is a tendency to explain elegance in terms of what it is not. "Elegance is the art of not astonishing," said Jean Cocteau. Elegance is not ostentatious, never vulgar. Elegance, in tune with the Bauhaus principle of modern architecture, says that less is more. Nowhere is this more telling than with women of means and the jewelry they wear.

In Washington, I was helping Virginia Regan, a young New Yorker who works at the Museum of Modern Art, to get ready to attend a dinner at the White House. She was planning to wear a poppy-colored dress by Carolina Herrera that made her look as though she were floating in flower petals. "How shall I wear my hair?" she asked. I suggested a small neat head with her dark brown hair rolled back on both sides and finished with a chignon. She deliberated before her jewelry case and with my encouragement selected a pair of pearl earrings. That was all.

The next day, she told me how many compliments she had received; everyone told her how beautiful and how elegant she looked.

On another occasion in Washington, I was doing the hair of Baroness Sandra di Portanova of Houston, who was going to a party given by Vice President and Mrs. George Bush. Her husband, Baron Enrico, is an heir to the Cullen oil billions and his and his wife's style of living reflects his good fortune and his desire to spread it around. They have magnificent homes in Texas and Acapulco, fly around the world in a private jet. He once tried and failed to buy "21" in New York as a gift for his wife, whom he has given fabulous jewels.

I often think to myself that a million dollars must seem to them like a dollar to me. With it all, they are friendly and considerate. The baron usually greets me at the door of their hotel suite with an eager handshake and offers me champagne. He invites me to go shooting with them in Texas and Mexico.

Baroness di Portanova wants to look elegant and in good taste. Guessing that the other women at the Bush party would be wearing their hair up, I suggested she keep hers soft and to her shoulders. Her black dress was by Dior. In front of her on the dressing table was a box of diamonds.

"Please, Mrs. Portanova," I said. "You are so beautiful. Just put one clip on the side of your lovely dark hair and one necklace. That's all." She looked breathtaking.

Several months later, she invited me to Washington again to do her hair for a party the Portanovas were giving for Helene von Damm, President Reagan's appointee as ambassador to Austria. As I combed Mrs. Portanova, she practiced reciting a poem she had composed for the occasion.

She was planning to wear a brocade dress by Oscar de la Renta with a mink-bordered stole, and she had selected a pair of gold and diamond combs from Cartier to put in her hair.

I brushed her hair up and to the center, giving a smooth line in front and making it loose and fluffy toward the back. With such an elaborate feeling to the dress and the hairdo, I decided it was best to omit the combs.

Most women are a little insecure about dressing for a big party. Hoping to be the center of attention, they are afraid of not doing enough to attract notice. What they should guard against is doing too much. A tried-and-true rule to follow is this: After you are dressed, take a good hard look in the mirror and subtract a piece of jewelry, or two.

I have never seen as many gems as I did in London in June 1981 at the wedding of Lady Diana and the Prince of Wales. I was doing the hair of my English clients and I couldn't believe the heirloom jewelry they wore—earrings, bracelets of every size, necklaces, stomachers that had been in the family for centuries, and tiaras, which are difficult to secure on the hair because they are so stiff and heavy.

All the glory that was England must be displayed for events like a royal wedding or a coronation, historic pageants that make great theater. The weight of tradition and the spirit behind them make it possible for such glitter to be elegant.

Elegance never looks *nouveau riche* or as though it just came from the store. Two clients from out of town arrived at the salon one afternoon proudly sporting the Vuitton handbags they had just bought at Saks Fifth Avenue. I advised them to take them home and polish the leather handles before wearing so they wouldn't look so new.

Elegance stands the test of time, which is why elegant women put clothes away to rest and then retrieve them years later, and why photographs of elegant women don't look dated.

Rosamund Bernier, who lectures to a packed auditorium at the Metropolitan Museum of Art, is noted for the brilliance of her presentation and the elegance of her person. I was so excited by her lecture on Catherine the Great that I rushed up to the podium and asked her to let me do her hair at my salon. For her lecture on Queen Christina of Sweden, who often dressed in male clothing, Mrs. Bernier found a fifteen-year-old Grès outfit of trousers and tunic that was reminiscent of a Renaissance page's costume. In her closet is a thirty-year-old Balenciaga, still serviceable.

A portrait of Sarah Bernhardt in the museum collection synthesizes elegance more than any words can. The divine Sarah lounges against a mass of pillows in a long white satin dress that swathes what Alexandre Dumas described as her "broomlike body" in seductive folds. At the neckline, wristbone and hem are drifts of ostrich feathers. The dress bypasses the fads of its era, covers the physical imperfections of the actress who played the *femme fatale* on and offstage. She would be considered alluring and fashionable were she alive today and wearing the same dress. Were it not for the artist's signature, Georges Clairin, and the date, 1876, it would be impossible to pin the woman or the fashion to a specific time.

Elegance is not the same as chic, which is more of the moment, the latest word. There's a certain type of woman who is photographed regularly by *Women's Wear Daily* and the *New York Times*. Tall, thin as a board and rich, she spends a fortune on clothes. She's a barometer of fashion in New York and Paris. People look at her and say, "Oh, she's wearing the new Saint Laurent. Isn't she chic?"

They don't say "Isn't she elegant?" as they did about Barbara Paley. I remember seeing Mrs. Paley from the window of the salon one morning walking on Madison Avenue. She had on black and white houndstooth-check pants, a white blouse and a black cashmere cardigan, black patent leather shoes and a little bag over her shoulder. Everyone was turning about to look at her. She didn't have to wear a Saint Laurent to be elegant.

And yet, Mrs. Paley did wear clothes by name designers like Halston, Norell, Givenchy, enhancing their reputations by her patronage rather than the other way around. She took from the newest fashions, though never the extreme versions or colors, and put her imprint upon them. She wore caftans to premieres, and made it look ladylike to go out in the evening as well as in the daytime in pants when that vogue was controversial.

One would never have called her *très chic*, however. To be absolutely *dans le vent* in fashion, mirroring every detail of a designer's vision for that season, is not the same as being elegant.

A woman who keeps up with the Concorde set can't be seen twice in the same dress. Butlers call their opposite numbers to find out what madame is going to wear, which designer, which color. It used to be easy for them in France when they could also call the couture house and find out that madame bought that certain model. A couturier like Madame Grès never made the exact same dress twice; she'd vary the top, change the skirt. Now that high society wears designer ready-to-wear, you see as many as four women at a party in the same dress. It's like the uniform of the evening.

One of the maxims with which I was trained in Paris was "Perfection is the enemy of elegance." To look as though you just came out of a box from Saint Laurent with the tags still pinned to the merchandise is to miss the point of elegance, and is dull besides. A woman who always wants everything about herself to be just so, never a hair out of place, never a spot of dust on her white gloves, who looks like a little doll in the shop window, is *précieuse*—a little precious, slightly affected.

I prefer a woman with flair, which is an ingredient of elegance. With flair, something has to be slightly off-kilter somewhere.

Christian Dior was quoted as saying a woman couldn't look sexy and elegant at the same time. I think he was wrong and that Jacqueline de Ribes was right when she said, "It's just more difficult."

Alfred Hitchcock, the movie director, described Grace Kelly's appeal as "sexual elegance." Hitchcock chose sophisticated blondes as the heroines of his films, "the drawing-room type, the real ladies who become sexy once they're in the bedroom." Catherine Deneuve fits the bill, too—a little frosty on the outside, the sensuality smoldering underneath.

Marlene Dietrich had a bisexual elegance that seemed wicked in the Thirties, especially to Americans, but is very much in fashion today. Her Germanic kind of sexiness implied that the woman might be attracted to other women as well as men. Dietrich in pants, Dietrich in white tie and tails and a top hat, Dietrich smoking through a long cigarette holder, Dietrich showing her beautiful legs—the sexiness in every gesture was controlled. Restraint is an essential of elegance.

Dietrich played the chic prostitute, sleek and tough, and some men love that. Auburn-haired Katharine Hepburn, also cool and elegant, and a pioneer wearer of men's pants, was an American thoroughbred type, not hard but boyishly hard to get. And some men love that, too.

To be both sexy and elegant, the sexiness must be played in a minor key: When it's too strong, the elegance disappears. But sexiness alone is hard to sustain. Think of Marilyn Monroe and Brigitte Bardot, those pure sex symbols of the Fifties and early Sixties. The TV treat of the Christmas 1982 season in France was a retrospective about Bardot's life. "Five hours of pout and mane tossing," according to the *New York Times* correspondent, who termed it "a cruel enterprise." At forty-eight years of age, B.B. was trying to look and act as she did at twenty-six. Monroe was spared that fate by dying young, but she obviously had seen what was ahead for her.

Sexiness plus elegance is longer-lasting. Princess Grace was lovely and desirable to the day she died. Anouk Aimée's classical beauty hasn't changed in twenty years. To look at her is to love her: the softness and intelligence in her brown eyes, the refinement of her nose, the sensuality of her lips, the neck like a swan that I can't help wanting to kiss. The way she holds her head, on an angle sometimes, with the hair falling gently toward her face. The grace of her movements, her manner—she's so nice to everyone—and the classic style of her clothes.

In the same category are society women like Mrs. Michael Kaiser (former model Betsy Pickering) and Mrs. Philip Harari of London. Both have *un petit point* of sexiness. Mrs. Harari has that red hair and a sexy walk. So does Terry Allen Kramer, partner in the investment banking firm of Allen

& Company and a producer of Broadway hit shows. Mrs. Kramer has chestnut hair and a dynamite manner.

I treasure a photograph of Barbara Paley arriving at a party. The wind blowing around the entrance made her Halston caftan seem to caress her body, outlining its slender but curvy shape. I teased her about how sexy she looked and she said, "Oh, Marc, do you really think so?"

Deep down, every woman wants to be thought sexy. A woman will say to me, "Make me look sexy, because I'm going out this evening with someone special." The obvious thing to do would be something like combing the hair back and severely to one side, sexy the way they show a streetwalker in the movies and on the stage. There it's fun because it's part of the show, but I don't think a woman should go to a party like that. It wouldn't guarantee the result she wants. I would rather be more subtle and do her hair so she feels very feminine, young-looking and desirable; I prefer that she not show too much flesh, but leave more to the imagination.

Bold sexy is such an easy look to create that many women automatically go for that, but they don't understand men if they do. Tight jeans are sexy and most men will look at the derriere of a girl in tight jeans, and then at her face, and probably think about going to bed with her or taking her skiing for the weekend and then to bed. But will they think of taking her to a three-star restaurant? Not unless she has, as we say in French, *du chien*—seductive elegance.

It's funny how American fashion magazines, which used to try to teach something about taste and elegance, now emphasize sex. Not just *Cosmopolitan*, which has long been a joke with its cover photographs of girls with their breasts falling out of their dresses, but the others as well. Its readers would be much happier, I am sure, if instead of concentrating on looking sexy, they learned how to flirt.

Flirting is an elegant art and so much fun, too. *La manière*—that way a Frenchwoman has of walking past a man at a party and letting him know she's available. Or flirting across a room with a glass of wine in her hand and her eyes saying, *Tu me plaît, tu es mon type*—You appeal to me, you're my type.

The man lifts his glass and smiles, making the gesture of drinking to her beauty. The woman smiles back, even if she's with another man. They know it won't go any further, but it makes for such agreeable sensations, if only for the moment.

I wonder if some women are scared of flirting or if they just don't have the knack. It's a skill that improves with constant practice. After a woman gets married here, she loses the experience of *la coquetterie*, if she ever had it. Americans take flirting too seriously.

More than once, I've had a man get up from the table and come over to me and ask, "Are you looking at my wife?" I'll say, "Sir, you are a very lucky man. Your wife is very attractive and I can't take my eyes off her. That's all." Usually, he laughs and invites me to the table for a drink.

Flirting offers such opportunities for eloquence without speaking a word. A woman can say so much with her eyes, with a penetrating look. At a party, people will wonder about a woman neither young nor beautiful who has the most interesting man there paying her court. She has the gift of making him feel like a king by keeping her eyes riveted on his, giving him her total attention.

Many businesswomen seem hesitant to use feminine wiles. I don't mean in the office or at the business conference, although I can't see what harm it would do to flirt a little at a business lunch. Some women carry their business around with them all the time, and not just the business but the attitude of being equal with men in all respects. Even when they go out in the evening, they have to compete, to let a man know they don't need him to take them out for dinner. They give orders as they do in the office, and boast about how smart they are, how much money they've made, how important their business deals are. Then they complain that there are no real men around. It won't cost them equal pay and opportunities or their independence to flirt a bit, and they might find they are enjoying life more.

Let men light your cigarettes and open doors for you. It's so elegant when a man does that, or when he pulls out a chair for a woman to sit on.

Let the man take the lead. A businesswoman came up to me at a cocktail party and said, "You have the cutest ass I ever saw." Couldn't she have found a more elegant way to get her point across?

Beauty you are born with, elegance you can acquire.

I, for one, find it much more pleasant to be in the company of a woman who has a good sense of humor than with a great beauty. I'd rather see character when I look into a woman's eyes than the empty expression of a doll.

There are so many ways of being attractive; perfect looks are not the only one. Charm is more potent than exquisite features. But women exaggerate the importance of beauty. One will complain that she hates her nose because it is flat, but somewhere there is a man who loves flat noses. *Pour chaque casserole, il y a une couvercle*—for every pot there is a cover.

A beautiful woman is at a disadvantage in comparison with one less generously endowed by nature. A man will never accept her looking unattractive for a moment. What did I see in her? he will ask himself. A beautiful woman is often trapped by her beauty. She may have low self-esteem because she believes she is only liked for her appearance and not respected as a total human being. Like an actress, she lives in fear of disappointing her audience. Everyone has a bad day now and then, but it's hard for a beautiful woman to take it in her stride.

I feel sorry for women who live by their beauty alone, such as those models and actresses who can only play themselves when they were young and who will never get to do character roles. Life comes to them as long as they are beautiful. One day, they notice that people have stopped telling them how beautiful they are. Truck drivers stop whistling, something they hated when it happened and miss when it stops.

The French have an expression, *une belle laide*—a beautiful ugly woman, literally, but it actually refers to one who has a certain something, who appeals despite her lack of physical attractiveness.

How does she manage this contradiction? By developing a style. Diana Vreeland, the supreme example, once said of style, "It helps to get you down the stairs," meaning the grand entrance, making sure you are noticed, that you stand out in a crowd.

Her style is rather eccentric, with her red rooms, black clothes and manner of speaking like a Delphic oracle. On the arm of Bill Blass, she arrives at a party looking like Queen Elizabeth I; another time she is the Empress T"Zu-shi.

Not every woman has the audacity for that kind of style. Another way to draw attention is to develop *beaucoup de classe*, to have savoir faire, to know how to put oneself together. In that way, a woman can class herself close to a beautiful one. She can approach elegance.

If nature didn't spoil you with looks when you were born, it's up to you to discover your personality. A beautiful woman can be loved for her beauty, but it may not last. A woman who is a type, who has style, can endure until her last breath. If she is smart, a beautiful woman will start cultivating elegance while she is young so she will have it when her beauty fades.

Madame Grès, the most elegant couturiere in business today, described an elegant woman for an interviewer from *Connoisseur* magazine: "She is generally soberly and simply dressed when it's necessary but she also knows how to be fanciful without being eccentric, sophisticated but with temperance. She knows what to wear in any circumstance; she is at ease everywhere. She has taste and sensitivity and recognizes quality."

Mrs. Paley always knew what was the right thing to wear. She might ask, "What do you think?" but she would do what she had decided. It's true she had worked for *Vogue*, but there are many fashion editors who aren't elegant. Whatever is new they wear, regardless of how it becomes them.

Behind the success of the socialite fashion designers is, I think, the propaganda that elegance can be acquired by stepping into an elegant woman's clothes. It worked for Chanel, who rose from humble beginnings to become a high-society figure, but it doesn't work for every socialite who dresses exquisitely. There's a big difference between creating a style for oneself and being a designer for other women.

Mary McFadden has designed some very original and feminine clothes. She went about it like an artist, reworking themes from the art of Africa, the Middle East and the Orient. Even if she weren't the daughter of a social family, her designs, particularly the feminine pleatings, could stand on their own.

Carolina Herrera comes out of the tradition of the very rich, very elegant South American woman. Her mother-in-law, Mimi Herrera of Caracas, is the prototype, commuting between Venezuela, Paris and New York in the old days with trunks filled with ball gowns.

Carolina is an expert on the grand entrance or "drop dead" elegance that forces admiration in the most crowded room. "It's very important to keep the focus on your face," she once explained to an interviewer. A dress with exquisite detail in the skirt is lost when the room is packed with people. So she concentrated on the sleeves. Her sculptured creations rising out of the shoulder to frame the face recall—to those who have the memory of elegance in the Fifties—the dresses of pure shape from the late Balenciaga, the high priest of the architectural school of fashion design.

Gloria Vanderbilt, on the other hand, has lent her name to the lowest common denominator of fashion, jeans. What does a woman get when she buys them? Good fit, perhaps, but not the individual style of Gloria Vanderbilt.

Then there is Betsy Bloomingdale and the little robe she designed for Swirl. She got the idea from a visit to a hospital. The robe is made of thin terry cloth in pretty colors trimmed with flowers, cut like a long T-shirt that opens in back and wraps after the arms are inserted in two holes at the top. It's a charming, sexy garment to wear over a bathing suit or for breakfast. Mrs. Bloomingdale has great personal flair, an eye for the practical as well as the chic. She embarked on this venture for her own amusement and without the slightest illusion that she is a designer.

An elegant woman has a sense of the right thing—she knows what suits her and she sticks with it. She doesn't care about the label in the dress and she doesn't try to look like someone else, because she knows she can never be that other person. If women would only try to discover themselves and express their individuality instead of trying to copy another's, or dressing to impress other women, which I suspect they do more often than they dress to please men.

An elegant woman understands who she is and accepts what she is, inside and out. This means she has to be honest with herself and extremely critical. She has a full-length triple mirror in a well-lighted area of her bedroom or bathroom as well as a double hand mirror with a magnifying glass on one side. She never leaves home without subjecting herself to scrutiny in those mirrors—front, back and both profiles—as though she were passing army inspection. And she never buys clothing without studying herself very carefully in a triple mirror in the store's dressing room. To verify her decision, she sits down to see if the dress still fits well about the hips and shoulders. Above all, she should do this with a strapless dress to ascertain whether someone viewing her from the back when she is at a dinner table will be put off by puffs of flesh oozing over the bodice.

She must be ruthless with herself, capable of saying as she looks at her back, "There is something a little vulgar about my derriere, too low-slung, and the way the legs are joined to the hips. The only way I can wear pants is with a tunic or a long jacket to cover my rear and just show my legs." Or, as she tries on a pair of shoes, "These are lovely on the model in the photograph, but on my feet they look like water skiis."

Just from walking on the street, I can see that most women don't do this. At most, they take a quick glance straight on, narrowing their eyes to help along the self-deception.

Elegance requires a lifetime of discipline. The great *elégantes* are like athletes in training. They keep in top form with daily exercise. They watch what they eat. That doesn't mean starving themselves, because to be thin as a razor blade is unnatural. Elegant women control temptation to overindulge in food or drink. They learn the nutritional value of foods and take pleasure from small portions. A clean plate is not a sign of elegance. Nor is a fondness for alcoholic and carbonated beverages. Elegant women hardly touch the stuff, at most a drink before dinner, a glass of wine with dinner. And they are impeccable about their persons. Talking about elegance, Mrs. Paley said, "Neatness, which is grooming after all, is definitely the most important requirement."

It takes much more than clothes to make a woman elegant.

Carriage: She stands straight and sits erect at the dinner table unless she leans across slightly to look into a man's eyes.

My ladies from Connecticut and Long Island have this stately carriage, as do elegant Parisiennes and highborn Englishwomen. They say it was drummed into them when they were children by their nannies, who taught them that slouching was sinful, the mark of a furtive character. In some of the schools for women in New England, such as Smith College, which Nancy Reagan attended, they were photographed for posture faults, lined up naked in profile under a spotlight, and graded accordingly.

The way a woman holds herself communicates a lot about her self-assurance. Impressive carriage forces eyes to turn to her when she enters a room. It can even subdue an arrogant headwaiter in a restaurant.

Elegant posture can be learned: shoulders down, hips tucked under, head up and pushed back like a flower on a stalk. In Paris, the models I knew used to practice in their fourth-floor walk-ups, striding with telephone books on their heads. The test was whether they could sit down without the book falling to the floor.

The Sound of Her Voice: A husky voice can be sexy à la Marlene

Dietrich, but not when it can be mistaken for a man's. A masculine voice in a woman is supposedly the result of heavy smoking and drinking. But there's the decibel count, as well. Too many women shout instead of speaking in low, modulated tones.

Then there's the accent, which can be a giveaway that the background doesn't match the clothes, or the face. I once approached a beautiful model in Montreal. When she opened her mouth, I started to laugh. It was unkind, but I couldn't help it.

It used to be said about the wife of a certain tycoon that you could take the girl out of the Bronx but not the Bronx out of the girl. She was beautiful, expensively clothed and jeweled, near perfection until she spoke. Why she never took elocution lessons was a mystery considering she could have improved her elegance factor 60 percent; *My Fair Lady* put forth the proposition that a flower girl could be passed off as a duchess by changing her speech.

Perhaps some women don't realize what a liability their voices are because they don't hear them. With the wide choice of inexpensive electronic equipment today, that's no excuse. Buy a tape recorder, listen and do something about what you hear, if necessary.

Give a lot of preparation to the message you leave on your answering machine. You don't have to go so far as one woman who hired an actor to sound as though she had an English butler, but practice until the recording sounds like the woman you aspire to be. Answering machines open up new opportunities and risks for courtship. If you give your telephone number to a man and your machine doesn't sound so great when he calls, he may lose the picture he had of you.

A beguiling voice on the telephone can be like a violin with good tone. And it can be misleading. Once when I was sick in bed and my television set was out of order, I called a repair service and spoke to a woman with a sweet, French-accented voice. I had a picture in my mind of an adorable Parisienne. After I recovered, I called her and asked her to meet me for a drink. Not wanting to overdo it the first time (like taking her to La Grenouille), I invited her to meet me at a more modest French restaurant on Second Avenue. "I will wear a safari jacket and a white scarf," I said. "I will wear a navy blue dress with a white flower," she said.

When I saw her, I thought, *A short Mae West*. But the elegant thing to do was to go through with it. So we had a drink and dinner, and when she asked me to go to her apartment for a Cognac, I remembered I had a friend who had just been operated on at Doctors Hospital.

It isn't enough to fix the sound of your voice. Vocabulary is important, too. How can a man fall in love with a woman who says, "Oh, yeah"? She could just as well say, "Oh, yes."

Elegant women are never profane, never use barnyard language. They say "shoot" or something like that, just as an elegant Frenchwoman would bite her tongue before she would say *"merde."* She might say *"mercredi"* (which means Wednesday), with a long stress on the first syllable, or *"Cambronne"* (after the French general who commanded the forces at Waterloo and, when asked to acknowledge defeat, replied, "The Old Guard dies but it never surrenders"; his name became the elegant substitute for the word he might have said).

It has been chic for certain French jet setters and actresses to use English four-letter words; *voilà,* there's the difference between chic and elegance, almost as chic as using cocaine, a stupid habit that took hold on both sides of the Atlantic.

Smoking: It may be bad for health, but if a woman must smoke, she ought to do it elegantly, the way women did when they first took up the filthy habit early in the century. They smoked after dinner, and in the company of friends—but never in the street.

I saw a fashion socialite whose photograph appears at least once a week in *Women's Wear Daily* coming out of an apartment building one morning with a lighted cigarette in her hand. When she got to the corner, she took a nervous puff and threw the cigarette into the gutter. That canceled out her elegance immediately.

I am fascinated to observe Poppi Thomas smoke. The widow of Joseph A. Thomas, the investment banker, she is one of the most elegant women I have known. She lifts the cigarette in its holder to the corner of her mouth with such grace, inhales so softly and exhales so delicately that smoke never gets in anyone's eyes.

Manners: An elegant woman has one set of manners for everyone, regardless of their occupations, station in life or how well she knows them. She doesn't wait to find out if they are "somebody" before deciding how to treat them. As Wilson Mizner, a Palm Beach social figure of the Twenties, said, "Be nice to the people you meet on the way up, for you may be meeting them on the way down."

Elegant manners do not consist of engraved stationery but of the thoughtfulness behind the notes of appreciation for a gift, no matter how trifling, a good time at a party or a helpful act. I can't imagine women like Mrs. Paley, Mrs. Bloomingdale and Mrs. Reagan ever being too busy to remember to say thank you. A telephone call is acceptable, but nowhere as elegant as a handwritten note.

An elegant person would not respond to a personal invitation to a private party through her secretary.

An elegantly mannered person will never greet a friend with "You look tired" when silence would be golden, or with "You've lost weight" when "You look wonderful" is so much more graceful.

9

CONVERSATIONS
WITH ELEGANT WOMEN

D oes elegance have any meaning for today? Is it worth the effort to attain?

There's no need to become obsessed with elegance. Where is the fun of life if you can't take it easy once in a while?

And yet I would say yes to elegance as a goal to be pursued with a joyful spirit, knowing that, unlike youth and beauty, momentary things, the rewards of elegance always lie ahead.

Even if one never runs the full course, to approach elegance is quite enough, too.

How does a woman do that if she wasn't born to advantages of wealth and tasteful surroundings? I talked about that with Reva Ostrow, one of the most successful fashion entrepreneurs in New York and a woman who lives an elegant life entirely of her own making. Her handbag-manufacturing business has afforded her an apartment on Fifth Avenue, designed and executed according to her highly individual taste by Ward Bennett, and a property in upstate New York.

She is a striking woman, tall and slender with a blaze of white strands dramatizing her natural black hair.

MARC: What's the cost of elegance?

REVA: I think the most important thing about being elegant is not to be too fashionable. Buy classic, good, well-made beautiful things, not too high-fashion, that will last, and to which you can always add, and that you will always look well in.

You can't talk about elegance without putting in the word *classical*. The classic is what maintains itself: Brooks Brothers khaki pants, the Hermès "Grace Kelly" bag.

MARC: One of the most elegant women I've ever known is Simone Letourneur, who works in my checkroom. People turn to look at her when she boards the bus. Women who come to the salon ask where she bought her clothes. "It's nothing, I got it at Alexander's," she'll say. Of course, she had years of exposure to beautiful things in Paris. But, in general, do you think a woman can be elegant without a lot of money?

REVA: My theory is you don't have to be rich to be elegant and you don't have to be rich to be classic. It helps, though, in areas. However, you really don't need it, because I think a lot of people consider me reasonably elegant and they did when I was eighteen. The quest that I had was recognizing I had it in me to be as elegant as Mrs. Paley. I just didn't have her resources. But I had the ambition.

I can far more afford things now than I could before and I buy more traditional and more classical and what I consider more elegant clothing now, and far less fashionable. Elegance, the really true one-hundred-percent thoroughbred elegance, comes to you when you are more secure, because until then you can be elegant, you can be classic, but there is an element missing. You're not pure enough and you're not sure enough to be plain enough.

MARC: Maybe that's why elegance has been called the privilege of age.

REVA: A year ago, I was still wearing puffed sleeves, one of the benchmarks of early Eighties fashion, and I was still doing a few little damages. I was making errors. I was not totally sure, so I couldn't walk out in a little short-sleeved black linen blouse and a black skirt and a red belt and feel as elegant as I did in my Chloé or my Trigère. Now I can. A lot of elegance has to do with your frame of mind.

MARC: You're saying you won't have the puffed sleeves?

REVA: I won't wear anything that high-fashion anymore. Before, I was not secure enough to be one hundred percent, in my estimation, elegant. I felt, because of the lack of security, that I needed more fashion—to project me, to make me stand out, to make me an entity.

Mrs. Paley never wore very high fashion. She wore expensive, beautiful designer clothes, but she picked the most classical of those things. If you look at the really stunning, superb, elegant Frenchwomen, they are classical. They are not wearing the extreme of the moment. That's fashion, not elegance. I really believe in fashion, but not for me anymore. I've arrived at a point in my life where, when I walk down the street, I remember I've got a head on my shoulders, and I think of my profile and I think of my hair and I think of what I've accomplished, and all of a sudden I don't need the puffed sleeves anymore.

MARC: How would you tell other women to arrive at that point?

REVA: I'd say a lot of years on the couch and a great drive not to be nervous. A mother who loves you very much will give you that automatically.

MARC: How do you see the current emphasis on designer labels?

REVA: Years ago, Neiman-Marcus and Saks Fifth Avenue never showed labels except their own. Then came the promotion of line-for-line copies from Paris at Ohrbach's in the Sixties. That made designer names very important. When the American designers saw the French doing it, they jumped on the bandwagon.

It's been terrific for business except that women have lost their individuality. If they're not wearing a designer name, they don't think they're dressing right. They have lost their ability to pick what they like. Their taste level has dissipated into "I have to have a Calvin Klein or an Anne Klein or a Geoffrey Beene." So if they see fabulous dresses by less publicized designers, they cannot buy them. They become immobile.

And it isn't just in a certain group. Designer labels have moved down to the working class, the blue-collar worker; everyone has been brainwashed. But the problem is that you don't have many elegant people designing with elegant taste anymore.

MARC: Tell me about yourself and how you got to be elegant.

REVA: I was born in Brooklyn, raised in Queens. I wanted to be an artist when I was young, but somewhere along the line I realized I didn't have the talent.

I sewed very well. In the early grades in school when we did samplers and aprons, I really excelled. I did fabulous, fine embroidery. At the age of nine, I was winning knitting contests and sewing contests.

When I got to be about thirteen, I got interested in clothes and, not having very much money, I started to make my own skirts. In those days, we wore dirndls. You buy two lengths of fabric, sew them together, and shir one end and add a waistband. It was then I decided I wanted to be a dress designer.

I went to Washington Irving High School in Manhattan and every single day for four years I was on a subway train from Queens at seven-thirty in the morning and I never came late to school one day, and I was never absent.

You have to understand that there is a certain amount of discipline that helps you conquer anything you want to do.

MARC: Including elegance?

REVA: Yes.

MARC: What happened next?

REVA: I graduated from high school with honors, but the scholarship I needed to attend design school fell through, so I meandered around and never did get a designing job.

I became a trimming buyer at Pauline Trigère and I sewed for myself. I made incredibly beautiful clothing. I could copy anything in the world and you would not know it wasn't the original. It was a labor of love, and I was able to wear Jacques Fath and be always very, very well dressed. Very poor but very well dressed.

I spent my Saturdays shopping, looking around. My eye was just developing, an eye for line and purity.

MARC: Then you think you can develop "it," or whatever they call taste, intuition about elegance.

REVA: I think X amount has to be in you, but I don't know how much X stands for. You don't teach anyone talented how to draw or paint, but you can develop what's in them. If you have it, it can be developed. Some people don't need developing. Picasso never went to school.

MARC: But he worked at it all the time.

REVA: Of course, you never let up. I always wanted to better myself.

MARC: But how do you develop this instinct, this knowledge, if you aren't wealthy, if you aren't surrounded by beautiful things?

REVA: You have to be inquisitive, which most people are not. They plow through life not knowing, not seeing, not learning.

I am always looking—at store windows, at buildings, at people in the street, at cars. I'm always seeing, I'm always learning, so that gives me a foundation. I didn't stop when I got to live in Manhattan.

If you only see a little cotton blouse in Lerner's and you don't go to Lord and Taylor, and then you don't go to Saks Fifth Avenue, and you don't go to Bergdorf Goodman and Henri Bendel, then you don't know. If you don't look at Dior and at Bill Blass and this one and this one and this one, and have a comparison, then you don't know.

MARC: Aren't there a lot of people who look and don't know?

REVA: Not if they've done enough looking over the years.

MARC: Still, isn't there more to it than just comparison shopping?

REVA: Yes, and it's what the younger generation today that has grown up without seeing elegance around it has to do if it wants to recognize it.

I used to go to the New York Public Library and take out the old copies of *Vogue*, *Harper's Bazaar* and *Vanity Fair* and study them. If you want to see elegant clothes, you must go back to the Thirties. And kids today can also find it in the magazines of the Fifties, even the early Sixties.

I also took out books on costume design and spent days tracing early Greek and Egyptian costumes. I was doing it for schoolwork, essays on the history of clothing in different countries, but that was how I was training my eye to linear proportion.

MARC: I have always done that in museums.

REVA: So have I. The costume collections of the Metropolitan Museum of Art and the Brooklyn Museum show you examples of great design but are also probably the only places where one can see what clothes were like when they were made with real quality. Of course, there are costume collections in the museums of most major cities.

And also, I went to the thrift shops on Third Avenue and bought clothes and accessories of great quality for nothing. Silk chemise dresses with drawnwork, eighteen-button gloves, wonderful shoes.

MARC: I think you also have to look at people.

REVA: You must observe people. Who do I like? Who don't I like? Am I dressing like someone I don't like? No, I'm dressing like someone I like, but I have basically bad taste. It's true. Most people won't admit that. They think they're doing fine. That's why they never get out of the rut they're in. They plow through life not knowing, not seeing, not learning.

MARC: What about asking a friend for advice? A friend who looks the way you'd like to look, who has taste. Ask her to go shopping with you.

REVA: Of course. But will you listen when she says, "Why don't you get one fabulous dress instead of five stupid ones?" Or, "Why don't you stop wearing that blue eye shadow?" And do you have an elegant friend? You see so few elegant people today. There aren't enough mentors around for young people.

MARC: Did you have any?

REVA: I had a friend who came from a little bit better family than mine—"better" meaning richer and snobbier and a little more mannered—and she called my attention to the way I spoke. Because elegance is a kind of breeding, speech, education, everything. I had an accent when I left Brooklyn, as everyone from Brooklyn does. She called my attention to the way President Roosevelt spoke on the radio. And that was all I needed. I decided to pronounce my words distinctly.

MARC: It's true. You can't stop with clothes, with hair, with furniture. You have to go all the way to polish yourself. But in the matter of clothes, did you have mentors?

REVA: You need someone to look up to and say, "She's fabulous. I want to look like her." Jackie Kennedy was a very strong mentor for this country in the early Sixties. I worked for Trigère. She's a personality with tremendous style that she brought from France.

I went to Paris. France gave me a new perspective on elegance. I saw that traditional sixteenth-arrondissement woman in her little-nothing outfit—elegant, sophisticated, old quiet money. Nothing flashy. I think that's hard to come by for Americans. Americans are not secure enough. We don't have that heritage, that kind of education. Elegance in France is a life-style.

MARC: You go to Paris often, don't you? How do you go?

REVA: I used to travel first-class on the morning flight from New York, but then they cut that out and put the Concorde in. So I take that. It's three and a half hours and I save that wear and tear, and the jet lag. And, of course, the class of people is much better.

MARC: There's an old farmer's saying, "You have to put it in the ground to make it grow." Would you agree then that you have to spend money to acquire elegance?

REVA: I would agree that quality is the best investment and that quality isn't cheap, although it isn't necessarily the most expensive either.

MARC: You don't have to spend five thousand dollars for a dress. You can do it with a cashmere sweater and skirt, and good boots.

REVA: I would rather have one good dress or one good pair of shoes than three or four of anything. But if I like a skirt, I buy two. I buy multiples, usually two of everything. One is in the cleaner's, one I wear. It simplifies my life.

MARC: And then you throw them out after a season?

REVA: Not at all. The average dress in my closet is five years old. I have a linen dress I've been wearing for about seven years and every year I pull it out and put it on. I hardly ever give anything away. I don't change with fashion. I buy classics. I put things away for a couple of years because I don't have the heart to throw them away and because they are expensive clothes. After I put them in the box for the Arthritis Foundation, I find myself picking out the good things and putting them back in the closet. A year later, I pull something out and say, "Gee, I'm glad I didn't give that away. That Saint Laurent smock looks so great this year. Last year it looked terrible."

I've been wearing the same dress New Year's Eve for about five years. People who come to my parties have seen one little dress I've had for four years, over and over. They don't seem to mind, and neither do I. I can do that because I buy such classics. I usually fill in with two good things a season.

MARC: Did you always do that, even when you were poor and learning?

REVA: In a sense, yes, because I always liked the classics even though they were avant-garde when I wore them. As you know, many of the great classics come out of a sporting tradition, and when I was a kid I rode horseback, which was an elegant sport, riding English saddle, that is. Unfortunately, today they've gotten away from the classics and introduced fashion to riding, and the clothes are hideous.

At sixteen I was built like a boy and I wore jeans around the stable when nobody wore jeans. I wore pants, man-tailored chinos that fit beautifully, with a turtleneck sweater and stocks with the neckband, when no one was wearing them. And a trench coat that a friend who was a model brought back from Paris. I never wore them to work but as daytime clothes on Saturday when I came to Manhattan from Queens to go shopping at Bloomingdale's. Twenty years later, my best girlfriend said to me, "I was embarrassed to be seen with you." Because in the Forties the only women who wore pants in Manhattan were Katharine Hepburn and Greta Garbo—and Reva Ostrow. I was way ahead on a lot of fashion, but it was classic.

MARC: I don't think I've seen you in pants.

REVA: Women wear pants because they want to be men. Not physically men, but to have the privileges of men. There's a definite psychological thing about women who wear pants constantly. I don't mean in the country or weekends, for comfort. Women who stay in pants are treading on men's territory. They're willing to lose their identity with a symbol. Pants mean power. You're dressing like a man. You're putting on his attire. Men don't wear skirts, do they?

Pants are not comfortable. They're always wrinkled. Women wear pants because they're too lazy to put stockings on, and they don't want to wear a girdle. Pants gave women the outlet of no shoes, no stockings, no undergarments. It's the first initiated slob act of the era.

MARC: Businesswomen don't wear pants to the office too much, but they seem to have made a uniform of the pinstriped man's suit, with a skirt.

REVA: The executive woman is trying to be a carbon copy of the executive man, in her attire, so that she doesn't threaten him. If she wore a dress, she would become sexual and therefore not be able to work. That's insanity.

If men are going to be threatened by a woman's brains, it won't help to mask herself in a string tie and a tailored suit. It's outrageous. Women are squelching their personalities, they are living fearfully in a corporate structure, petrified of the men instead of just being human beings.

MARC: But you don't wear the uniform.

REVA: If you are in your own business, you can maintain your individuality. Pauline Trigère, Mollie Parnis, Mary Wells of Wells, Rich, Greene—these are individual, fabulous women. But when women are not in their own businesses and are in the corporate structure, they have a tendency to be substitute men.

My first suit, which I got at sixteen, was a gray and white pinstripe flannel, man-tailored, with one kick pleat in the front of the skirt. I wore it with the yellow turtleneck sweater that I used to ride in. Yellow was a hunt color. Nobody I knew did things like that.

MARC: A sense of color comes into this, doesn't it?

REVA: Yes, although I wear very few colors and they have been with me since I was sixteen. My suits have always been gray. My first evening gown was red. My second evening gown was red. My third evening gown was black. My fourth evening gown was black. I have never had anything but a red or a black evening gown.

Basically, I have always worn gray, black and red and a little beige. And now I'm starting to wear a bright blue, but only over a black blouse and skirt. I have black shoes and gray shoes and my life is very simple. Everything goes together and that way I don't need too many things.

MARC: Those are the colors of your apartment—gray, black, red and white.

REVA: Yes, I live in no color. I feel that people are the color. This apartment is a stunning background for people. There's nothing to interfere with what they're wearing. Women shine in my apartment; each one stands out because there is nothing to interfere with them.

MARC: But it sounds as though you had "it" from the beginning.

REVA: I was elegant and chic when I was young, but not like I am today. I can put on a plain black dress and comb my hair and walk down the street and hold my head like this and everybody will stop. It's my profile. My head is classic, and until I realized it was, I couldn't pull off what I pull off today.

I always thought I was ugly and unattractive as a young girl. I had two cousins who were blond and blue-eyed and won beauty contests. I suffered painfully, as a young person. But I maximized. I achieved a look. And now I'm deliriously happy with the way I look. But it took thirty years of watching and studying—people, proportions, shapes, anything—and working and accomplishing. Only recently have I come to realize how good I am.

MARC: And you did it all by yourself.

REVA: Yes. The business, and the apartment on Fifth Avenue and the house in the country.

MARC: And the elegance.

REVA: Elegance is security, assurance.

I'm aware of it when I dress for dinner. I put on a necklace and earrings and a bracelet. Then something tells me the bracelet is too much. So I take it off, and the next thing I know, the necklace follows. Sometimes, the earrings go, too. I feel a surge—of regret, maybe—but I realize now it's too much and I don't need it.

I first knew Mrs. Michael Kaiser as Betsy Pickering, one of the beautiful models from the U.S. who came to Paris in the Fifties with the newspaper and magazine editors to have the clothes from the semiannual *haute couture* showings photographed against French backgrounds for their readers. What a sensation these tall, long-legged American beauties caused everywhere they went, and especially among the hairdressers who prepared them for the camera.

I had opened my salon in New York by the time she stopped modeling to marry Hari Theodoracopulos, a Greek shipping man, and since then she had been a client of mine and of Raphael on my staff. A few years ago, she sent Michael Kaiser, the photographer, whom she had married after her divorce from Mr. Theodoracopulos, to me to have his beard trimmed. I cut the hair of her teen-age sons when they are home on vacation from boarding school.

Like Mrs. Paley, Betsy Kaiser was named to the International Best-Dressed List's Hall of Fame, an honor reserved for perennial winners. She has that rare quality of sexy elegance, more so as she approaches fifty than she did at twenty-one. We talked about all this one morning in her sunny apartment on Fifth Avenue. A brunette with gray-blue eyes, she was wearing a black gabardine skirt and a black cashmere sweater with sleeves loosely cut as in a fencer's shirt. Her aristocratic feet were shod in high-heeled black patent leather shoes with yellow toes.

The walls of the dining room are covered with her husband's prize collection of photographs—Richard Avedon's portrait of James Galanos in a dinner jacket open to reveal several inches of bare chest; Henri Cartier-Bresson's Paris scenes; and several Michael Kaisers, including two portraits of a woman on a beach in bikini bottom and T-shirt, her hair much the worse for sun and salt. "Do you know who she is?" Betsy asked, and laughed when I said, "It can't be you?"

Betsy's bath and dressing room, designed by David Hicks, is completely mirrored—walls and ceiling—and is equipped with a professional hair dryer and lots of drawer and closet space for rollers, clips and hairbrushes; in short, a private beauty salon.

BETSY: You know I can't stand going to hairdressing salons. I feel it's such a waste of time and I don't like being with all those women. Not that I don't have very good women friends. But I just can't spend my life in a beauty salon, which I would have to do if I hadn't learned to do my own hair when I was modeling.

I have to wash my hair once every two days, or once a day in the summertime because I'm exercising so much. But I have this very naturally curly hair, so I really need very good direction from a hairdresser. You've always told me what to do with my hair.

I need a very good haircut, which is the most important thing, and now, good hair coloring. We're experimenting a little bit, aren't we? You want me to let it go gray.

MARC: You were doing that and then you changed your mind.

BETSY: After I started turning gray about four years ago, I just dyed the first inch on the hairline and never touched the rest, but then when I cut my hair about a year ago, I let it go and it was quite a shock. I don't mind gray hair, but mine was so kinky and I looked so washed out in the morning without makeup.

MARC: So what is this you've done with yourself?

BETSY: Remember, I asked your advice and you told me about Loving Care? This is the dark brown. I didn't do the forty-five minutes; I put it on for fifteen or twenty minutes.

MARC: I think it's too plain. You should bring a little warmth to it. But it's good, in that if you look closely you can see some muted gray hairs underneath. That's what in France we call "maquillage." You don't dye the hair, you just make it up.

BETSY: That's it, exactly. Makeup. I think you should change your hair coloring like you change your rouge. I might let it go gray again. It's nice to know I can do that in the sun and salt water. I might just do this every once in a while with a different color since it's so easy. The colors are so marvelous.

This rinse gives my own natural color a depth and it also colors the gray, and I think it's giving me body.

MARC: Your hair is very fine and porous. Therefore, if you leave it on too long, it will be too hard-looking. It's better that you make up your hair very slightly.

BETSY: There are so many marvelous things to work with now. I just wash my hair and set it, and take the electric comb to it or the blow dryer.

Guillaume showed me how to use the electric comb years ago and that has been a revolution. If your hair is overset, if it doesn't work out, you just take the electric comb to it and it loosens up. And then Alexandre, when he came out with the hairpieces, that saved my hair for a while.

Do you realize how many bad hairdressers there are? As many as bad doctors. One of the great hairdressers of Paris, in 1959 when I was doing the *Vogue* collections, teased my hair so much that it broke off at the roots, the size of quarters.

MARC: I know who you mean. When he saw a woman like you, like Suzy Parker, he went wild. He wanted to do his best, his very best. Some guys, when they have such a beautiful creature in their hands, they go overboard. Once in a while, we all do a great catastrophe.

BETSY: But my dear, this is also one, two, three o'clock in the morning. That was when we started to shoot the collections. Remember?

MARC: Those were the days. Tell me, what do you think of modeling as a career now? If you had a daughter, a Brooke Shields, would you want her to model?

BETSY: I adored modeling. It gave me an opportunity to travel. And at one point I wanted to be a fashion designer, so I loved all the glamour and the clothes. That was very exciting. But I don't think I would want my daughter, if I had one, to be a model today. I would definitely insist on her finishing her education. I went to Sarah Lawrence for three months and left. Fortunately, I was successful immediately. I was traveling two or three times a year to Europe.

I worked until 1963, when I married. My sons were born in '65 and '66. That took care of the Sixties. The crazy Sixties. I was wearing this marvelous mane and streaking my hair.

MARC: You wore your hair long for quite a while.

BETSY: Shoulder length or below. It was great because, with my curly hair, it was easier to manage. Or I could pull it back. But five or six years ago, the long hair just didn't have the body it used to. And it was aging me. You kept recommending I cut it. It was passé. And finally I did, to this length, just below the earlobes. I wanted to have a new look. Long hair does age you.

I do respect your opinion. No matter how much taste she has, a woman needs a good hairdresser, and a good designer.

MARC: But she has to know what's right for her. For instance, I don't see you going out in the evening in décolleté dresses very much, although your skin is very lovely. You seem to be covered up most of the time.

BETSY: There's nothing like a little cover-up for more seduction. It's the cut of the dress that counts. Men love to see a back. They love very sensuous fabrics and colors.

MARC: I think a woman is more sexy seen through cover than with everything out, but some women think otherwise. I know a businesswoman who tells me she always gets a bigger order if she goes with her boobs showing.

BETSY: My husband thinks, and I agree with him, that there is nothing more sexy than a woman in a suit and a strand of pearls, no blouse. That's the way the French do it, very elegant and yet so sexy. Men like conservative-looking women.

MARC: It makes a man want to discover what's underneath.

BETSY: A slip underneath, or a camisole, and you wear those marvelous long panties, step-ins they call them, and stockings and very elegant shoes. Lingerie is very important.

MARC: One of the clients told her daughter, "You'd better wear beautiful underwear if you go to Monsieur Marc, because you have to get undressed." Isn't that sweet? She meant the checkroom, of course.

BETSY: Being sexy is not just the clothes, it's the way the eyes sparkle, the way her teeth sparkle. Her hair must be fresh and well cut. It has to look natural, whether it's dyed or not. It has to suit the woman. That's why the hairdresser is very important.

MARC: You say you exercise a lot.

BETSY: A woman has to maintain her body, not only because it's her body but I think it helps her mind. Indeed it does. It just gives you more enthusiasm. That's all part of growing older gracefully. Always keep your enthusiasm.

MARC: Do you follow an exercise regime?

BETSY: I have a stationary bicycle in my bedroom that I ride while listening to the news or to music. I work out regularly on Nautilus machines at a fitness center. I walk and play tennis. I'm an addict about exercise. If I don't do it, I feel terrible. I don't think properly. I become depressed.

MARC: Do you have to think about your weight? You don't look as though you've gained any since you were a model.

BETSY: I started thinking about it ten years ago when I gained ten or fifteen pounds after I stopped smoking. I had been smoking three packs a day and I had no energy. And my dentist told me I would have no enamel left on my teeth because I was brushing them all the time. So I thought, This is ridiculous, and I stopped.

After thirty-five, there's no such thing as never having to worry about your weight. One has to watch. I've always liked very healthy food and I never used to gain weight, but now I watch how many pieces of bread I have, or, when I want to go on a diet, I don't have bread and butter, and I don't have sauces. I have a marvelous salad, and chicken breasts and fish. There are so many things available today.

MARC: What about alcohol?

BETSY: I'll have a scotch if people are here, or when I'm out, which is a few times a week. Everything in moderation. One has to become aware, one has to moderate.

MARC: How much do you weigh?

BETSY: Between 125 and 128, and I'm five foot nine. But I'm small-boned and when I was 135, I looked like a linebacker. I didn't gain in my hips. I gained in my upper back and my bosom. That is the most difficult place to lose it. I gained fifty pounds with each child and I didn't feel well with that extra weight. Plus, the clothes are so expensive today and I wanted to get back into my Galanos again.

MARC: You don't wear much makeup. Most women past twenty-two tend to put on more. I don't think they realize they are doing it.

BETSY: Men hate makeup on your skin, plus they hate it more on their clothes. But they adore to have a woman make up her eyes. I pile on the mascara. I use more eye makeup than I ever used as I'm getting older, and less on the skin because it won't carry heavy makeup. I think a woman should reevaluate her makeup about every eight years. When my hair was gray, I made my eyebrows much darker. Yesterday when I colored my hair, the dark eyebrows were not right.

I think gray-brown eye shadow is the prettiest and that's what I usually put on in the morning. Madeleine Mono makes a very good eye pencil, very soft, and I put the brown in there on top of the cream eye shadow. In the evening, I put a little bit more color, purple or green on the brown.

MARC: I can't stand women who put blue or pink over their eyes, particularly the other day I saw an overbleached blonde with hair like straw and too short for her age, her makeup I could have cut with a knife, and she had pink pencil over her eyes.

BETSY: Once in a while in the evening when you have your makeup on, you take your rouge brush and put a little pink on the bone over the eyes and it's pretty.

MARC: But not frosted, I hope.

BETSY: The one who uses iridescent shadow is the same type who will paint the toenails of the dog.

MARC: What do you use on the skin?

BETSY: I use either Orentreich or Laszlo cream as a base and Clinique powder over that, applied very lightly with one of those French down puffs. Although sometimes not. If I'm coming out from under a dryer, I won't use powder. It depends on my skin that day whether or not I use powder. If my face doesn't have that moist look, I spray it very lightly with a mist of Evian.

When it's very cold in New York and all the steam heat is on, your skin gets dried out.

But there's nothing that can help a face that is not rested.

MARC: It used to be that a Frenchwoman wouldn't go out if her face didn't look right, if she didn't have the right thing to wear. She would rather stay home.

BETSY: I think she should, except that if something is very important, you make time to be rested. How do you cover up aging? You can't cover it up. You can only improve the quality of your life with proper exercise and diet and what goes into your mind. Your life shows in your face. If you relax within yourself, you will just look fine, and still sexy because you have everything inside you.

Some women cannot grow older gracefully, so their makeup gets heavier, the face-lift is too much, and they get frantic about their age. Emotionally, they're very immature.

MARC: Do you think it is possible to be elegant, or to work toward elegance, if you don't have any money?

BETSY: Absolutely. Even in the Fifties, when I didn't have much money, I started buying Galanos clothes, and fortunately I have them all. And except for a few I gave to the Brooklyn Museum, I wear them. I did a ball for two thousand teen-agers to benefit the Youth Counseling League, the Gold and Silver Ball, and for that I took out a Galanos dress that was eighteen years old.

Most women would not think of wearing an old dress. For me, something four years old is brand-new. Luckily, I have the closet space.

MARC: When you were modeling, you could get designer clothes wholesale, which isn't something the average woman can do. It's a privilege of being a model, like the airline pass is for the stewardess. Did designers ever give you clothes?

BETSY: Never. Once in a while we could buy a sample, but they were usually so shot.

MARC: But what direction would you tell someone to go who didn't have money and didn't have that privilege?

BETSY: Blouses and skirts. They're the best investment she can make and there are so many places she can go to find things at a discount. Or if she is handy, or if she knows someone who can sew, she can get a very fine piece of fabric and have a plain good straight skirt made, invest in a good belt or buy one of those on sale, and wear the skirt with a change of blouse or sweater. A straight skirt lasts forever.

I just bought a black suit from Jimmy Galanos. Now this is something they'll do for you if you buy from the designer salon in a store with Blass or de la Renta, too, or a French couture house. Jimmy made the suit with a short skirt. Then he made a pair of tuxedo pants with the satin stripe down the side. I didn't have satin on the lapels of the jacket, figuring I could always put a satin scarf at the neck. Then he made me a long skirt, and a sleeveless crisscross blouse trimmed in the satin. With the one jacket, the short skirt, the long skirt and the pair of pants, I could really travel for a month. I could wear a turtleneck underneath it, a white blouse, the blouse he made, add boots. And shawls—one of the best things that have come along for dressing something up or changing the look.

Invest in a suit and it lasts ten years; you wear it with a sweater or a blouse or plain, which is divine. I love expensive clothes because they look so well, but I'm very careful with what I buy and I keep reverting back.

And also, I do not send these clothes out to the dry cleaner. I have them spot-cleaned.

MARC: The cleaners here take the life out of the material. I have clients who send their clothes to Paris to be cleaned. I send my ski clothes to France to be cleaned and waterproofed, and when I go to Paris, one client gives me all her gloves to take to the cleaner over there.

BETSY: Hanging clothes is very important. If you have to cover something, you must never do it with plastic. Use old sheets or cloths. Hangers are another big investment. If you cannot afford good ones, wrap the regular hangers with tissue paper. And let the clothes air out before you put them away.

MARC: There are so many women who buy the most expensive designer clothes and wear them just so, and yet they don't have that quality called "elegance," that quality you have.

BETSY: Most women are very insecure about the way they dress. They'll say, "Jimmy Galanos showed this stocking with this shoe with this outfit," and they think they have to wear it that way. They can't mix. They can't comprehend that every outfit has to change according to your body, climate, personality. There are days when you want to put on a sweater. Another day you feel like putting on a silk blouse.

MARC: Yet you, having been a model, are the person who used to come out in the way the designer showed the clothes.

BETSY: When Diana Vreeland was doing the Fashion Group shows, she used to let me add my own earrings or stockings. I would accessorize myself and then she had me accessorize other people.

MARC: That's the sense of elegance. What you feel like, you put on.

BETSY: It's like cooking. You feel like fish; it depends on what's at the market, what's in the air, what your personality is that day, how it tastes as you cook it.

But that's why so many designers are making so much money, because these women have to see the whole outfit right in front of them, the dress and all the accessories.

The greatest revolution in fashion has been the separates. The young men and women are taking them and putting them together the way they feel. It's marvelous to see my boys dress. They wear secondhand clothes, like Canadian Air Force jackets. They're on intimate terms with a mail-order shop in California. One of my sons bought a black cashmere coat for forty-five dollars in some place called Andy's Chee-pees in the Village, the most beautiful black cashmere coat you've ever seen.

The kids aren't intimidated by all these designer clothes. They don't have the money to buy them. So they look original; they are so chic.

MARC: What fragrance do you wear?

BETSY: As little as possible. Today everything is so perfumed—tissues, soap, shampoos. I buy everything scent-free. I put fragrance on my clothes, not on my skin. I believe in trying to stay with one fragrance. I love Jimmy's perfume, "Galanos." And then I love Shelley Marks's "Pot Pourri." It's a bath oil that I use when I bathe, but I also put some on a little cotton ball and tuck it in my pantyhose. He has this tiny little shop on Madison Avenue. I've seen Cary Grant in there. And I sat next to Michael Caine at a party and he said to me, "I know what you have on."

Monsieur Marc's
List of the Most Elegant Women

SIMPLY ELEGANT

Rosamund Bernier (Mrs. John Russell)
Evangeline Bruce (Mrs. David)
Aimée de Heeren (Mrs. Rodman)
Audrey Hepburn
Carolina Herrera (Mrs. Reinaldo)
Mildred Hilson (Mrs. Edwin)
Françoise de Lobkowicz (Princesse Edouard)
Gisèle Masson (Mrs. Charles)
Jacqueline de Ribes (Vicomtesse Edouard)
Geraldine Stutz

SEXY ELEGANT

Anouk Aimée
Capucine
Maryll Lanvin (Mme. Bernard)
Catherine Deneuve
Diana Harari (Mrs. Philip)
Betsy Kaiser (Mrs. Michael)

Mercedes Kellogg (Mrs. Francis)
Terry Allen Kramer (Mrs. Irwin)
Simone Letourneur
Louise Rouet (Mme. Jacques)

FOREVER IN MY MEMORY

Barbara Paley (Mrs. William)
Gloria Guinness (Mrs. Loel)
Louise de Vilmorin

Inelegance Is . . .

Designer jeans
Dacron suits (with or without a designer label)
Open-toe shoes without a pedicure
Motto pillows
Stretch limousines with darkened glass windows
Fuchsia hair
Cleavage
Eyeglasses in the hair
Walkmans in public places
Chewing gum
Smoking in the street
Eating in the street or in public transportation
Using a secretary to extend, accept or refuse a personal invitation
Not saying thank you for a gift, an evening, a weekend
Name-dropping
Place-dropping
Rubbing shoulders (corporate country club America's answer to the
    jet-set kiss)
Apologizing to someone you meet at other people's parties for not
    inviting them to your own
Waiting to see if a person you meet for the first time is "someone"
    before you extend your best manners
Having two sets of manners
Telling a spouse or lover about a previous spouse or lover. (Better do
    as Edith Piaf advised in "A Quoi Se Sert L'Amour": Make believe
    your current love is both your first and your last.

10

IN AND OUT OF
FASHION

A

AGE

I've always thought Americans put the wrong emphasis on age with their worship of youth and dread of losing it. The fault may be in the language. In French, *Quel âge avez-vous?* literally means only "What age do you have?" In English, "How *old* are you?" has a mournful sound. No wonder the answer is often an understatement. Even bread is referred to as one day *old* when "baked yesterday" would be more accurate and pleasant to hear.

Recognizing that life is a continuous process of becoming and that youth is the least exciting part, the French appreciate a woman of experience. Not until thirty can a woman be interesting; at forty, she is mature like a good red Burgundy or Bordeaux wine. She has learned to put herself together, she has been to a few restaurants and traveled a bit, and, it is assumed, she is familiar with passion.

In the film *La Vie Continue*, Annie Girardot plays a widow in her forties, with the lines and puffy spots showing in her face, going about the business of life as a very sexual being. To me, the sexiest woman on or off the screen is Jeanne Moreau, in her fifties. Every time I look at Moreau, I want to hold her in my arms and never let go. Or Capucine, in her youth one of Givenchy's favorite models, an actress at fifty. In *The Trail of the Pink Panther* with Peter Sellers, she played Inspector Clouseau's wife.

How can a Brooke Shields, sweet adolescent that she is, possibly be as interesting as women like that, or like Sophia Loren, Jane Fonda, Raquel Welch? The French do not, after all, have a monopoly on feminine sexiness past forty.

Despite the Brooke Shields phenomenon, there are signs that nymphets may be on the way out of American fashion, or at least stepping aside to let in women who could be their mothers or more.

On prime-time television, where Charlie's Angels kept male viewers glued to their sets in the Seventies, actresses like fiftyish Rita Moreno and Joan Collins and sixty-eight-year-old Jane Wyman are playing the parts of smart, aggressive, well-turned-out women of power whose sex objects happen to be much younger men. As far as I know, this is a case of fiction imitating life.

In the real world of the Eighties, women are exercising power at relatively young ages. One is not surprised to meet a female vice-president of a bank or a president of a division of an industrial or entertainment company who is in her thirties.

But women at the half-century mark and beyond are also enjoying recognition, some in new careers and social experiences: Jacqueline Onassis as a book editor; Carmen dell'Orifice, one of the most elegant models of the Sixties, back before the cameras with white hair and a figure as slender as ever; Dorian Leigh, the model for Revlon's "Fire and Ice" promotion in the Fifties, who later ran a model agency in Paris, is now a party caterer and food consultant in Connecticut.

Helen Gurley Brown, editor of *Cosmopolitan*, gives advice on how to be sexy at sixty. Vera Newman, designer of scarves and table linens under the Vera label, drives sports cars and celebrates her seventy-fifth birthday in a discotheque.

If a woman takes care of herself, she can bloom at almost any age, but she should dress and act in a manner appropriate to her level.

There comes a time when, as the French say, things are not where they used to be. Chins, necks, upper arms, breasts and behinds follow the law of gravity. It's very rare that a body stays as firm as it was at twenty or twenty-five. We enjoy life a little more with food and wine; some of us exercise a little less. Our shapes expand.

Even the woman who diets, exercises, worries away her flesh and spares no expense for cosmetic surgery can't completely avoid drooping. Little cushions of fat develop at the base of the neck even if her posture is superb; they also appear around the armpits and overlap the top of a strapless dress. Upper arms are seldom immune to the passage of time. Before a woman twice twenty or more buys a dress without sleeves, or one of those bare-shouldered and one-shoulder evening dresses that designers who serve fashionable socialites keep turning out, she should try it on in front of the triple mirror and wave at herself. If the flesh of the upper arm moves, she should take off the dress. Are there freckles on her chest from too much sunbathing in her youth, or other blotches of age? Does she have hollows at her collarbones? (We call them "saltcellars" in French.) If so, let her forget about décolleté, for false notes like these will ruin the effect she worked so hard to achieve with an expensive dress and jewelry and a beautiful hairdo.

At the benefit of the fall 1982 season, the Belle Époque dinner at the Metropolitan Museum of Art, the sexiest-looking women were covered up: Raquel Welch in an André Laug python-printed sequined dress that showed only her sensual face and the curvy outline of her body; Cristina Ferrare DeLorean in a long-sleeved sequined chiffon blouse over black pants; Lynn Wyatt in a taffeta dress by Cardin with a stand-up ruffle along the left side and a shirred bodice.

Cover-up is more provocative than an expanse of flesh. There's more excitement for a man in discovery than in knowing that what he sees of a beautifully wrapped package is what he gets.

With concealment, a woman can selectively accentuate her best features—her face and hair; her silhouette; her legs, which are her most enduring physical asset, provided they were good to begin with, of course. Was anything ever as alluring as the women of Vietnam and China, before the Communists put them in proletarian drab, in their straight-line tunics slit up the sides to reveal a flash of shapely ankle, calf and thigh? Even when she's tottering, a woman can still play up her legs with lacy stockings and delicate shoes. Much prettier than a V plunging down a leathery chest is a neckline draped to bare a smooth back, another part of a woman's anatomy that stays young-looking longer than the rest.

B

BAGS

You can always tell an elegant woman by her handbag and shoes. She regards them as gilt-edged investments, accessories she cannot afford to skimp on.

Handbags last longer than shoes, are less subject to the caprices of fashion and make excellent gifts. A young woman striving toward elegance on a limited budget should educate the men in her life to present her with a beautiful bag at Christmas or for her birthday.

Simplicity and quality of the leather and fabric are the important things to look for in choosing a bag. These and the sturdiness of the workmanship were what originally drew fashionable women to Gucci in the Fifties. If one looks hard, one may find a few designs not marred by the double-G initials that made Gucci a status symbol for conspicuous consumers and now are shunned by the chic.

Hermès markings are on the inside, and its designs more refined, but current prices are astronomical. The quilted handbags with chain handles carrying the Chanel label, also on the inside, are terribly expensive and the affordable copies lose in translation. Sexual elegance was Gabrielle Chanel's forte; the chain handles, besides being graceful and long-wearing, convey an erotic message to those primed to receive one.

Bags by Reva are practical and reasonably priced but can only be bought in the most exclusive outlets in the U.S. Reva uses mostly fabrics such as ultrasuede for her bags, which are deceptively roomy and pack flat into a suitcase. The elegance is in their slim line and lack of decoration.

Women who lead busy lives often use their handbags as filing cabinets, and this leads to unsightly consequences—a moderate-size bag bulging with its contents, or what appears to be a horse bucket slung over the shoulder. A well-designed bag usually has hidden capacity.

Another possibility is to carry a briefcase for business papers and keep the handbag for eyeglasses, wallet, makeup and keys. In the last few years, briefcases have become a fashion item, and the same standards apply as for handbags—simplicity and quality. The silhouette should be slim, the construction sturdy, the handles and clasp graceful. A Samsonite attaché case is beyond the pale, for women or men. (See NATURAL.)

How a woman carries her handbag is a clue to her elegance quotient. A bag with short handles should be carried over the lower arm by the side of the body, never in front. To hold the straps in the palm of the hand and dangle the bag as you walk is not only inelegant but inviting to purse snatchers, a factor to be considered in most major cities of the world these days.

Shoulder bags have gone through many image phases in the last twenty years. Whether one looks like a streetwalker, a flight attendant, a policewoman or an elegant creature depends on the quality of the bag, its size and proportion to the wearer, and her carriage. If she holds herself erect and walks so that the bag swings slightly from the shoulder, it adds a charming flirtatious air. But a new defense tactic against muggers is to place the strap around the neck and then swing the bag under the armpit.

A bag cannot be too classic and conservative as far as design and color, except for sports and resort wear.

For evening, a bit of glitter is permissible, but if the glitter isn't real gold, as in the clasp of the bag, better go for sobriety. Gold and silver *minaudières* that can be carried in the palm of the hand are in the category of jewels as to both workmanship and price. A perfectly plain satin or envelope bag is always correct. Unless it's a family heirloom, petit point marks you as a member of the American Express seventeen-day tour to three major capitals.

BARGAINS

Women who have "it"—flair, taste, knowledge of fashion—do very well buying clothes on sale. They are dedicated shoppers, and having studied the quality of items as they arrive in the stores at the beginning of the season, wait for them to be reduced (and sometimes, knowing there will be another reduction, wait further). When the price is right for them, they pounce. Of course, they run the risk of losing the prize.

But theirs is a special talent. Sales are a delusion for most women, like the slot machines in a gambling casino. Tempted more by the slashed prices on the ticket than by the value of the garment and its becomingness to them, they make their biggest mistakes and end up losing more than they save.

As for bargain hunters off the beaten track, they can be deceived by a phony designer label or a designer's mistake that the merchant took off his hands and is reselling on the cheap.

Unless you are very sure of yourself, bargain hunter beware.

BELTS

Another accessory with restorative powers for old familiar clothing—to convert a chemise to a dress with a defined waistline; to shorten a dress by making a *blouson* top.

You can't blame a woman for wanting to show off a tiny waist. But if the hips below are broad, what's the point? Here's where a three-way mirror can straighten her out.

BIKINI

Diana Vreeland may have had a point when she said, years ago, "The bikini is the greatest thing since the atom bomb." The fallout has been catastrophic. The bikini can be sexy on the right body, a Bo Derek or someone pretty close to a 10. On someone else, disaster.

Why don't women accept that they can be better sirens in one-piece suits? A maillot makes a good body look sensational, and is kind to a mediocre one. Unfortunately, manufacturers ruined the one-piece suit when they cut it high on the sides. It makes the wearer look as though she hasn't graduated yet from diapers.

BOOTS

Boots can be elegant and sexy with midcalf-length skirts, if they fit close to the leg and have regular high heels. No triangular or other oddly shaped heels, no pointed toes, no white boots of any kind, none of those boots with an accordion droop.

For a feminine, sporty look, pants can be rolled up and over boots. Ankle-high boots go with pants in the country; fur boots are fun for après-ski.

Beautiful leather and suede are worth the price; plastic not even for free, or in bad weather.

C

COLOR

Color is almost a sixth sense, and therefore a highly personal and emotional topic. If your mother told you green was unlucky, if your husband likes you only in blue, if your lover left you on a day when you were wearing gray and if you were fired in a pink suit, there isn't much to talk about as far as color, is there?

But one can make certain general observations. Elegant women avoid strong colors, while women whose first priority is being noticed won't wear anything else.

Vivid colors look good in the summer, in tropical climates and around the Christmas tree. Bright pink winter coats on a city street remind me of hunters lost in the woods.

You can never go astray with black, navy blue, gray or beige, or with any of those colors (or noncolors) in combination with white or with a scarf in predominantly soft tones of another shade, such as mauve or rose.

Carolina Herrera once said that "black is safe, and brown is chic." I think black is always chic and brown is not the color to wear to earn compliments. In any case, steer clear of brown unless you have a wonderfully creamy complexion. As an alternative to black, navy blue can be chic and it has uniquely flattering properties for both women and men of almost any skin and hair tone. Navy goes well with white or green; brown with beige or light blue.

Red is a color of several moods—erotic, youthful, reckless, a color of celebration. Supremely elegant women like the late Gloria Guinness choose red as their third color after black and gray. Red is Nancy Reagan's favorite; it suits her effervescent personality and looks most becoming with her honey-toned hair.

Women who are contemplating turning blond should reflect on how limiting that shade of hair can be. Dark hair knows no bounds as to color, but a blonde must be careful not to look cheap. Black is beautiful for her and so are pastels and white, provided she has a suntan; otherwise she will look washed out.

Certain colors shoot into fashion like meteors for a season by designer decree, which is just when a clever woman will let them pass. Why should she be lost in a neon-green or electric-yellow crowd?

Khaki and loden green are forever chic but should be bypassed if your complexion is sallow or your hair on the dull side.

Particular discretion is called for in buying colored furs. Red or tawny fox can be sexy and elegant on a blonde or redhead; on a brunette it's déclassé. The same applies to spotted furs, most of which have been withdrawn from the market as endangered species although fake-fur versions are everywhere. (See NATURAL.)

White and very pale shades of fox and mink have a place at royal receptions, debutante parties, and charity balls in Palm Beach. However, if you can have only one mink, don't let it be white. Conservative shades of brown and black mink are universally becoming. A mink coat is the best all-around security blanket. It goes with everything, is the warmest of elegant furs and after it's served its time on the outside can be used as the lining for a raincoat. Sable is more elegant but costlier, and so is fisher, except that it isn't particularly flattering except to a redhead.

CONCORDE

A Concorde flight bag is still a bit of a status symbol even though it is possible to buy one without crossing the Atlantic in the supersonic plane. Carry-on luggage for subsonic flights, however, should be made of unmarked canvas, leather or nylon faille with only name tags for identification. After all, why advertise a commercial airline when the chic way to travel is by private jet, or, for short distances—say from New York to Southampton for lunch, or from Paris to the farm in Normandy—a helicopter of one's own?

D

DESIGNERS

The fashion designers of modern times who understood women best have been female. Two of the most creative were Gabrielle Chanel and Alix Grès. Strangely enough, the proof of Chanel's genius is in the copying, while Madame Grès's is in her uniqueness. I don't believe any woman ever felt betrayed by Chanel or Grès, whereas with other designers she may have felt sacrificed to their desire to gain attention for themselves.

Chanel, in particular, duplicated for others her experience as a *demimondaine*. She invented sportswear—and costume jewelry. She was the first to dress women in men's trousers and to make working-class wool jersey fashionable. Yves Saint Laurent, the darling of the fashion press and the hard-chic ladies, is constantly recycling Chanel's ideas.

The suit with the unstructured jacket and braided trimming that she brought back into fashion when she reopened her *maison de couture* at 31 rue Cambon in 1954 became the uniform of the *haute bourgeoisie* in France and America. Anyone can wear it. A woman with short legs can have the skirt made longer and the jacket shorter; a woman with long legs can do the reverse. Chanel put a chain inside the jacket at the hem so that it would never ride up or down when the wearer moved.

Nancy Reagan is the most famous of the loyal fans Adolfo has won with his version of the Chanel suit. Adolfo didn't just copy Chanel; he added his own interpretation, mostly with very lightweight knitted fabrics that are particularly suited to the American climate and its overheated rooms. It is amusing to observe the checkroom at Monsieur Marc on one of those weeks in fall and spring when the ladies in the Adolfos eye the ladies in the Chanels. To the connoisseur, there is no mistaking one for the other.

Chanel died in 1971 at the age of eighty-seven, and for the next eleven years her house kept turning out ladylike clothes according to her vision. Some young designers were hired to rejuvenate the line. They padded the shoulders, shortened and narrowed the skirts and made the necklines of blouses plunge. The result was a 1980s hooker look, but not as elegant as the girls who used to work the Madeleine and the Champs-Elysées districts in their Chanels during the Fifties. Considering the prices—$3,000 for a ready-made, $6,000 to $15,000 for a custom Chanel—it was a disaster. Karl Lagerfeld took over as "artistic director" for spring 1983 and beat a tactical retreat to classic lines.

Madame Grès is still going strong in her establishment at 1 rue de la Paix at eighty years plus. Few living designers understand sexual elegance as she does. Put a skinny woman in one of her "amusing little suits" and a man yearns to undress her. Madame Grès's secret is to make him guess at the body underneath the clothes. She does this with draping and a bias cut that cannot be imitated. Women who own Grès evening dresses guard them like family silver. One of her 1936 models can be worn today without adjustment.

Like the great artist she is, Madame Grès never stops seeking perfection. I observe her when I do the coiffures for the showing of her collection in New York. She will try a dress on a dozen models and reject them all until she finds the one whose breast is just high enough, waist small enough, hips gently rounded enough for a certain evening dress.

So much for creativity, which used to be the driving force behind the French *haute couture*. Marc Bohan of Christian Dior, Yves Saint Laurent and Hubert de Givenchy still make clothes to measure for a small, rarefied clientele, but mostly the Paris couturiers are in the business of selling fashion, meaning a certain level of taste with seasonal changes, through ready-to-wear and other franchised outlets for their names.

Seventy percent of Hubert de Givenchy's customers are American, which is why the celebration of the thirtieth anniversary of the founding of his *maison de couture* was held in New York rather than in Paris in May 1982. And what a celebration that was, with bicoastal society and their French friends gathering to pay homage to *le Grand Hubert*.

The ladies are crazy about him. How could they help it? He is as tall as a basketball player; *distingué* with his blue eyes, silvery hair and aristocratic bearing; and ever so rich. Givenchy has a house on the Left Bank for which he reportedly paid millions, a seventeenth-century château for weekends, a ski chalet at Mégève. Though he gives no hint of being the marrying kind, many of these women keep hoping they can succeed where others have failed. To convert Givenchy or one of the other wealthy bachelor princes of the fashion world to wedlock is a challenge, like climbing Annapurna. After all, there is always the example of Oscar de la Renta and Françoise de Langlade to cheer them on. The de la Rentas were married in 1967 and have lived happily ever after, combining their talents—his as a designer, her as a hostess.

For originality in fashion these days, one has to look to designers like Mary McFadden and Norma Kamali in New York, to Giorgio Armani in Milan, and to the Japanese designers in Tokyo and Paris. Like Chanel, McFadden and Kamali interpret their experiences as women for particular audiences. Armani has a typically Italian flair for tailoring, which he expresses with an avant-garde sophistication. The look can be copied, but not the fit, which is the essence of his style.

The Japanese are the most innovative with their concept of clothing in one size for all. Loose-fitting pieces can be wrapped, cinched or left to hang free. The Western designer's preoccupation with enhancing a woman's body does not concern them. In Japanese costume and art, the neck is the only part of the body left bare to be appreciated. And what a sensuous part that is.

The woman who wears clothes by Issey Miyake, Yohji Yomamoto, Mitsuhiro Matsuda and Rei Kawakubo has to pay more attention to her face and her hair.

DOGS

A dog is a great asset in making social contacts, particularly in the city, where fear and shyness build barriers. A woman whose mother instilled in her never to talk to strangers feels free to respond to the friendly interest of a fellow canine-lover when she takes her dog for an airing.

A dog owner should therefore give at least as much thought to dressing for the walk in the park as for achieving success in a corporate jungle. A sporty note is the best: well-fitting pants and boots; or a pleated wool skirt, twin sweater set and moccasins; an amusing fur parka, perhaps. A mink-coated dog walker seen shortly after dawn heralds a mistress determined to keep warm and a pet fortunate to be living at a stylish address.

As for dressing the dog, almost anything is *de trop*—above all, painted paw nails and jeweled collars. Fur coats are an embarrassment; a raincoat for a poodle or a Yorkshire terrier may be a necessity since those breeds dislike going out in the rain.

Fashions in breeds change every decade or so. Poodles are out, York-shire terriers are in, not only for their air of *chic negligé* but because they are good company besides, and easy to train. *Le tout Paris's* passion for dachshunds has never quite made it across the Atlantic. There is, however, a Franco-American understanding about King Charles spaniels.

On the whole, big dogs are the chic of the Eighties, like Bill Blass's golden retrievers. Personally, I am crazy about hunting dogs and have a weakness for women who share my enthusiasm. But since not all men are of the same mind, a large dog can be a liability to a single woman. Some gentlemen callers don't like to meet a hound of the same size.

E

EYEBROWS

What is the most distinctive feature of Brooke Shields? Not her preco-ciousness, not her thick light chestnut hair, not her sweet disposition. These are noticeable traits, but it's her eyebrows—unusually straight and wide over her pale blue eyes—that make Brooke's face memorable.

The shape and color of eyes give a face its particular look; the eyebrows give expression. Like a hairdo, eyebrows can be dated to a certain period in fashion and many women don't realize how much their eyebrows can make them look passé even as they wear the latest clothing and hairstyles.

Pencil-thin eyebrows announce the Thirties and the movie sirens like Greta Garbo, Marlene Dietrich and Mae West, who wore them against a similarly artificial background of Art Deco. Male actors of the same era with particular savoir faire, like Ronald Colman and Adolph Menjou, sported pencil moustaches.

A more natural look with the eyebrows tweezed only underneath has been the contemporary fashion. Some models leave the area above the nose unplucked, or artfully tweezed so that a few faint hairs are visible.

Sometimes nature apportions eyebrows considerably lighter or darker than one's hair. If the contrast is disturbing—very dark eyebrows can be a bit forbidding on a woman—don't hesitate to improve on nature. But exercise utmost care, because the porousness of eyebrow hair is very different from that on top of the head.

To lighten eyebrows, apply a mild mixture of peroxide and ammonia with a nail brush or cuticle stick wrapped with cotton at the tip. Leave for a few seconds and wash off quickly with lukewarm water. Eyebrows can be darkened with hair coloring, but, again, speed is essential. Never go as far as black; even a jet-haired woman should stop at dark brown for her eyebrows.

EYEGLASSES

A woman who really cares about her looks and has trouble with her vision should get herself fitted for contact lenses. If she cannot wear this form of corrective lens, however, glasses can be feminine and even sexy when they concentrate attention on the eyes in such a way as to stir a man's desire to remove them and discover what the wearer is really like. The frames must be thin—wire or tortoiseshell—never colored or trimmed with rhinestones or initials, and sized in proper proportion to the wearer's features.

Oversize glasses, whether clear or tinted for sun, are outdated, especially when they go with a teased lion's mane or are pushed on top of the head. Aviator glasses belong in a box with artifacts of the Seventies.

Women who chain their half-glasses around their necks are proclaiming that they have surrendered to the absentmindedness of advancing age. Men never make passes at such old girls who wear glasses. One can keep track of spectacles when not in use by tucking them into a pocket. Once opticians perfected the bifocal lens with an invisible line of separation, there was no excuse for half-glasses.

For reading theater programs and to carry in an evening bag, a lorgnette is elegant, particularly if it's an heirloom. Louise Rouet, the enchanting auburn-haired wife of the director of Christian Dior, uses one that belonged to her grandmother and snaps open and shut like a fan.

F

FACE-LIFTS

I claim no expertise on this subject and admit once again to a bias for the natural.

Cosmetic surgery has become almost as popular as the blow dry and not just among the Concorde crowd. Half a million Americans a year, men as well as women, undergo some form of corrective facial surgery. Since the cost of a few strategic nips and tucks is equivalent to that of a mink jacket or coat, price is no deterrent.

Women talk about their face-lifts more openly than about hair coloring. One very warmhearted millionairess offered three friends the opportunity to have their eyes "done" the same time as hers. They recuperated together at her triplex apartment, spending a week swathed in bandages, playing bridge and being nourished on *cuisine minceur* by her French cook. It was like a little girl's slumber party, one guest said.

The day after her husband left her, a woman I knew flew to Brazil to put herself under the knife of Dr. Ivo Pitanguy, the noted sculptor of *beau monde* flesh. She had the works—face, buttocks, breasts—and she must have decided it was worth every cent of the divorce settlement she spent on the excursion. Less than a year later, I received an announcement of her second wedding.

Most clients who talk to me about their face-lifts say they are pleased with the results. Of course, they run a risk. Not only may the surgeon have had a bad day or not be as competent as believed, but there is always the possibility of complications: damage to facial nerves, scarring, infection, and even cardiac arrest, which is what happened to one fashion leader just as the surgeon completed the last tuck. Another suffered an emotional breakdown after discovering she could no longer close her eyes.

Some of us fight desperately to deny the passage of time, but even those who accept it do not always have the good fortune to age with physical grace. If a woman's face has developed serious flaws such as heavy pouches under the eyes, a double chin like an English bull, turkeylike wattles in the neck, and she is advised that these can be improved by surgery, then she should go ahead, by all means, if it will make her happier. But let her have it done with moderation, keeping her personality intact, assured that her eyes and her expression will remain human. She can ask to subtract ten years but not twenty. An older face often appears weary and drained. The goal of a face-lift should be to look rested. If she becomes dissatisfied in a few years, frightened of every new line and sag, and goes back again and again for redoing, she will end up with a face that may be smooth and unwrinkled but lacks vitality.

Everyone knows who the big customers are for facial surgery, not because of the telltale seams behind the ears, in the scalp and under the chin, but from the photographs in the fashion and society pages. There's no mistaking the wide-open eyes of a China doll, the wax cheeks puffed with silicone, and the masklike expression. Skinny from rigorous dieting and exercise, their hair youthfully styled, clad in designer clothes, these women look as real as mannequins in Bergdorf's window. As far as I can tell, they like it that way. Personally, I think a line or two gives a face necessary character.

I recall when I first came to America, plastic surgery was mainly a matter of nose sculpture. When Barbra Streisand burst on the scene in the mid-Sixties and became a star practically overnight, part of her singularity was her refusal to bob her nose. For a while it seemed as though her refreshing look of Nefertiti-from-Brooklyn might be widely copied. Unfortunately, it now appears that a whole generation of women, who were then children or teen-agers, were taken to cosmetic surgeons by their mothers. Where, I wonder, are the young women with interesting noses? In another twenty years, will there by any with laughter lines around their eyes and wrinkled brows? Will the grandmothers of A.D. 2003 all have uniformly incisive chins?

The *beau monde* has always had its little home remedies to try in conjunction with cosmetic surgery. One that was popular for a while was to put Preparation H, the hemorrhoid-relief product, under the eyes to reduce bagging, particularly after a hard night of partying.

Another trick, which works only for women, was to wear the hair severely pulled back to force the eyes into the *oeil de biche*, or doe's eye, that was so popular in Paris in the Fifties.

Though it's too late to start repairing a face ravaged by time and overindulgence with the following methods, a twenty-five-year-old could adopt the wrinkle-forestalling regime of women who really work at elegance all their lives.

Stay out of the sun, or at least protect yourself with a hat and a sunblock preparation.

Don't smoke; abstain from alcohol and carbonated beverages; exercise regularly; and follow a balanced, nutritious pattern of eating.

If you are considering cosmetic surgery, select a surgeon certified by the American Society of Plastic and Reconstructive Surgeons, 233 North Michigan Avenue, Suite 1900, Chicago, Illinois 60601 (312-856-1834). These are physicians who have taken years of advanced training in plastic surgery as compared with many trained in other specialties, like ear, nose and throat, who have added cosmetic surgery to their practices.

FRAGRANCE

America has certainly become a fragrant society, I often think to myself as I walk to the salon in the morning and feel saturated with the scent of women, and men, rushing to their offices. It's a far cry from my early days in this country, when too much perfume was considered vulgar, unwholesome and rather alien. Many Americans believed, with some justification, that Europeans used scent as a substitute for regular bathing.

But all that has changed. America has been "educated" to drench itself in fragrance, not just perfume, which at $80 to $150 an ounce for a status brand is a costly luxury, but in affordable scented soaps, bath oils, shampoos, lotions and *eaux de toilette*. To counteract the complaint that a drop of luxurious perfume didn't last very long, the fragrance industry developed a long-lasting technology. It has succeeded all too well. Some fragrances can't be gotten rid of with less than extraordinary means, such as fumigation.

The purpose of anointing oneself with fragrance is twofold: (1) to attract a member of the opposite sex (or the same, depending on one's sexual preference) and (2) to make oneself feel better. A marketing vice-president for Charles of the Ritz referred to this as "narcissism, or glorifying one's existence."

Actually, to really bathe in the stuff is a foolish act of aggression that can repel the very people one wishes to attract. Some of us are allergic to strong scent. Certain perfumes make me physically uneasy and more than once I've found myself sneezing and yawning in the presence of a heavily fragranced dinner companion. "Don't you feel well?" she will ask. "I didn't have much sleep last night," I'll answer. If I were truthful, I'd say, "I can't wait to leave you."

You have overdosed on fragrance if

• The elevator you have just left is so suffused with your scent that passengers who never saw you know you were there.

• You can smell your fragrance around you fifteen minutes after applying it, without sniffing your skin.

• Someone at the opposite end of a sofa can smell you.

• Someone at the next desk to yours in the office is aware of your presence without looking up. To force your fragrance on a co-worker who finds it offensive is grounds for complaint to the industrial-relations department.

Businesswomen should really rethink the custom of spraying themselves with their purse vials before going to midafternoon conferences. It may bolster their confidence, but it can be counterproductive if the others at the meeting don't happen to be as fond of the scent as the wearer.

I would disregard the advice of fragrance manufacturers to slather yourself with their products. For a daytime working environment, confine yourself to a scented body shampoo or *gelée* in the shower and a dab of perfume in your bra or other underwear. Perfume lavishly applied to the skin will turn sour when you perspire.

In the evening when you are going out to play, you can apply perfume to the pulse points—inner side of the wrists, crooks of the elbows, base of the throat, earlobes—in addition to the aforementioned daubing of the underwear. Another seductive habit due for revival is to place a drop of perfume on your handkerchief.

Better invest in good perfume and use it judiciously rather than large quantities of toilet water, which seldom duplicates in exact tone your favorite scent. If anything, it sometimes has a more strident note.

Keep fragrance away from heat and sunlight, which alter the color and aroma. Constant daubing of your skin with the bottle stopper adds body acids to the product. Pour off a small quantity from a large bottle of perfume to keep in a container on your dressing tray and store the original in a drawer or other cool place.

Women with dark hair can wear almost any fragrance; blondes had best stick to lighter scents.

Perfume rarely smells the same on two individuals, but various brands are perceived as sporty, young, exotic or sophisticated, generally as a result of their combination of ingredients, and also because of the influence of their advertising campaigns.

Certain classics endure as favorites of elegant women: "Chanel No. 5" (though never in a hot climate), "Joy" by Patou, "Mitsuoko" and "L'Heure Bleue" by Guerlain, "Cabochard" by Grès; and for a lighter feeling, "Y" and "Rive Gauche" by Yves Saint Laurent, "Calandre" by Paco Rabanne, "Madame Rochas" by Marcel Rochas, and Robert Piguet's "Fracas," a best-kept secret among fashionable women. "Fracas" is one of the least expensive luxury fragrances and is not widely advertised.

Saint Laurent's "Opium" seems to be on the road to classic status as an Oriental musk scent. Estée Lauder's "Cinnabar," introduced at the same time, has an uncanny resemblance to "Opium," but the Saint Laurent scent has a more elegant note.

Most of these happen to be French fragrances, although there is a coterie of followers for Revlon's "Norell" and Estée Lauder's "Private Collection."

Mixing fragrances to create a very individual scent is the mark of the truly elegant woman. Seldom do they give out their formulas.

It's important to realize the effect of your own body scent in combination with the fragrance. Never buy a fragrance impulsively. Test it at the counter on your wrist or lower arm and wear it for half a day before deciding.

FUN

When applied to fashion, as in a category of furs that includes Mongolian goats, tinted rabbits, and rodents not raised on Canadian ranches, or to a specific outfit or hairdo, *fun* usually means inexpensive or freaky. The same word in French, *amusant* or *amusant et insignifiant*, usually goes with sexy chic or even elegance.

Just make sure that you're the one having fun rather than a designer or a hairdresser at your expense.

G

GLOVES

Around the time hats began to disappear in the Sixties, gloves lost their significance in women's wardrobes. It's a shame because gloves are a contact point for elegance and femininity, and many young women don't realize the flirtatious possibilities they offer. The gesture of removing a pair of gloves can be very seductive. Dropping a glove used to be a sure way of opening an acquaintance, but today a woman can't count on having hers picked up by anyone but herself.

Fall and winter gloves should be made of glacé kidskin of the best quality and workmanship, an expensive investment, but there is no alternative. No design other than self-stitching, and only neutral colors like black, brown, navy, gray, taupe, beige—and white for formal evening occasions; silk or cashmere linings for cold weather.

A little more leeway for sport—woolknit with suede palms and backs; nylon never, nor transparent crochet. Cotton gloves will do in warm weather, in dark colors to absorb the newsprint for a businesswoman who reads the *New York Times* and the *Wall Street Journal* on the way to the office in the morning.

The traditional etiquette about gloves, which may be unknown to younger women, still holds. Gloves are never worn indoors except for a formal reception or a ball, at which point they are not removed for shaking hands. They are taken off for eating.

GROOMING

Impeccable grooming is basic to elegance, which has as much to do with clean hair, polished shoes, unwrinkled skirts and unchipped fingernails as any distinctive item of clothing. It begins with conviction and is furthered by the triple mirror. The elegant woman never leaves her home looking *n'importe comment* (it doesn't matter how), because she knows it does matter. Never would she be seen in dirty blue jeans and sneakers or uncombed hair, even to go to the corner for a newspaper or a container of yogurt. A client once reported to me, "I've seen Mrs. Paley at seven A.M. and she looked the same as she does at four P.M."

Give advance thought to what you will wear to an important party or meeting. Lay everything out on the bed and study them. Have a dress rehearsal so you'll notice if a lining is hanging out, if you've put on weight and the buttons look as though they might pop. Do the colors go together? Is the outfit as becoming as you thought when you bought it?

H

HANDS

Hands are one of the most expressive parts of a woman's personality but are never to be used for talking.

To put your hands to your face is an aging gesture. Perhaps it's a subconscious attempt to cover the blemishes of time; rarely do young women do it.

Fingernails a half-inch long are an achievement for the manicurist but are not elegant except on Balinese dancers. Nails should be filed into oval shapes, never square, extending slightly past the base of the fingers. Polish can be clear or colored, but never frosted.

Some women who are successful in disguising their age as far as their faces and figures are concerned are bothered by unsightly spots and arthritic gnarls on their hands, the one part of the body that resists cosmetic improvement.

Some fade-cream products may be effective, but on the whole the only thing to do is to keep the nails beautifully manicured and to hide the affliction by playing with a lace-edged linen handkerchief.

Wearing white gloves at all times, even indoors, is not a satisfactory solution to the impossible problem of aging hands. They only call attention to what is being hidden.

HATS

What a pity it is that hats went out of style. They contribute so much to an aura of elegance. Using a hat to complete an image, or to disguise the familiarity of a dress, suit or coat several seasons old, is practically a lost art for women who developed their fashion consciousness in the late Sixties and the Seventies. Fortunately, young women have taken it up again, at least in a sporty way, influenced by Diane Keaton in *Annie Hall* and the "preppy" custom among high-school and university students of wearing men's fedoras. (See TUXEDO for my sentiments on women in male attire.)

Mrs. Vernon Taylor, a chic Coloradoan who is an expert skier and horsewoman, has created a legend about herself with her extensive collection of hats. She cuts an unforgettable figure on the slopes of Vail with a plumed fedora and a cape. Novice skiers are advised not to copy her.

On a dressier note, nothing can compete with the effectiveness of a turban on an oval face, or with the surefire romanticism of a light straw hat with an undulating brim, woman's best ally in the war against the harmful properties of sunlight. A fur beret can last for years, one of those blue-chip fashion investments.

A Parisienne trick with knitted stocking caps is to place wads of cotton on either side of the head to give a better shape (and additional warmth) before putting on the cap. Keep your secret when removing the cap by grabbing cotton and knit from underneath and rolling them up together.

Some businesswomen find that a hat is a subtle weapon in the battle to obtain recognition in the corporate world. A hat insinuates authority and importance. Would a male chauvinist be as likely to put down a woman who came to a conference in a hat as he might if she appeared bareheaded with a flip? Probably not, although this raises a problem about hats. There's a difference between looking like a self-assured elegant woman and a battle-ax. Remember, too, that hats are staples in a comedian's box of props.

Most women buy hats at a bar in a department store where they take a quick glance at themselves in a hand mirror or in a mirror mounted on the counter in the midst of jostling customers. Since proper proportion is the key, not only of the brim and the crown to the facial features but of the hat to the entire body, it is essential to study yourself in a full-length mirror just as you must with a new hairdo. Walk away and come back to the mirror to sense the impression you give from afar.

A hat usually requires second thoughts about makeup—a touch more dramatic, perhaps. A brighter shade of lipstick with a glossy finish, certainly. More color on the cheeks if the brim casts the upper part of the face in shadow. If, as a result, the eyes appear sunken, you might correct with eye-shadow highlights on the bone ridge, and a light penciling of fake lower lashes. (See VEILS.)

I

INDIVIDUALITY

That's what's missing in so many American women. They follow what somebody else does about fashion, somebody else's hairdo.

A woman should find her own look, her own style. That's something Frenchwomen know. They always like to look different from other women, not the same. Even if a certain color is in style, they try it on in a store and know right away if it isn't right for them. In America, the saleswoman says, "Brown is what they're wearing this season," Who are "they" to decide?

What's right is what looks right on you, and that's not necessarily what a designer decided. How ridiculous a short woman looks in a short dress, especially if she's no longer young. She looks like an ice skater out of place and season.

Just because a designer cuts his skirts short one season—maybe just to get attention and because he doesn't have any other ideas—doesn't mean you have to take all your clothes and follow suit. When he decides to lengthen them for winter, you will be frantically running around looking for extra fabric.

You can go close to fashion, but don't go to the extreme. See what fashion says and go in the direction that is best for you. Unless you have a fortune, don't even think of taking every twist and turn.

INITIALS

Wearing someone else's initials (or name) may be in fashion but it isn't elegant. If anything, it's a sign of insecurity: Who am I but an advertising billboard for another's product?

Yet displaying your own monogram prominently on all your possessions, a preppy custom as I understand it, is rather ostentatious, particularly if you were endowed with more than one middle name, or have a family name beginning with a snobbish *de* or *von*.

What it comes down to is this: Wear only your initials, but discreetly—for identification on belongings that may be lost or stolen such as wallets and suitcases, and also where they won't show very often, as on lingerie, handkerchiefs and a tailored shirt.

J

JEANS

On Worth Avenue in Palm Beach, one of the world's most luxurious shopping streets, they can tell the tourists from the winter residents by the designer blue jeans the visitors wear. The designers whose names are plastered on the outsiders' backsides are not the same designers who come for personal appearances in January and February and to be feted at Martha's and Sara Fredericks's exclusive shops on the avenue: Givenchy, Valentino, Galanos, Bill Blass, Trigère, Mary McFadden and the like.

Blue jeans may have enriched Gloria Vanderbilt and Calvin Klein, but they have never been chic. Even if she liked the fit, a woman of taste would probably take a razor blade to the label. The only acceptable names are the nearly invisible Levi's label, after the original manufacturer of the denim work clothes, or the somewhat larger tag of L. L. Bean.

Blue jeans with fitted boots can be sexy on a tall, skinny girl. Her legs must be thin to give the stovepipe look. If she's the least bit heavy, she looks like a sausage. If most blue-jeans wearers saw themselves from the back in motion, I'm sure they'd go home to change. I, for one, want to cross the street and look somewhere else.

Blue jeans in the city or in the first-class section of a 747 on an international flight were a Seventies affectation supposed to show affiliation with the arts, left-wing political chic or youthful spirit. Corduroy and khaki are more attractive for ordinary leisure that doesn't involve hard physical activity. Blue jeans belong in the country or on a ranch, where they were born.

K

KISSING

I like to kiss my clients when they leave for vacation and when they come back: once on each cheek, which is the European way; on only one cheek is American. Fashion society does a lot of gesturing over the shoulder or make-believe kissing. It seems to me that if you're glad to see someone, you touch-kiss. Otherwise, don't do it at all. One has to be sensitive and take the cue about who likes to be kissed and who would rather not. From the first meeting, I have kissed Nancy Reagan as I always do Betsy Bloomingdale.

Princesses prefer to be kissed on the hand, rather than the cheek. An American client who thought she spoke French used to raise her hand high and say, *"Baisez-moi!"* I doubt she was aware that her command was for something stronger than just kissing her hand.

Hand-kissing is a dying tradition I do my best to keep alive. It's an elegant gesture of respect a man can pay a woman and an opportunity for physical contact. There is a language of looking into the eyes and squeezing the hand that dates back, I'm sure, to the time when there were no telephones for communication.

One never kisses a hand when meeting in the street, or a gloved hand at any time.

KNEES

The knee is one of the ugliest parts of the female anatomy if left by itself. When the thighs above are covered by Bermuda shorts, and the calves below by socks, the bare knees glower like a pair of English pug dogs. What makes minishorts and mini-miniskirts for tennis potentially sexy is the fact that the knees are overlooked as the eye climbs to more erogenous zones. But forget about minis unless your thighs are smooth and shapely.

Knee socks can have an ethnic chic when the knee itself is clothed, as with knickers for cross-country skiing.

KNICKERS

A sensible uniform of the advanced cross-country skier, knickers look silly unless you are very skilled at this type of Nordic exercise.

Knickers have a certain sporty chic when worn by someone with a cute derriere and slender calves and ankles. Otherwise they magnify figure flaws.

With eighteenth-century court dress for inspiration, Galanos has tried to be elegant with knickers. Nancy Reagan wore his black satin ones with rhinestone closings under a black chiffon skirt at the dinner she and the president gave at the American Embassy in Paris in June 1982 for President and Mrs. François Mitterand. A severe-looking left-wing intellectual, Danielle Mitterand came in a white embroidered suit and ruffled blouse. The dinner invitation specified informal dress, a cryptic instruction that is very clear to men but usually throws women into fits of anxiety.

L

LEATHER

A woman should think three times before wearing leather, particularly those aviator clothes and Nazi storm trooper outfits some designers keep presenting as part of the macho look that is their vision of the contemporary female.

If she meets the standard for women in male clothing (see TUXEDO) and combines the leather with a cashmere turtleneck in a soft color and a bright scarf, then it can pass for hard chic. Otherwise, it's just depressing.

Leather pants look good when you bring them home from the store. After a month or two, they need the equivalent of a face-lift because leather stretches, especially after being worn on a long automobile ride. If you sit for more than an hour, the heat of your backside stretches the leather, and when you get up to walk, the leather looks like a dried prune.

LINGERIE

A woman should adopt the motto of the United States Marine Corps, *always prepared,* as far as underwear is concerned. Who knows when she may be called upon to undress, for any one of a number of reasons including a visit to the doctor?

Lingerie is very important to a man because it tells a lot about what kind of woman she is underneath and whether she cares enough to want to look divine just for him.

Lingerie should be appropriate to her personality. Black looks good on almost everyone, although better on brunettes than blondes. White or flesh tone suits blondes better, but if too plain, it looks antiseptic. I prefer white with a floral pattern, slightly see-through and with an edging of lace. Too much lace reminds me of the French cancan. Although beige and brown are popular among Frenchwomen, if the skin is too pale, the wearer looks as though she just got out of the hospital. Women seem to go for the jungle prints and vivid shades like purple and red that manufacturers and stores push on them, but I don't. I like simplicity, delicacy and refinement.

Of course, sexy underwear alone won't make a woman sexy. It's up to the man to do that.

Still, it doesn't hurt to choose garters attached to stockings, which may never replace pantyhose but are coming back into fashion, and for good measure a satin and lace chemise. I'd much rather see a woman running around the house in a man's pajama top or a man's shirt than in a dressing gown.

La Duchesse Anne in the Rue du Faubourg Saint Honoré has those pure silk T-shirts and long culottes that are the warmest, most elegant underwear for winter, in black, white or skin tone.

M

MAKEUP

Most of the women of bicoastal society have become expert about makeup. They consult cosmetic artists as they do their hairdressers for big occasions and they have taken instruction as well to learn how to put the best face forward at all times. I strongly recommend a consultation or two with a facial expert like Pablo Manzoni, who was associated for many years with Elizabeth Arden and now has his own salon in the Ritz Tower Hotel in New York. For a woman who has any aspirations to be in fashion, it's an investment as important as tennis or skiing lessons, though far less rigorous and expensive.

The value of this professional assistance is to help create a natural look. The painted face is a theatrical look, fine for an evening in TriBeCa or any other occasion when a woman purposely sets out to have a little fun with fashion. Otherwise it is both cheapening and aging. I've never known a man who liked heavy makeup on the woman he was with.

Cosmetics manufacturers obviously can't increase their profits by promoting a classic look, but that in fact is the most elegant. True, a continuous stream of new products over the last twenty years—such as blushers, lip glosses and highlighters—have dramatically changed the way women achieve that look, but the goal of naturalness and simplicity remains the same. This season's newest shade of lipstick won't make any difference.

On the other hand, there's a lot to be learned from cosmetic and fragrance advertising, not necessarily about the products. With certain high-fashion models or actresses, clothes and background settings, an aura is created. The Chanel campaign featuring Catherine Deneuve was a visual education in the classic French elegance I so admire. Estée Lauder ads establish the rich-lady look of American fashion socialites and their environment of antiques and fine crystal. I know a woman who furnished her living room from the Lauder ads.

What you won't learn from the ads is how the models achieved their fresh, dewy look. One tip from knowledgeable women is to spray the face with water, a fine mist of Evian. Some spray before putting on foundation, then pat dry. Others spray to set their makeup after it is completed.

Apply foundation with a damp sponge, using downward strokes on the cheeks, horizontal strokes under the eyes. Translucent powder over the foundation gives a more finished look.

One of the worst forms of modern propaganda has been that blushers can sculpture the face, almost as though the brush were equal to the cosmetic surgeon's knife. Russet patches on a woman's cheeks, no matter how skillfully brushed on, are as unnatural as her grandmother's twin spots of rouge. The prettiest blush on a woman's cheeks is the faintest.

During the day, makeup should be very light—just enough to give a little color to the complexion. For evening under artificial light or dinner by candlelight, one can be a bit stronger. That doesn't mean vivid color after dark but rather discreet highlighting of eyes and perhaps a deepening of lip tones. Some women who only use lip gloss by day will mix lipstick and gloss at night.

There are only two basic shades of eye shadow that are flattering: smoky brown for dark eyes and smoky gray for blue eyes. Both are to be used in conjunction with mascara and with highlighters on the bony tissue below the eyebrows. Skillful makeup artists can mix the basic shades with dark blue, green or purple, but if I could, I would ban bright blue and green eye shadow, the cliché of middle-aged Middle America. I'd also ban all frosted shades and iridescents. Eye shadow should not be applied uniformly to the whole lid but concentrated on the outer corner.

Eye liner is one of those unwelcome reminders of the Sixties, and all those would-be Cleopatras (as though Elizabeth Taylor needed eye liner with those incredible violet eyes). Pablo still uses eye liner but is careful to say it must be smudged, a trick that requires an even steadier hand than straight penciling.

Just because an aging face is a tired-looking face, most women think they can hold back the years by increasing the amount of makeup they wear. They should do just the reverse. Don't believe that suntan out of a bottle is rejuvenating or that bright cheekbones divert attention from the parenthesis lines around the mouth and the furrows between the eyebrows.

Remember that the blush of youth is a soft one unless the person has a fever.

Women who have reached the bifocal stage or beyond must be sure to put on their glasses after they have applied their makeup, study themselves carefully and then remove probably half.

M

MOCCASINS

A species of footwear that carries more social weight than any other.

Like everything else in the Gucci idiom, the moccasins with the metal bar across the instep and the metal rope inserted in the stacked heel have lost cachet through conspicuous overconsumption.

The classic moccasins in the L. L. Bean catalog—Bluchers, rubber, camp, Indian—as well as the Sperry Top-Sider, all of which come only in tan and brown, have a preppy connotation. Integrity of styling and sturdy workmanship make them the most appropriate for weekends in the city, exurbia and deep country.

The DeBusschère moccasins of soft kid with contrast piping sold through Belgian Shoes, Inc., in New York are a code for Old Guard conservatism. Seen, for example, on a stroller on Worth Avenue in Palm Beach, they signal a visitor from *vieux riche* Hobe Sound to the north.

The pastel kid moccasins in the Hélène Arpels boutique on Madison Avenue, where the most elegant feet are shod, are precious examples of *haut chic*, with prices to match—$245 a pair.

N

NATURAL

Only fabrics made from natural fibers can be elegant: wool, cotton, silk. Maintenance is more expensive than for the so-called carefree fabrics in both time and money. It begins with buying a steam iron and hunting for a competent professional dry cleaner.

Ultrasuede, a man-made fabric that Halston introduced to high fashion, is beloved by the same ladies who are reluctant to part with their flip hairdos. They sing the praises of its practicality—washable and wrinkle-resistant.

Fake fur can be fun if worn with audacity and if it doesn't look like a bathroom rug. Molded plastic luggage goes with polyester knit clothing—both look and feel unnatural.

On the other hand, what could be more natural than hair under a woman's arms and on her legs? In some European circles, it's considered sexy and fashionable. In America in the Seventies, some women thought they were making a political statement by not shaving their armpits.

This is one instance where I prefer artifice for aesthetic reasons. Don't male ballet dancers have clean-shaven bodies?

O

OYSTER

An aphrodisiac best consumed with champagne and background music of gypsy violins, although in these days of polluted waters you're taking your life in your hands.

The name of a classic, status watch, the Rolex "oyster perpetual," which has a gold and steel frame and, as its name indicates, is supposed to be waterproof and unbreakable. (See WATCHES.)

P

PANTS

Very few women know how to wear pants elegantly. The pants must be cut straight, almost like a long skirt, and should move free of the leg. If they move with the leg, they are too tight, like a cowboy's. That's sexy inelegance.

Just because pants make you feel free doesn't mean you should sit with your legs spread apart. Cross your legs as though you were wearing a skirt.

There comes a time when a woman can't find pants to fit her. Not necessarily because she's fat. A bony woman can be too broad. Or the crotch of ready-made pants hits her behind in an unflattering line. In profile, the line should fall more or less directly from the waist to the shoe. A pronounced shape to the backside means they're too snug. When you're deciding on length, be sure to put on the shoe or boot you'll regularly be wearing with the pants.

Study yourself in a three-way mirror. If it tells you bad news, give up pants except for digging in the garden. With a skirt and blouse, you'll get twice as many admiring looks as you will in badly fitting pants.

PLOUC

A useful word. Means tacky in French.

Q

QUILTED

Puffy down coats in iridescent colors are an abomination, particularly in the city when the temperature hits 50 degrees. The wearers look as though they are waddling around in their bedcovers.

This is a case of subversion of a classic style. The traditional Chinese quilted jackets and coats were gracefully slim, with their mandarin collars and frog closings, as were the versions made in France at couture houses like Christian Dior with their inner paddings of cotton, wool or silk. Even the proletarian blue uniforms of the People's Republic of China that tourists brought back as gifts were moderately stuffed in comparison with the capitalist imitations that followed. The culprit was down.

L. L. Bean's Northwoods goose-down vests and jackets will survive as legitimate country and campus attire. As for the rest, I won't take comfort until they disappear.

R

RUFFLES

The ladies love them so why shouldn't manufacturers give them ruffles and more ruffles even if it does show a lack of imagination?

It didn't take much to add a stiff frill to a blouse to produce a Volkswagen fashion even the home sewer can manage. The test of the designer's art is in the rippling grace of the ruffles and their strategic placement.

Women feel feminine in ruffles and think they disguise a multitude of figure faults, but in fact they're wrong on a heavy woman or a masculine-looking one, although a ruffled neck and cuff make an Amazon or a woman with a severe face look regal.

S

SCARVES

It really is true what they say about Frenchwomen: that apart from their ability to make an omelet with one egg if need be, they have an extraordinary flair for elegant sleight of hand with a scarf.

In Paris one recent summer, they were wearing roses at the neck fashioned from scarves. This is how they did it:

Take a scarf with contrast piping—a twenty-six-inch square is the best size—fold in half and then half again. Twist from both ends tightly to make a cord, then tie around the neck, knotting twice tightly. Flick the ends to open into the shape of rose petals.

There is no end to what can be done with a scarf to freshen your wardrobe. The only limits are your imagination. As with anything involving manual dexterity, practice improves skill. One of the interesting new ways is to drape a large scarf around the shoulders as a cape and knot on one shoulder. The difference between chic and ordinary results is in the slightly off-kilter look of the knot.

A Hermès scarf tied under the chin, when worn with a mink coat, Hermès bag, sling-back pumps and an aura of "Joy," makes a jet-set look. Most women with their heads wrapped in scarves look like Queen Elizabeth II, symbol of the English country look.

T

THIN

Despite the masochism of bicoastal society women, thin is grossly overrated. Southerners and European women agree with me. As a man, I prefer a Venus de Milo. Plump women are much more amusing than skinny women, much more alive, much more fun to be with. And they can still be chic. Mrs. Douglas Fairbanks, Jr., is one who is *bien proportionée*. A pretty woman, very stylish and a great hostess in New York and Palm Beach, she always has wicked stories to tell.

On the other hand, it is not possible to be really obese and in fashion. Designers don't cut sizes larger than 10.

Foreigners visiting the U.S. for the first time always comment on the number of freakishly fat women and men they see once they leave New York, and find this puzzling in a nation so preoccupied with dieting. I'm sure it must relate to the snack habit and to the portions of food served in restaurants—plates heaped high in no-star eating places, fashionably meager portions in the ones the food critics rave about.

TUXEDO

To wear men's clothing successfully, a woman has to be very feminine and sexy-looking. Otherwise, she looks like a eunuch.

The tuxedo—*le smoking*, as French designers like Yves Saint Laurent call it—is a case in point. Paris and Seventh Avenue were both pushing the look in 1982 around the time the film *Victor/Victoria,* starring Julie Andrews, was released. She looked wholesomely sexy in black tie and dinner jacket, though Catherine Deneuve looked much better.

There should be something a little perverse about a woman in a man's dinner suit, like Marlene Dietrich, who set the standard with her blond hair, husky voice and those incredible legs.

One of my clients, a beautiful Frenchwoman with long blond hair, brought the first Saint Laurent *smoking* to New York to wear to a movie premiere back in the Seventies. She asked me to comb her hair at her apartment. Saint Laurent had shown the *smoking* with a see-through blouse and suspenders with a rhinestone stripe down the middle. She didn't bother with the blouse, just a black bow tie around her neck and the suspenders, which she wanted precisely anchored to her nipples. She asked me to fix them for her with Scotch tape.

"What a fantastic idea. Are you sure you want to do it?" I asked a bit hesitantly.

"What's the matter, haven't you ever touched a breast before?" she taunted me.

Not one like that. She was perfectly sculptured.

Saint Laurent keeps reviving his own themes. For fall 1982 he shortened the jacket of his *smoking,* widened the lapels and also showed it with skirts. Marc Bohan of Christian Dior took the classic dinner jacket and interpreted it with a long black skirt, black satin cummerbund and a black bow tie on a white charmeuse blouse. "A bit mannish in a sexy, feminine way," he said.

The New York houses like Calvin Klein and Anne Klein adapted the look by exaggerating the shoulders of the jackets, shortening the skirts above the knees or cutting the pants above the ankles and showing them with sheer stockings and high-heeled shoes.

The kids took the style up right away, wore it to the dance clubs with Forties hairdos and made it very witty. That was in September. By November, the stocky women were out in force in their tuxedoes, then the ladies of two times twenty with streaked blond hair, and finally the gray-haired ones with Sassoon hairdos. One could only sigh, and pray for this fad to pass.

TYROLEAN

I have a particular fondness for the Austrian alpine style because it is associated with my favorite sport. For hunting in the Tyrol, you wear loden, an all-weather wool that actually improves with age. The costume is very classic and there is a specific tradition attached to every part of it—the cape, the buttons, the different colors. The feather in the band of the hat is supposed to come from game you shot yourself.

The collarless jacket with contrast piping, flower-print lining and medallion buttons is one of the few non-British ethnic fashions in the preppy style. L. L. Bean sells two or three versions appropriate for dressing up in the country. Of course, it's not the same as if you bought yours in Austria and had a vest whose buttons proved your marksmanship.

U

UNIFORMS

I wish young businesswomen felt secure enough to give up their uniforms—the pinstriped or other hard-finish man-tailored suit with skirt, foulard bow tie, leather shoulder bag and bulging briefcase. Even flight attendants are more interestingly dressed; airline marketing executives are shrewd enough to sense that passengers are more comfortable with hostesses in normal sportswear.

Some businesswomen try to tease a little by wearing very high-heeled shoes, bright nail polish and long hair, unbuttoning their shirts and leaving a thin gold chain in the V. That makes a joke out of the uniform in a way. But what does it prove except that they are afraid to show their individuality, that they aren't sure of themselves as women?

Those who are really confident about their ability and their positions could wear something feminine—a skirt and a cashmere cardigan over a blouse, perhaps, or a suit that's less tailored (a Chanel for example), or simply a well-cut wool dress.

V

VEILS

There's something mysterious about the look of a woman's eyes through a veil. Not the full-length veil that symbolized the Islamic revolution led by the Ayatollah Khomeini that took Iran back into the dark ages, but the little netting a French or Italian woman would have the wit to wear to one of those competitive cocktail parties in New York.

The delicate face veil attached to a small pillbox or cloche, or stretched across the bridge of the nose and anchored with a bow at the crown, represents the most refined elegance. The impulse it stirs in a man to lift the veil and kiss the woman beneath is compelling.

W

WATCHES

The Cartier tank watch has the status of a classic; its successor, the Santos, less so because it was too quickly "in." The Cartier round, gold onion and the Bucheron styles with distinctive leather banding and hidden closing are elegant.

Rolex watches suffer somewhat from the Gucci fate—overexposure. (See OYSTER.)

Traditionally, a woman never wears a wristwatch with an evening dress; Cinderella knows when midnight strikes without looking at a timepiece. But a businesswoman with a tightly scheduled existence would probably feel lost without one.

X

XMAS

The abbreviation fits a three-month commercial promotion but is otherwise not an elegant way to wish anyone a joyful holiday celebration. I sign my greetings *Joyeux Noël*, but "Merry Christmas" is always appreciated.

Y

YACHT

As J. P. Morgan said, "If you have to ask how much it costs to run a yacht, you can't afford one." The same applies to the upkeep of Porthault and Pratesi linens.

There are ways to tell if someone is very rich without asking. Does he or she own a yacht or racehorses? Does she receive packets of swatches and sketches from the Paris *hauts couturiers* at the beginning of the fall and spring seasons?

Never refer to a yacht as anything but a boat in polite conversation unless you mean the presidential yacht U.S.S. *Sequoia,* which is now in the hands of a nonprofit organization. The owner of a yacht and the guests who serve as crew during the sail are called "sailors."

Every sport has its fashion code. Those screaming shades of yellow, orange and green, which are inelegant everywhere else, are *de rigueur* on a boat for oilskin coats, parkas and other such foul-weather clothing.

Z

ZIRCON

Although zircon is a mineral, zircon gemstones fall into the same category as rhinestones as far as I am concerned—they're not the diamonds they pretend to be, and are therefore suspect.

Chanel made obviously fake costume jewelry chic, but that was in the context of her design concept. In general, paste is . . . (see PLOUC).

11

THE ELEGANT MAN

The principles of elegance for women apply equally to men, including the conviction that elegance is a worthwhile pursuit, and even an opportunistic one.

In a competitive world, as any businessman will tell you, the first tactic in getting a job, advancing in a job or making a deal is to attract respectful notice to yourself. As the old saying goes, Clothes make the man. If all the world's a circus, as it has been in terms of fashion for so long, the clearest way to stand out is by being quietly elegant.

Men have a much easier time than women in doing this. There is a strong element of classicism in elegance, and there's no shortage of classic clothing for men. Even the most aggressively fashionable men's designers are feeling very classic in the Eighties as they announce that elegance is back in style. Actually, among men who have really run the world in recent years, elegance never went out of style as it did for so many fashion-conscious women.

All a man has to do then, if he wants to approach elegance but is unsure of his taste and knowledge, is go for the classic model in every category of clothing and he can feel quite confident about his appearance.

If a man is young and starting out on the road to elegance, he can play around with developing a highly individualistic style. There were never so many opportunities to do that, drawing on resources from every part of the world, especially the mainspring of male elegance, England.

Young men have the time and the physical grace to make mistakes, an enjoyable part of acquiring style. The middle-aged man who hasn't had the practice and doesn't want to make the effort to develop an eye can look awfully stupid when he experiments with faddish trends—e.g. the bearded forty-year-old with a tinted blow-dry hairdo, wearing designer jeans and leather jacket, his bare feet in Gucci loafers and his wrist encircled by a silver bracelet engraved with the message I'M NOT A HERPES SUFFERER.

If a man can be eccentric with a note of elegance like Tom Wolfe, the writer, with his white suits and jazzy southern-gentleman look, bravo! But if he lacks the intuition and knowledge that keeps the stylish eccentric from becoming a freak, let him be quietly classic all the way.

Style can be a very tricky business if you don't have a flair for the unconventional. André Oliver can declare that the patterns of the tie and the silk square in the pocket must not match, but if a man doesn't have taste and the ability to coordinate color, he will look like a Christmas tree.

I believe that only an Englishman can mix patterns: a tweed jacket with plaid pants, a striped shirt, and a tie in still a fourth pattern. The duke of Windsor set the style for all time, but in London a group of designers and boutique owners are packaging this special talent in ready-to-wear clothes.

The Italians have a different talent, more suave and flashy than the English, witness the "American gangster" look by Giorgio Armani, which is another approach to the classics. Italian tailors are superb craftsmen, but they have to be kept on a curb rein if elegance is your goal, which you wouldn't have to think of doing in Savile Row.

The French have always worshiped English tailoring and sports clothes. Pierre Cardin made a revolution in men's clothes in the Sixties by translating the Edwardian English gentleman's hacking jacket, with its natural shoulder, nipped-in waist and pronounced flare below the waistline, and the flared stovepipe trousers into a fashion that took over the world.

The French snobbism of the Eighties is to add the American classics to the English and charge a high price for the Parisian seal of approval. Kim d'Estainville, a social personality who escorts elegant women like Hélène Rochas and Marella Agnelli, stocks his Hemisphere boutiques with $50 Levi's, J. C. Penney work shirts, Wyoming ranchers' jackets, Hickey Freemen suits, Lacoste alligator shirts and Burberry raincoats, and penny loafers.

For an industry that lives by novelty, classic may be only a fad for the Eighties; for the elegant man, the question is, "So what else is new?"

According to Beau Brummell, who might be considered the inventor of elegance in modern times, the worst thing a man could do was to dress so that people turned around to look at him in the street. Cardinal principle of elegance: The elegant man, like the elegant woman, is never too fashionable.

On the other hand, Brummell spared no expense or effort to attain perfection. He had the finest linen, wool and leather; the best tailor, hairdresser and valets to serve him. I would rather not recall that he died bankrupt and mad, because I also subscribe to that principle of elegance which makes quality paramount. I believe that the best is always the soundest investment, and that a gentleman never deviates from that standard.

I always wanted the best quality, even when I couldn't afford it. I worked and saved for it, and in America I learned to borrow. My first car was an MG, my second a Mercedes. These days I drive a BMW. My camera is a Leica, far from new. My sweaters are cashmere. I'd rather have one or two things that are the finest of their kind than several of lesser quality. If I don't like the way something is made, if I don't like the way it feels, if it offends my sense of quality, I won't buy it.

It was Beau Brummell who got men out of knee britches in the early 1800s and into unwrinkled trousers. He was the pioneer of the starched collar and of polished leather boots, but, more than that, of the idea of simplicity and elegance achieved through cut and perfect fit.

Modern technology hasn't been able to improve on these principles. Polyester may not wrinkle but it sags and is incapable of taking an elegant shape; it doesn't breathe. Pants and jackets made of good material of natural fiber and well cut and sewed don't crease.

American ready-made clothes for men have vastly improved in recent years. The suit jackets have lengthened, the pants slimmed down, and the tailors who finish the bottoms in the stores have learned to mark them so they fall below the tops of the shoes. European women used to say that American men looked as though they had too much water in their basements, a reference to their wearing their pants too short, with their socks showing.

But although it is possible to buy a suit of good quality and fit off the rack in a men's shop, I still think there is no better investment than having a suit made to measure by a good tailor. I admit that prices have risen since I ordered some of the suits in my wardrobe. One expects to pay at least $1,000 for a custom-made suit in New York or London. But consider its life expectancy. One counts by decades instead of years, and in Savile Row, suits are taken in for refurbishing when they wear out in spots.

I am still wearing clothes I had made at Kilgour, French & Stanbury in the Fifties. Armando Orsini, one of the most dapper restauranteurs in New York, has a vast collection of suits, seventy hanging in his closet at last count. Most were made by Cifonelli in Rome. When Armando Orsini is on duty at his restaurant, he changes suits three times a day: from informal attire in the office in the morning to a light-colored suit to greet the luncheon crowd, then again to attend a cocktail party, and then into a dark suit for the dinner hour. He never has to send them to the cleaner for pressing.

Don't they go out of style? "I never follow fashion in the real sense," he says. "I never take up a fad." He had ten or fifteen suits with narrow lapels that he put away to rest for a few years until they looked new again, and he never went overboard on lapels wider than four inches.

Lapels should be in proportion to a man's overall size. Narrow lapels on a broad-shouldered individual look as though he doesn't have enough money to make it. Wide lapels on a bantam give the impression he is apologizing for being small.

The silhouettes of custom-tailored suits are less likely to go out of style, because they are made for the individual and so much depends on body type. Englishmen and upper-class Europeans have a tight way of carrying themselves, which is one reason double-breasted suits are popular over there. So do older American aristocrats, although I discovered that may be because many of them wear corsets. They'll tell you it's for their backs, which they injured playing polo or some other gentlemanly sport. As a rule, American men hold their bodies more loosely and this is why the natural-shoulder, single-breasted suit with a free-and-easy cut is favored here and is actually most becoming.

American influence has made itself felt internationally in lighter fabrics (the most elegant still come from the British Isles, however) and in the lighter-weight buckram under the front of the jacket. These days a suit that looks like armor tends to be worn by a businessman from Lille.

When I consider how many women have told me they have fallen in love with men whom they saw for the first time from the back, I believe that the shoulders alone justify the price of a made-to-measure suit. No factory can duplicate the loving care of human hands in the setting of a shoulder and the working of a sleeve into an armhole. One woman assures me that she can always tell an Italian tailor's handiwork by the sexual arrogance of the shoulders.

Cuffed trousers have always had an elegant edge over cuffless. But a short man doesn't need the added horizontal line and would do better having the bottoms of his pants legs turned under.

Formal Evenings

When an invitation reads "black tie," men know what is expected of them. Women, however, wonder whether they should wear short or long dresses, glittery or plain. How formal will the tone be for this particular evening?

For a man, "black tie" signifies a black suit, the lapels of the jacket faced with black satin or ribbed faille and with a black stripe in satin or flat braid down the sides of the trousers. This outfit is called a "dining suit" by some Savile Row tailors (who are also promoting a midnight-blue barathea that looks black under artificial light), "*un smoking*" in French, and a "tuxedo" in American English, in tribute to the exclusive club in Tuxedo, New York, where it was made socially acceptable in 1886 after it was worn by a member of the Lorillard tobacco family. He caused a bit of furor because the tailcoat was standard dress at that time for formal occasions, and this jacket, adapted by Henry Poole, the London tailor, from a smoking jacket, was considered too casual. But it caught on to become the classic attire for formal occasions that do not call for "white tie."

Unless they circulate in high society or the diplomatic world, or are members of La Confrérie des Chevaliers du Tastevin, most reasonably well-dressed men can get by without owning a pair of tails and white-tie accouterments, but they must have at least one tuxedo—which they refer to as a "dinner jacket"—in their wardrobes. To call a tuxedo a tuxedo is as damning as referring to draperies as drapes, I understand, though far be it from me to grasp such fine distinctions of the American language.

The importance of the black dinner jacket in a man's wardrobe cannot be overemphasized. It is his social passport, the barometer of his sartorial taste and an opportunity for looking elegant. Therefore, if there is one suit in his closet that should be made to measure, it's the *smoking*.

The late Serge Obolensky, social lion of New York society, used to advise his less fortunate White Russian friends to equip themselves with the best custom-tailored *smokings* they could manage because it would be the best investment they could make in America. It proved to be that for various diamond salesmen and public-relations men like Obolensky who relied on their charm and elegance to open doors to business and to marriage with American society women.

Even I, who have followed quite a different course, have three such suits, one made in Italy, one by Cardin in Paris, a third at Kilgour, French & Stanbury. I don't think you can hold a candle to an English tailor for evening clothes. I also have a white-tie-and-tails outfit from Lanvin in Paris and, the most beautifully made of all, one for which I paid $5 at a thrift shop to wear to a costume party. I never go on a trip of any length without taking one of my *smokings;* I never know what occasion may present itself.

There are a few immutable rules concerning black tie.

• The lapels of the jacket should be fully faced with satin or ribbed faille rather than bound along the edges.

• Lapels can be peaked, notched or part of a shawl collar.

• The jacket can be either single or double-breasted without vents, but since it will give service for many years, the simplest style is the wisest. Double-breasted jackets with an audacious nip at the waist have a certain chic, but the single-breasted models last better through the thickening most men's bodies take on around the middle as they age.

• Black velvet is too dandyish for city wear and public receptions. It belongs, if at all, at a casual dress-up party at home, or a romantic evening *à deux* with Cristal champagne and caviar. A velvet jacket with satin revers worn with a wing-collar shirt and embroidered striped vest is a Milanese designer's flight of fancy, not to be taken seriously.

• With the black dinner jacket, one wears a cummerbund or a waistcoat, preferably to match the fabric of the lapels.

• Shoes should be patent leather or highly polished black leather, which is in high favor since most patent today is synthetic.

• Socks are black silk or lisle.

• The strictly classic shirt is white, starched and with a pleated front worn with studs. It feels like armor. In the old days when men wore starched collars even for business, they were disciplined to suffering, but the modern man is allowed a little leeway and soft shirts with studs or ordinary buttons are acceptable.

I like white silk shirts with pleated fronts because of the pleasant sensation of silk between my body and the jacket. When I move, everything moves with me. Lanvin and Cardin, in Paris, and Carlo Palazzi have extensive collections of silk evening shirts, which must be laundered by hand. I consider myself lucky to have a competent woman taking care of mine.

Ruffles are unforgivable except when worn by waiters in second-rate restaurants. Blue ruffled shirts belong on Liberace.

• The bow tie, in black satin or grosgrain, should be tied by hand rather than pretied in the store. The size should be moderate, and proportionate to the shape of the wearer's face.

• The wing collar with black tie, symbol of male elegance in the Thirties, has made a comeback as a camp style for the young, who may accentuate the look with brilliantined hair slicked straight back. André Oliver wears it with distinction for slightly more formal occasions.

The wing collar offers no room for compromise. The collar must be made of stiffly starched cotton and attached after the wearer has put on his starched white shirt with piqué bib. After one wearing, the collar has to be laundered. It is a standing collar that reveals the band of the black tie in back; the tips of the collar fold back just above the bowknot. If the tips are anything but crisp (as happens with a poor laundering job or with the new shirts that have attached wing collars), the wearer looks bedraggled. A ready-made bow tie is out of the question because the clip is visible at the back. A waistcoat completes the ensemble, never a cummerbund.

What this all adds up to is sober, refined and classic: the only way for a man to look elegant in formal evening clothes.

That's clear enough for invitations to private dinner parties and public events in the city. But what does "black tie" mean in a resort? In Nassau, black tie goes with white jackets, but in Palm Beach the jackets are black. At a benefit staged by a department store in the Florida resort, the only man in white jacket and wing collar was the president of the store, who obviously struck the wrong note. How was he to have known?

According to Danny Zarem, manager of the André Oliver men's shop in New York, an outpost of the Pierre Cardin empire, Palm Beach is very much affected by the presence of Douglas Fairbanks, Jr., a most elegant man, or, as we say in French, *tiré à quatre épingles*. His sartorial orientation is British. "English tradition was white in Bombay and the tropics, but otherwise you owned one great dinner jacket that you took around the world, no matter how heavy it was," Zarem said. A white jacket should be approached with extreme caution, he added. "It has the connotation of a bandleader, and only someone with enormous style can wear it and not look like a bandleader. A man can look so much sillier in white than black. There is nothing worse than people without taste taking liberties with the black-tie look," he said.

In Newport, Rhode Island, during the summer, young men may wear a white jacket with madras pants and call it "black tie" dressing, or a madras jacket with black pants. In Southampton, Long Island, black tie might be worn with black jacket and red pants.

Young men of prep-school and university age have been taking to "creative black tie," which can be anything from a red or madras tie and cummerbund with a black jacket at a country-club dance to following the precedent set by Woody Allen, who appeared at a black-tie opening looking conventional in every respect except for the white sneakers on his feet. At the Gold and Silver Ball in New York, some prep-school juniors and seniors matched Keds and Adidas to their first black-tie dinner suits. A slightly older group affects cowboy boots with black tie at the opera.

If you are young, or acknowledged as an eccentric genius, these touches are fine, particularly if it is understood that the occasion doesn't call for elegance on your part. But if you are none of the above and want to be properly dressed for a formal occasion, especially one at which you can't tell how far from the norm the other guests will go, stick to the classic black jacket and tie. As Zarem says, "If you stray, there's the danger of getting tacky."

As for movie stars, TV directors and heads of recording companies who appear at weddings, award ceremonies and other such formal events in custom-made dinner jackets with their shirt collars open, that's tacky and arrogant besides. It shows a lack of respect for the hosts and the other guests. An elegant person thinks not only of himself but of others as well.

There is a particular elegance associated with certain sports, and it is a pleasure, if one has the opportunity, to conform to their customs. For a formal dinner in a castle near Salzburg during the hunting season, I invested in the Austrian version of *le smoking*, a jacket of loden-green melton cloth as soft as velvet, collarless and with the lapels, cuffs and pockets hand-stitched in a leaf motif, and fastened at the waist by chain-link silver buttons. I wore it with black pants and a white shirt, deviating from strict custom in only one respect: Disliking the requisite pink tie, I cut a piece of Tyrolean floral-print ribbon from a package that happened to be in my room and fashioned a bow tie for myself.

The Navy Blazer

Another great classic of British tradition, beloved of all nationalities, is the navy blue blazer, *le passe-partout* or master key of an elegant man's wardrobe.

"The ideal form of refinement," according to an advertisement for a blazer in the Ralph Lauren "Chaps" line, which is true enough except that the jacket in question was made of Dacron polyester and wool, which canceled out the elegance on the spot. The navy blazer should be made of pure wool or cashmere, and preferably custom-tailored.

The navy blazer goes everywhere four seasons of the year, both for prescribed social occasions and for those when a man is not certain about the uniform of the day or evening in the environment in which he is suddenly cast.

With black trousers and a bow tie, he will look very dressed in his blazer, even to the point of covering his chagrin at not having his black dinner jacket in his suitcase on a quick trip abroad. He will wear it with white flannel pants on an evening ashore from a yacht anchored off the French Riviera, with charcoal-gray trousers to a Sunday dinner in New York, and to Sunday lunch with a Dutch banker at Château Neercanne on the outskirts of Maastricht. The banker will be in a blazer, too, with a cashmere pullover and rep tie. At the polo matches in Palm Beach in February, the young society crowd (male and female) wears blazers with chinos and Top-Siders (sockless, of course). A Dior blazer, custom-fitted blue jeans, and moccasins polished to reflect the wearer's face are the current chic of younger jet setters.

The tone is set by what goes on at the legs and the neckline. With a seasonal change of pants (from flannel to gabardine, from wide-wale corduroy to linen) and a decision about his shirt collar and tie (buttoned up with a discreet knit or striped silk, or open with a foulard at the neck), a man can always be confident that he is correctly dressed in his blazer.

A change of metal buttons will do wonders to raise the tone of a ready-made blazer. Buttons carrying the insignia of a university or a regiment, or the Austrian silver buttons signifying success in the hunt, are acceptable only if they legitimately belong to the wearer; otherwise, he can always fall back on his monogram or on neutral ground such as buttons made of antique coins.

Shirts

As a man who works in shirtsleeves, I find the dress shirt as important in my wardrobe as the pinstriped suit is to the banker. Even if this were not the case, I would still consider shirts a major form of masculine self-expression and therefore worthwhile to invest in the best quality of natural-fiber fabric and in fit.

Though the market is flooded with beautiful, ready-made shirts of every conceivable style and designer label, I would still continue to have mine made to order (mostly at Carlo Palazzi in Rome, Sulka in Paris, and Turnbull & Asser in London). I have slender arms that look lost in a ready-made shirt; and with my European orientation, I like a shirt shaped to my body rather than flapping loose in the American tradition. But it seems to me that most men can benefit from a custom fit to the collar, which should be scaled to the proper height in front and back and not just to the circumference of the neck. And how can anyone feel well dressed without a good fit at the wrist?

Colors and patterns must be discreet (no barbershop stripes or racetrack checks) and the same goes for the monogram, which should be placed on the body of the shirt at the left side, or on the left pocket for men who must have one. I think initials look silly on the sleeve, and unbearably ostentatious on the cuff. The whole idea of a shirt monogram is that it is personal and should be seen only by someone close to you.

As for short-sleeved dress shirts, a man who will wear one of those is a man who will wear polyester suits. It is not only more elegant but more practical to roll up the sleeves of a dress shirt to the elbow, because then you can roll them down to put on your jacket. With short sleeves, the wrists hang out from under the jacket looking like a chicken leg without feathers.

Casual wear is another matter, although the elegant man will almost always vote for long sleeves. I can recall seeing Hubert de Givenchy strolling on a Sunday afternoon in 80-degree heat on Madison Avenue in New York in impeccable chinos and a pink cotton shirt open at the neck, the sleeves cuffed neatly at his elbows. Even in a sportier model, such as a denim shirt with epaulets, long sleeves look better than short.

For country wear, sailing, tennis or golf, an all-cotton knit, solid or with narrow horizontal stripes, with cap sleeves is proper attire. Unfortunately, it is almost impossible to find one that doesn't have the Lacoste alligator or the Ralph Lauren polo player (or the Brooks Brothers fleece).

Candidly speaking, the knits look great on someone who is young and has a good body. If a man doesn't have the shape and if he is smart, he will choose camouflage—wear a T-shirt under a *blouson* or other loose or unbuttoned shirt. But how many men will take the trouble, or have the courage, to study themselves in a full-length three-way mirror (the same essential as for a woman) and admit to sloped shoulders, fleshy tires and budding breasts—and act their age?

Neckties

You can tell a lot about a man's taste by his neckties, even if he only wears what his wife buys him (his selection of a mate is even more revealing).

Everything there is to be said about ties can be summed up in one word—*sober*. Widths may vary over the years, but patterns remain classic: stripes, geometrics, dots, paisleys, and only on a small scale. Colors are muted. The more elegant the man, the less expressive his necktie. William Paley's are dark blue.

Knitted four-in-hands and patterned silk bow ties (knotted by hand) pep up a tweed jacket, add a sporting note to a blazer.

A wave of informality originating in international film and rock-music circles and their jet-set groupies and now penetrating the country club set is pushing the notion of open-collar chic. The bare neck is like bare feet—inelegant except in genuinely casual settings. When venturing into unfamiliar social waters, play safe and wear a tie. If you see, after you arrive, that the atmosphere is very relaxed and you are urged to remove your tie, you can do so.

Underwear

I simply cannot understand the American man's love affair with boxer shorts. And I don't see how, when he takes off his trousers and parades around in front of a woman in boxer shorts and over-the-calf socks, he can expect more than a stifled yawn. He'd be better off with nothing, or wrapped in a towel, or, still better, in a silk dressing gown.

I myself find the Swiss cotton briefs I buy in Paris most satisfactory. I wear only white, resisting the purely commercial fad for colored and patterned underwear that is supposed to have saved the industry from collapse. It is unthinkable that a man with any taste or sophistication would wear briefs with the Playboy bunny trademark, any more than he would buy leopard-printed bikini underpants.

I may be accused of carrying the principles of elegance too far. The loud bikini briefs are amusing, and why shouldn't a man have a little private fun? I suppose if he finds himself with a married woman when her husband walks in, he can always announce that he is the masseur—or grab a towel and ask, "Which way is the beach?"

The big chic among European men is the American bedtime classic, Brooks Brothers cotton broadcloth pajamas (in cotton flannel with a navy tartan pattern for the country in winter). These are of the same baggy class as the boxer shorts, but for once I can see the point of comfort here. Of course, for virile chic, nothing matches the comfort of sleeping nude, with a Sulka paisley-printed cashmere robe to jump into when the alarm goes off.

Hats

One can make a case for hats on the basis of health. As much as a third of one's body heat escapes through the top of the head if one goes hatless on a cold day.

But that's not the compelling reason that younger men have taken to wearing hats again. They realize what opportunities were lost when hats went out of style. Tipping one's hat to a woman is an elegant gesture that gives a man an air of distinction, and a great feeling besides.

There is a lost etiquette to men's hats.

They should be removed in the elevator of an apartment house, hotel or a public building unless it's so crowded as to make it physically awkward.

A man tips his hat in passing a woman in the street and removes it if he stops to talk to her. If he shakes hands, he should also remove his right glove. I prefer a little kiss to a handshake.

Men don't buy hats, it is said, because they feel foolish wearing them. If so, that must be because they don't know how to pick shapes becoming to their faces. In keeping with the casual style of living today, tweed hats and sportier felt models—such as a fedora with a soft, unbanded brim—go with city clothes and make men who are accustomed to going bareheaded feel more relaxed about wearing a hat.

I must own about fifty hats, including several versions of the classic English sports cap and a vintage black Borsalino in which I look like a dapper banker with the brim rolled up, and like a character in a gangster movie with the brim down. When I wear my black homburg, a very fine fur felt with a rolled brim, with my navy cashmere coat, gray gloves tucked into the upper left-hand pocket and white scarf, I feel like a million dollars. People tell me I look like a diplomat.

One Man's List
of Inelegant Fashions and Fads

(no matter how chic they may be in certain circles)

• *Patchwork pants.* Perhaps if I had never seen a circus clown I wouldn't mind them so much. "Lilly" flower prints and animal-embroidered corduroys are in the same category.

• *Socklessness.* Wearing no socks with Top-Siders or sneakers is reasonable on a boat, but otherwise it's bad for the feet and unkind to the noses of other guests. The fad of going sockless to a dressed-up party is a ridiculous affectation.

• *Designer blue jeans.* If anything, these are worse on a man than on a woman, although the reasons for disapproving them are the same. (See JEANS in chapter 10.)

• *Other macho manifestations,* such as leather, and chest hair showing through an unbuttoned shirt.

• *Initials and emblems other than your own.* (See same heading in chapter 10.)

• *Diamond jewelry.* Some of the pillars of society between the two coasts wear rings, cuff links and shirt studs set with diamonds, on the theory, I suppose, that if you have it, enjoy flaunting it. But that's not elegance. And besides, if a survey by a national women's magazine is to be believed, diamond pinkie rings (and gold chains) "turn off" the majority of women. Discreet gold jewelry, such as cuff links set with mother-of-pearl for formal evening wear, is the outer limit of masculine jewelry.

• *Mink coats.* Sporty furs like sheepskin, wolf, raccoon and seal are chic on the ski slopes, for après-ski or other snow and woodsy settings. If a man must have mink, it's only elegant as a lining and collar of a melton or cashmere coat in a truly cold climate like Leningrad in January.

A Basic Wardrobe of International Classics for an Elegant Man

1 navy wool or cashmere blazer
1 black smoking/tuxedo/dinner suit with black tie
1 navy pinstripe suit
1 gray flannel suit
1 beige gabardine suit (for summer)
1 safari suit from Abercrombie & Fitch for summer weekends and
     for safaris in Africa and India
1 Austrian loden coat (for stormy weather)
1 Burberry raincoat (trench coat or plain model; the Hermès fold-
     able version in silk is still more elegant)
1 navy-blue cashmere coat
1 Scottish tweed jacket
1 charcoal-gray flannel pants
Several pairs of corduroy, white denim, blue denim jeans by Levi
     Strauss, Lee or L. L. Bean, plus 1 pair Brooks Brothers khaki pants
     and white or pastel linen pants for summer
1 pair black leather laced shoes
1 pair brown leather laced shoes
1 pair good leather boots
1 pair moccasins, not tasseled
1 cashmere V-neck sweater
1 Shetland cableknit pullover or cardigan
A wardrobe of made-to-measure shirts

1   dozen white linen hand-rolled handkerchiefs, useful for mopping
     up spilled champagne from a lady's dress, or to make tourni-
     quets for an unexpected hunting accident
1   or more hats; if only one, a packable fedora

Hands

Clients have talked to me over the years about the traits they find most attractive in men. A handsome face is seldom mentioned. French women
often say, *"Le chic, le cheque et le choc"*—his fashionable appearance, his
checkbook and the electricity that can pass between a man and a woman.
Most American women tell me they are drawn to intelligence, a sense of
humor and the look in his eyes.

More often than not, they say that hands are the part of the body they
notice on first acquaintance. There isn't anything a man can do about the
size and shape of his hands or the amount of hair that grows on the backs,
but he can see that his fingernails are neatly clipped and scrupulously
clean. A man who clips his nails in the presence of others is hopelessly inelegant.

It isn't a bad idea to have manicures to further the cause of the well-
groomed hand, but the nails should be only buffed, never lacquered with
clear polish.

Scent

I can usually tell when the man from the gas company has been to my
apartment to read the gas meter by the scent of "Aramis" he leaves in the
kitchen.

Since the elegant man bathes regularly, there is no justification, as there
was in olden days, for him to douse himself with fragrance, despite the
macho propaganda from the perfume companies. His scent should be de-
tected only by women within kissing or dancing range. I put a drop or two
of my favorite, Guerlain's "Vetiver," on the back of my tie or on the back
of my T-shirt.

Hair

When Brigadier General James Dozier was released after forty-two days in
captivity at the hands of the Red Brigades in Italy in February 1982, he
went immediately to the nearest army hospital and had his red beard
shaved off and his hair clipped close to the scalp. With practically nothing
but a fringe of bristle on top, he looked ready to fight World War II all
over again. For the general, the haircut symbolized his return to safety and

his chosen occupation. To seal his freedom, he ordered a cheeseburger, French fries and a Coca-Cola.

As the decades of the Sixties and the Seventies reminded anyone who might have forgotten about Samson, hair is an essential part of a man's well-being, an expression of his personality. In those years, it became an issue that divided families and an act of rebellion. To think how four young men from Liverpool, the Beatles, started it all with their coiffures like Renaissance pages, which were rather moderate hairdos compared with what followed, like ponytails and braids. Long hair became associated with the leadership of youth, with opposition to war, with sexual freedom and with drugs.

When I came to America, all men looked to me as though they had come from the army or from jail. The crew cut was the typically American style. A year later, Elvis Presley, the idol of millions, had his locks shorn by an army barber, a tragedy for his fans but an affirmation of American military values. In Europe, the army was much more tolerant about hair, as long as it was well groomed.

As I told you earlier, I learned to cut hair from a men's barber, Pierre Jansen, in Brussels when I was a kid. At Guillaume, we all took our turns on artists like Jean Marais and Jean Cocteau when Otello, the colorist, who also cut their hair, was on vacation.

In New York in the late Sixties, after the influence of the younger generation had filtered upward to their fathers, a few clients began asking me if I would cut their husbands' hair. Regular barbers had a tendency to cut too much, particularly around the ears. It made for a military look—or as we used to say in France, it showed that the client was ready to get married the next day. The test of a well-groomed man is not to look like that.

Then the *New York Times* published an article saying that I was cutting men's hair in my salon and I was called to the New York State Department of Licensing Services and threatened with the closing down of my salon. A distinction was made in those days between the sexes as far as licenses went. Only barbers could cut men's hair.

There is so much nonsense regarding licenses, which follow different rules in each state. In New York, one had to be licensed to give a shampoo even though any individual could buy a product in a drugstore and give himself a shampoo. But a manicurist didn't need a license in New York, while in some states a hairdresser had to prove he or she could give manicures in order to get a license.

I couldn't believe what they were going to do to me. Hair is hair. Actually, I had no desire to take on a male clientele, but I gathered the licensing board had received complaints from barbers who feared I was going to take business away from them.

The inspectors at the licensing bureau were very stern. They lectured me on the necessity of knowing how to work on men clients. I told them I did. And to prove it, I said to one inspector, who had an unshaven look due to a dark complexion and heavy beard, "I could shave you." I told him of a trick I had learned from a Hungarian barber in Vienna, how to give a shave without soap. You wet the skin with a sponge and pull it taut so the hair is exposed and you can cut it against the growth with a long-bladed barber's razor. This technique gives a very close shave.

The inspectors were impressed. Then I said, "Do you know how to check whether a haircut is perfect?" Even a champion cutter can't see unless he puts a little talc on the hair. It makes the uneven hairs show up and he finishes the haircut by following the lines with his scissors. They hadn't known that either. Licensing is much stricter in Europe, I let them know; and besides, I had no intention of running a barbershop in my salon. Today, the technique wouldn't be of much use since most men don't want a "clean" haircut; they want to look as though they need to visit their barbers.

I was excused. Since then, unisex haircutting salons have become very common and the licensing boards more flexible.

I still don't seek out male clients, I just take on friends or the husbands and sons of clients, and from this has developed a group of businessmen, a few investment bankers, a filmmaker, a judge and two lawyers who come together from New Jersey after the salon is closed for the day. There are a few I see in their homes, such as William Paley and sometimes his guests, like Loel Guinness. It's the conversation with these men of stature that I appreciate. With Gerald van der Kemp, the curator of Giverny, who came with his wife, Florence, on a visit to New York, I discussed art and food. I recall Mr. Paley telling me once about a business deal involving the television networks in which CBS withdrew on a matter of principle for him, and its rival, NBC stepped in to its eventual loss. "Always stick to what you believe in, Marc, and in the end you will win," he told me.

I begin a haircut by studying the contours of the man's face and noting whether his hair is straight or curly. I feel his scalp to ascertain the shape of his head. On a first visit, I like to cut the hair dry so I can see how it acts in a natural state. After it is shampooed, I check to see how it falls when wet. I cut with scissors, never machine clippers, and sometimes a razor to thin out very thick hair, but even for that I prefer the tip of the scissors.

I prepare the client by giving him a hand mirror and asking him to look at himself in profile as well as full face. At this point, I have him keep his collar closed so that we can see where the hair reaches in back; otherwise, there is a tendency to cut too high. Before I put the scissors to his hair, he will open the collar.

I usually try to convince him to let his hair grow a little longer. One to one and a half inches all around is a good length for most men, with the line in back on a level with the chin. Cut shorter than that, the profile has an unbalanced look. Another measure is for the hair to almost touch the top of the collar.

Some men tell me this is too long, that their wives or girlfriends find the back of a man's neck sexy and object to having it covered.

Ears should be at least partly covered; not too much, of course, because men have to hear what women are saying to them. A man with big ears looks like an elephant without some hair to conceal their size. I, on the other hand, have small ears and a narrow face so I need some hair over the ears to give me width.

These are my suggestions, but if the client disagrees, I cut his hair the way he wants it. Some men prefer a cleaner cut, such as the classic English style worn by the duke of Edinburgh and the Prince of Wales, with a side part, the ears completely bare and the hair cut a bit above the ears as well.

The TV film *Brideshead Revisited* stimulated an interest among younger men in an even more cropped look at the sides and back, but with the hair kept long and full at the top, a lock falling over the forehead. A very pre–World War II look.

President Reagan has an American version of the classic English style. I have never touched his hair, and I consider him very well served by his barber. The president's hair always looks right, neither too short nor too long.

I usually propose to my clients that they have their hair parted on one side and combed to the other. Contrary to what some men believe, it is more flattering than having it combed straight back.

Some men try to compensate for receding hairlines by letting their hair grow long and bushy in back, which only accentuates what they are trying to hide. The hair around the face and at the back should be about the same fullness as at the top.

Sideburns. Although the shape of sideburns is a matter of personal taste, very long ones look passé after the excesses of the Seventies. The latest chic is no sideburns at all. Since I don't follow fads, mine are about the level of the center of my ears. The important thing in determining length and width is not to look at the sideburns per se but at the whole head. Taking a snapshot is a realistic way to judge a haircut.

Baldness. The man who wears two or three strands across his bare top has a desperate air about him. He should either accept his baldness or get a beautiful wig, in which case he will look younger but will have to accept a certain discipline. He will have to buy at least two so he can send one wig to be cleaned, styled and redyed periodically, and he may have to forsake certain pleasures, such as swimming, although some of the better products are supposed to stay on underwater. He should consider only a wig made of real hair; the synthetics are less expensive, of course, but the wearer inevitably looks like a character from Mme. Tussaud's Waxworks, a far worse fate than having no hair at all.

Shaving the head completely can be attractive provided the skull has a nicely rounded shape. Yul Brynner was a formidable sex symbol and Telly Savalas has his fans, too.

Curly hair. You have to rely on a good hairdresser to give curly hair a neat shape rather than attempting to have it straightened. The fact is that there is no way to straighten really curly hair without taking the natural life out of it. With the least humidity, the curl springs back. So why not leave it curly?

If it's a matter of an annoying wave in front, that can be relaxed with straightening, but be sure to have it done in winter when it will stay for two months or more. In summer, it's a waste of time and money.

Some young men with very straight hair have permanent waves and even add bleach. The curly, sunshine-streaked look is very big among actors, rock musicians and Oriental hairdressers.

Coloring. Growing gray has never bothered me—I started at seventeen—any more than I am disturbed about my hair getting thin. As long as I can drink wine and do what comes with it, I am happy. But it's the same for men as with women: If you get gray, it's threatening to some of your friends who are afraid to be gray themselves.

Frankly, I haven't noticed that the loss of hair color has held me back in any way. Certainly not professionally, and not with members of the opposite sex. I'm told that gray hair makes a man look *distingué.*

It's not the color or lack of color of his hair that makes a man interesting. Hubert de Givenchy, the idol of the fashion socialites, is gray. Yves Montand's hair is gray and a bit thin on top and he's past sixty. When he made his singing tour of the U.S. in the fall of 1982, the women in the audience were beside themselves, and the critics, male as well as female, rhapsodized about how sexy he was.

Liz Smith, the *New York Daily News* columnist, stated in print that William Paley was America's most eligible bachelor, the biggest catch in New York society. Mr. Paley is eighty and he doesn't color his hair.

Mr. Paley was the founder of CBS. Would he have felt he had to tint his hair if he had been an anchor man or a correspondent on his TV network? Being gray didn't hurt the ratings of Walter Cronkite, although he did feel he had to wear a hairpiece to hide his baldness. I think Mike Wallace would look less haggard if his hair weren't so dark.

Gray hair is much more elegant than hair that looks artificially colored, particularly very dark hair, which only proclaims that the man is afraid of losing his youth. One of the strangest sights I ever saw was a woman with beautifully coiffed gray hair and her industrialist husband of the same age with a full head of jet-black hair. I wonder if he ever looks in the mirror when they are together. I think a man should leave his hair natural. If a little gray appears and it unnerves him, he can use a rinse. But once the gray becomes dominant, he is asking for a lot of headaches if he tries to conceal it. Poorly tinted hair looks like the tail of a cow. Professional coloring is time-consuming because as soon as the roots show, he has to go back for retouching. A man doesn't have the possibilities for camouflage a woman does with her hair.

If, for whatever reason, he feels he cannot live with gray hair, he should be sure to leave his sideburns natural. Above all, he should not color his eyebrows or his moustache to match unless he wants to look like Groucho Marx. Or his beard, either. Facial hair is body hair, much more porous than the hair on top of the head. It takes color much faster and the results can be catastrophic.

Also, body hair is often a different color from the hair of the head and it can be very upsetting to some men, especially when they see white hairs sprouting in their beards. They are deathly afraid of being called graybeards, "an old and experienced man," according to the dictionary, or, worse still, being taken for Santa Claus.

I would advise them to accept their gray beards, and if they can't, to shave them off. Just consider the alternative. The beard grows so fast that if they dye it, there will always be a little growth of white hair showing. With each application of color, the rest of the hair becomes darker and darker, producing an obviously dyed look that defeats the purpose.

White hair has a tendency to develop a yellow cast. I recommend Revlon's Glis'n, a shampoo mixed with a rinse, once or twice a week. When you get up in the morning, shampoo the hair lightly, dry with a towel and apply the product, leaving it on for ten or fifteen minutes while you brush your teeth and shave. Don't be afraid if the hair looks navy blue. After rinsing in the shower, it will come out clear silver.

Beards. I grew a beard when I was in the occupation army in Germany, where it was allowed as long as it was neat. I shaved it off at Guillaume's request but kept a moustache.

After I came to New York, I made a bet with a friend and started to grow a beard again. One of the reasons I liked it was that when I went fishing, the mosquitoes didn't bite me. Beards keep the insects from penetrating the skin, and they go with the hunter/woodsman look anyway. My beard was dark blond like the hair of my head and then it became prematurely mottled with gray. I chose to have a goatee because of its distinguished connotation—the beard of diplomats, doctors and high army officers, or so I thought. After about ten years, it was time for a change. By then, everyone was wearing beards. When a fashion hits the streets, one must go on to something else.

Although beards are obviously *vieux jeu* for the Eighties, there's no reason why a man shouldn't have one if he feels like it. But he should be sure to keep it trimmed, and that demands a lot of attention. A full beard hides a round face or a double chin; a skinny face looks overwhelmed by a mat of bushy hair.

I kept a moustache, a neat little brush. Having had one all my adult life, I would feel naked without it. Originally, I grew it in the hope of looking like Errol Flynn.

A moustache is useful in camouflaging thin lips like mine, or bad teeth. If properly trimmed, it lends character and elegance to a man's face. Women used to say that to kiss a man without a moustache was like drinking soup without salt.

There are so many possibilities of expression with a moustache. What fun it must be to have a handlebar to twirl. But unless one deliberately chooses an eccentric style, I think a man has to pass them up these days.

Face-Lifts

This seems like an appropriate place to mention face-lifts. Cosmetic surgery for men has been popular in Europe for a long time and now it is catching on in the U.S. Many of my friends in the *haute coiffure* and in the theater have had their faces touched up a bit, and they assure me it's good for morale as well as necessary in their professions. Some of them hint rather pointedly that I might want to do the same one day, as they also wonder why I let my hair stay gray when they have had such success tinting theirs.

To which I say, Why not have a face-lift if you don't like what you see in the mirror in the morning? Go ahead, but don't overdo it; improve your looks, but don't lose your character in the bargain.

Personally, I believe a man can get away, far easier than a woman, with wearing the marks of life on his face. Women seem to be intrigued by men with interesting faces. In an outdoorsman, the weathered look is most attractive. But the man who spends his life indoors in a sedentary occupation may appear sallow and weary when his skin loses its youthful elasticity.

Yet, if fear of aging is the motive for repairing one's face, the evidence points now more than ever to the late-middle-aged and the young elderly man as being especially appealing to women, young as well as old.

And I do wonder, if everyone goes to the cosmetic surgeon, will it make for a kind of mass illegitimacy, where no one ever really knows what his father looked like?

12

THE ELEGANCE OF FOOD

There has always been a direct connection between fashion and food. Christian Dior wrote a book, *Cuisine Cousu-Main*—handmade cooking. It had a silver cover and some of the recipes called for caviar and the remains of a bottle of Dom Perignon. Dior was a gourmand who shortened his life with overindulgence. Pierre Cardin, a designer with a much more contemporary spirit, talks about the joys of going to market when he is in residence in the south of France where he can inhale the aroma of the tomatoes and melons. One of the world's wealthiest businessmen, Cardin likes to do his own cooking once in a while—to grill a steak and prepare a salad.

What do I talk about with my clients most of the time as I do their hair? About theater, the ballet, the latest museum shows, to be sure, but more likely about the best parts of living—the outdoors, hunting, gardening, and cooking. We exchange recipes, pass along the word about the newest restaurants and the latest critiques of the old standbys. Everyone seems to be cooking, at least once in a while, or keeping an interested eye on what goes on in the kitchen.

It may be chic to be slender, but it's unchic to invite people to one's home and give them less than a memorable experience. It's the "in" thing to say that an interesting mix of people is more important to the success of a party than *haute cuisine,* but I agree only if it means that the best food doesn't have to be complicated, and that the hostess should concern herself more with a convivial atmosphere than with clockwork perfection.

There are fashions, or rather fads, in cuisine, and one must acknowledge that American eating habits have changed radically for the better in the last twenty years. However, the principles of elegance still apply. Trendy food doesn't last. Whatever happened to Beef Wellington, the cliché of the Sixties? In the Seventies, everything was pureed or undercooked to the point of being raw, thanks to the *nouvelle cuisine* rage and a Cuisinart in every kitchen. Classic cooking goes on forever, simplified perhaps by newer ideas of health and fitness.

Mrs. Paley called me a man for all seasons because of my interest in so many things other than hair. We joked about which I cared for more—women or food. Actually, I mingle the two. Let's just say I cook for people I like; that's one of my ways of loving.

Conversation With an Elegant Woman About Fashion and Food

La Grenouille reminds us that an elegant dining experience embraces not only preparation but presentation and ambience as well. The menu is classic French cuisine; the flower arrangements look like still lifes from the palette of a French impressionist master.

And, of course, there is the hostess, the elegant Gisèle Masson, carrying on the tradition set by her husband, Charles, an apostle of Henri Soulé of Le Pavillon, who established French *haute cuisine* in America. Charles Masson died in 1975.

Their son Charles Masson, Jr., is associated with his mother. A charming young man with dark hair and his father's warm smile, he supervises the opening of the restaurant every morning, and he does the flowers. He and Mrs. Masson stop at the tables to have a word with everyone. It makes for a lovely family atmosphere.

The Massons' second son, Philippe, a guitarist, relieves Charles Jr. from time to time and helps out in emergencies.

La Grenouille is a high-fashion stronghold. Particularly at lunch, one is accustomed to seeing on the banquettes at the front of the restaurant John Fairchild; Grace Mirabella, editor of *Vogue*; several important designers; and some incredibly chic women who are usually speaking French. The bankers and big businessmen like to sit in the main part of the restaurant, which the fashion crowd considers Siberia.

On the afternoon I had lunch and conversation with Mrs. Masson, she was wearing a black double-breasted gabardine suit by Saint Laurent with gold buttons. She wore it without a blouse, her only jewelry black onyx and gold clip earrings.

MARC: Do you find it as strange as I do that most of the people who admire your restaurant so much don't pronounce its name correctly?

GISÈLE MASSON: No, they don't. They say Gruhn-wee.

MARC: Or *Grahn*-wee, which sounds as though they had a big night, *grande nuit* in French. When I hear that, I say, "Good for you." Seriously, though, I teach my clients how to pronounce La Grenouille. I tell them,

MARYLIN BENDER WITH MONSIEUR MARC

"Say noodles." Say Gruh-*noo*-yuh. Is it true the restaurant got its name from your husband calling you *ma grenouille?*

GISÈLE MASSON: He used to call me *ma petite grenouille*—my little frog. I hope not because he thought I looked like one.

MARC: In French, the love of women and the love of food are interchangeable. We say *mon petit poulet*—my little chicken; *mon petit chou*—my little cabbage.

GISÈLE MASSON: *Mon petit lapin*—my little rabbit.

MARC: One of the specialties of the house is *les grenouilles*—frogs' legs.

GISÈLE MASSON: Of course. They come from France. The tiny little frogs, very delicious.

MARC: So many of the restaurant people in New York are either from Brittany or the Pyrenees. And you?

GISÈLE MASSON: I'm from Paris, from Montparnasse, but I adore Brittany. My grandmother was from there. My husband was from Belfort.

MARC: When Charles Masson was alive, one never saw you in the restaurant.

GISÈLE MASSON: I was backstage. My husband hated finance and all that part of running a business, so I did it, even the union contracts. I let him handle the operation of the restaurant, and the flowers. That's what he loved and he didn't want to be bothered with the rest. He was right because an artist shouldn't have to worry about business.

MARC: So you are good about business. You are also one of the most elegant women in New York. Let's talk about how you got that way.

GISÈLE MASSON: I was born in fashion. On my mother's side, everybody was in fashion, not as designers but as seamstresses. My great-grandmother, my grandmother, my mother at twelve was a seamstress. Fashion was what I always wanted to do. I worked in Paris for a while at Robert Piguet and then I came to New York and worked at Christian Dior, but in the office. I loved it. The first day—it was between seasons and they were selling hats. I bought three. Then I kept spending more and more, everything on sale I bought. I adore fashion. I love the fabrics. I love the feathers. Everything.

MARC: I think of you as one of my gray-haired beauties. May I ask you how it is that you don't color your hair?

GISÈLE MASSON: I adore gray.

MARC: When did your hair lose color?

GISÈLE MASSON: When we opened the restaurant twenty years ago, I still had black hair, and then all of a sudden it switched. One day I woke up and I was gray. Or so I remember it.

MARC: Mrs. Hilson, Mrs. Mosbacher, they love their gray hair. So did Mrs. Paley. But some people hate it. When you started to become gray, did you ask your husband what he thought about it?

GISÈLE MASSON: Oh, no. I wouldn't have listened to him if he had said he didn't like it. You love your husband, but some things are personal. There are some things you cannot change, because if you try, you are not yourself anymore.

MARC: Have you ever had friends say, "Why don't you color your hair?"

GISÈLE MASSON: Of course. And I say, "I love gray." It's important, though, to develop a style for your gray hair. If I had long hair, gray would look miserable.

MARC: I wonder if it's because they don't have confidence in themselves that some people hate gray so much?

GISÈLE MASSON: It's because they think gray means old. I never felt that way. Never.

MARC: You are always *le dernier cri* [the last word]. Do you only wear designer clothes?

GISÈLE MASSON: I don't buy because they are designer clothes. I buy because of the way I feel when I put on the dress or suit. I close my eyes and I know. I feel the dress before I look, before I see it. If it feels good, I say yes. It must be like a second skin. I won't buy it just because it's fashionable.

MARC: Being here in the restaurant for lunch and dinner, you are on stage in a way. How do you decide what to wear on a given day?

GISÈLE MASSON: I decided to wear this today because I felt like spring and it's not spring. I wanted a snappy suit. I keep clothes forever. It seems I keep building more closets and more closets. I have a fur jacket I brought from France thirty-two years ago. It's mouton and it has big shoulders so it looks right now. I've kept all my Roger Vivier shoes, beautiful shoes you can't find now. I don't know that those toes and heels will come back, but I love them so. You could dance with Roger Vivier's shoes.

MARC: How do you feel about color?

GISÈLE MASSON: With white hair, I can't wear every color. I like black and white, navy blue and certain reds. I never wear brown. I look terrible in it. You have to have a certain complexion and color of eyes. And I think brown is not a color a man loves.

My husband hated black so I never wore black when he was alive. I think it made him sad.

MARC: So you do believe in asking a man's opinion after all.

GISÈLE MASSON: You have to keep in your style, but you have to please a man, make him happy. First of all, because it's a game that a woman should play with a man. Make your man happy and then he is very nice to you.

MARC: That's very French. American women dress to please themselves, I think, and for each other.

GISÈLE MASSON: *D'accord.*

MARC: Frenchwomen have imagination. They dress before a mirror, studying the whole angle. The profile, the back. The average American woman puts the dress on and doesn't ever look if it fits her or if it's the right color.

GISÈLE MASSON: It's a feeling. The mood you have. One day you're in a Russian mood, one day a Moroccan mood. I think European women like to tease a man. It's a nice game.

MARC: Is it possible to dress elegantly without money?

GISÈLE MASSON: It's more difficult. When I was in Paris, before I came to America, I had no money at all. I started making my dresses. And there are things you can do to improve an inexpensive dress.

MARC: Yes, I remember going with Nicole, a manicurist at Guillaume, to Galeries Lafayette. Two hours after she bought a dress, it was a different dress. She took the buttons off, changed the pocket, cut the bottom off because it was too long and made a loose little belt.

GISÈLE MASSON: I had a couture dress that I changed from back to front. I never wear it when the designer is around. He would be furious. It wasn't his fault. It was me. I had it made to order and it fit me beautifully, but when it was delivered, I was another person. It didn't look right on me. So I just switched it around.

MARC: Do you have the same style in your private life?

GISÈLE MASSON: At home I wear only caftans, jellabas. From the moment I wake up in the morning to when I entertain. I have some lovely Moroccan things I wear when I give a dinner in my apartment. A woman should never be seen in an apron, by the way, even when she is cooking.

MARC: Do you ever wear pants?

GISÈLE MASSON: Never. I hate slacks. Even when I'm in the country. I have a house in the northern part of Brittany, facing the islands of Jersey and Guernsey, at Les Sables-D'Or-Les Pins. It's very rough country and I go there in the summer, but even there I wear skirts and blouses.

MARC: Did you ever forbid women to wear pants in the restaurant as another woman restaurateur did? The excuse was that standards have to be kept up. Another French restaurateur wouldn't let people wear glasses pushed up in their hair.

GISÈLE MASSON: We never did that. Women can be very elegant in slacks. It's a matter of personality, and also of feeling. We do enforce a rule of dress for men. They have to wear jackets and ties, or an ascot.

MARC: Do you have any trouble doing that?

GISÈLE MASSON: We have about six Saint Laurent blazers and Cardin ties to give men who don't have jackets and ties, and there are some who have walked out because they don't want to put them on. It is their privilege.

I see some men looking very elegant with their shirts open halfway down their chest. They have a style of their own and that's okay. But another comes in with a big belly and you cannot say, "It's because you are fat that you can't come in here." To avoid complications, we have the rule.

MARC: What do you think of those Hollywood men who go to a black-tie event with an open collar, even when they go up to accept an award? Or men who go to the opera in blue jeans? Can't they dress properly?

GISÈLE MASSON: I don't understand it either. In the Seventies, people were dressing down, but here I have a feeling it's getting better.

MARC: Do you think there is such a thing as elegance left?

GISÈLE MASSON: Yes. We have men and women coming here looking so elegant. It's a pleasure. So many women are even wearing hats now.

MARC: La Grenouille is noted for its flowers. You have small arrangements on every table, though I notice the flowers are not scented, because that would interfere with the food. How do you feel about perfume and food?

GISÈLE MASSON: The scent must be imperceptible. I put perfume behind my ears and a few drops on my hair. My favorite is Caron's "Narcisse Blanc." You can only buy it in France. And I adore something they have that's like toilet water, "Bain de Champagne." The bottle looks like a bottle of champagne. It's so elegant. Caron has this little shop across from Dior. Valerian Rybar decorated it. *C'est formidable.*

MARC: You once told me you opened a restaurant so you wouldn't have to cook. Did you know how to cook?

GISÈLE MASSON: I never wanted to cook when my husband was alive because he was so critical. Although he had been a headwaiter at Le Pavillon, he had worked in the best restaurants in the world in Europe and he had such marvelous training. He was a perfect cook.

As a child he had worked in his parents' restaurant and he developed that taste. He could take anything and create something wonderful. We used to have a little restaurant in the Berkshires and during the duck season he would awaken me at four in the morning and say, "I have prepared a mallard." And I would think, *Oh, no.* But then I knew it would be perfect, so I got up and we had it at four in the morning.

Once I wanted to surprise him with a recipe I had read about shad. If you put sorrel inside, it dissolves all the bones, it said. I love shad, and wouldn't it be marvelous if you could eat it without all those tiny bones? So I made a shad for him and when he came home, I said, "Look what I've done." He took one bite and it was full of bones. He said, "*Ma pauvre Gisèle.*" He opened the closet that had the garbage can and threw it in.

When he died, slowly I started at home to cook, remembering everything I had observed. I developed good taste. My husband used to make me taste everything.

MARC: I think that is what many amateurs don't do enough of—taste.

GISÈLE MASSON: You must taste, and keep tasting, while you cook.

MARC: What do you like to make for yourself?

GISÈLE MASSON: I adore soup. When I take a day off, I make soup. Or I roast a chicken, with celery and onion and herbs inside. Then after it is roasted, I remove the fat and deglaze the pan with sauterne. I strain it and pour it over the chicken. And maybe add a few white grapes. It's delicious.

But when I'm all alone, I make this wonderful meal for myself. Borsch, a baked potato with butter and lots of caviar. And sherbet with slices of pink grapefruit and vodka poured over it for dessert.

It's a very satisfying meal and it makes you feel very happy. Of course, the champagne is on the table.

BORSCH MASSON

3 tablespoons butter
1 leek, trimmed and rinsed well
2 carrots, quartered
1 onion, sliced
2 ribs celery and leaves
1 large beet, peeled and cut in half
3 cups chicken consommé
1¼ pounds brisket of beef cut in chunks
4 chicken necks, cut in pieces

Melt butter; add carrots, onion, leek, celery and one-half of the beet cut into small sticks. Gently cook over low heat, stirring; do not brown. Add consommé. Add beef and chicken necks, salt and pepper to taste. Bring to a boil, cover and simmer one and a quarter hours, skimming the surface as necessary.

Strain the bouillon through a cheesecloth. Return to a clean kettle; add other half of beet, minced. Bring to a boil for fifteen minutes; strain again.

Serve hot with or without sour cream.

POTATO À LA RUSSE

Scrub one large Idaho potato, wrap in foil and bake in 450° oven for one hour. When cooked, remove foil, slit open the potato and add one tablespoon butter and two ounces Beluga caviar.

SORBET À LA VODKA

Line a tulip glass with five slices of pink grapefruit. Fill glass to the half with lemon sherbet. Pour one-half ounce vodka over the top.

My country house is in upstate New York in an area called the French Catskills because of the number of restaurateurs, chefs, caterers, wine merchants and others like myself from Manhattan's French-speaking colony who have made it their weekend retreat.

Typically, we make the two-and-a-half-hour drive on Friday evening (the restaurant people depart around 11:00 P.M.) and return to the city Sunday evening. Saturday night is the least chic night of the week in Manhattan, except for a few weekends in the winter. The fashionables are in the country, or, if kept in the city, stay at home, leaving the restaurants to the suburbanites and visitors from out of town.

Our little weekend group consists of Sirio Maccioni of Le Cirque; André Soltner of Lutèce; Gérard Reuther, the chef at Tucano; and Jacques Pépin, the culinary writer and lecturer, to name a few. The late Pierre Larré, of Larré's, is sorely missed.

We hunt and fish and ski together—once a year there is the U.S. Chef's ski race at nearby Hunter Mountain. After any of these activities, everyone repairs to one of the members' homes (we take turns acting as host) for a good meal. We sip cider, nibble on salami and cheese, and talk while the preparation of the dinner goes forward as a collaborative effort.

New York State is apple-growing country like Normandy, and the landscape of orchards and farms in certain areas reminds us of this heavenly province of France. Normans say their cider is the champagne of the apple—American hard cider is dismissed as mere apple juice—and my neighbors vie for the honor of champion cidermaker.

Famous as they may be for their three-star cuisine, for their own pleasure restaurant men prefer the simplest food, the bourgeois cooking of their childhood, a regional specialty or two.

From keeping my eyes and ears open during these informal seminars, I have learned a great deal about the preparation and enjoyment of food, and have acquired a small repertory of classic recipes that are easy for even a novice to make.

This is my favorite dish, a simple classic of French cuisine, perfect to serve at the most elegant dinner party or in the company of friends on a weekend in the country. To complete the meal, I serve a salad of watercress and arugula with oil and vinegar dressing, and Brie; for dessert, fresh raspberries with *crème fraîche*.

GIGOT D'AGNEAU (*Leg of Lamb*)

Find a good butcher who carries baby lamb and knows how to cut the leg European-style—i.e., don't let him sever the shank bone but leave some to use as a handle for cooking and carving, also leaving what we call "the mouse," the little muscle close to the bone. If you want to serve five—probably about seven pounds, ask the butcher to give you a gigot to serve seven. You will certainly want second help-ings and something for the leftover dish.

Preheat oven to 350°.

Remove all fat from the meat. Slash in six or eight places, inserting a peeled clove of garlic in each opening. Keep feeling the meat so you can avoid the bone when you make the slashes. Rub with a little vege-table oil as though you were giving the leg a massage.

Holding the bone as a handle, brown the leg on each side in a heavy skillet over high heat. We call this "sizzling" and it seals in the juices of the meat.

Place in a roasting pan with two carrots, scraped and cut in half, and one onion, peeled. Season lamb with a mixture of salt, black pepper, dried rosemary, marjoram and thyme that you have prepared in advance.

Place in preheated oven; allow twenty minutes a pound for the meat to be pink when sliced.

When meat is done, remove from oven and let rest for twenty min-utes before carving to preserve the juices inside the meat. Holding onto the shank bone, carve into thin slices with a long, sharp knife freshly sharpened with a steel.

While meat is resting, skim fat off roasting pan, place pan over burner on top of stove, add one-half cup white wine or vermouth and scrape particles clinging to pan. This is called "deglazing" and should be done with a wooden spoon. Transfer to a saucepan, add one or two cups of beef bouillon or, better, a lamb stock that you have pre-viously made with lamb bones, onion, celery, carrot and bouquet garni. Simmer for about ten to fifteen minutes; strain while pressing roasted carrot and onion against the mesh to extract juices. Reheat and serve with the lamb.

SECOND-DAY GIGOT

Dice leftover lamb. Boil one-half pound peeled potatoes in two cups chicken bouillon. Drain; leave in saucepan to steam dry. Add a little milk and pass through a food mill or strainer to make a puree. Add half a stick of butter, one egg yolk, a little milk and (optional) chopped, cooked leeks if you have any of those left over. Cook over slow fire to marry the ingredients. Add diced meat, one-eighth tea-spoon nutmeg, salt and pepper to taste. Add grated Gruyère cheese to create a *gratin*. Pass under the broiler for five minutes to brown.

FLAGEOLETS LYONNAISE

Soak one pound dry flageolets overnight in water to cover. Add a bouquet garni and cook in the water for one to one and one-quarter hours. Drain.

In another pan place four tablespoons butter and one onion, chopped fine. Cook until onion is translucent, being careful not to brown. Add three slices bacon, chopped fine. Stir. Add one eight-ounce can tomato sauce and half of a second can and the same amount of water. Bring to a boil. Add drained flageolets and cook for one hour over low heat, covered. Add salt, pepper and one teaspoon of Dijon mustard (the surprise ingredient that gives a piquant flavor). Serves eight.

I gave the recipe for Flageolets Lyonnaise to Mrs. William Paley and a few weeks later she said to me, "Let me tell you what I did with the leftovers."

MRS. PALEY'S FLAGEOLETS

To the leftover flageolets that have been resting in the refrigerator, add one spoonful of caviar and serve with a shot of vodka for lunch.

This dish for chicken with raisins and prunes is hearty peasant fare, satisfying for a cold winter evening after an afternoon of rigorous exercise.

POULET AUX PRUNEAUX   *Serves 4*

1 roasting chicken, 4 pounds (*reserve liver*)
1 cup raisins
1 cup prunes
1 cup Cognac
1 stick butter
1 large onion, diced
1 clove garlic, minced
½ cup corn oil
salt and pepper to taste

The night before, place the raisins and prunes in a bowl and cover with the Cognac. Cover and keep in a cool place; do not refrigerate. Marinate for at least twelve hours.

Preheat oven to 350°.

Melt two tablespoons butter in a skillet and sauté onion until medium gold. Chop the chicken liver (remove membrane), add to onion and cook for five minutes.

Drain the raisins and prunes over a cup and reserve the liquid. Add the fruits to the onion/liver mixture and stir over medium heat. Season to taste with salt and pepper. Add the minced garlic. Stir and cook for five minutes.

Pour the reserved liquid into the mixture; cover and lower heat. Simmer for thirty minutes. Let the mixture cool.

Stuff the chicken and truss. Salt and pepper to taste. Place six tablespoons of butter, cut into as many slices, over the chicken.

Place the chicken in a baking dish and pour one-half cup corn oil over it. Bake for twenty minutes; raise heat to 400° and bake twenty minutes more. Baste every ten minutes. Add a little water to the pan if necessary.

The following is an exceedingly simple but rather rich dessert. It can be made in the kitchen or at the table in a chafing dish.

BANANA FLAMBÉ

½ stick sweet butter
3 teaspoons granulated sugar
Juice of two oranges
6 bananas just barely ripened; peeled and quartered
1 jigger Cognac

Melt butter, add sugar to dissolve; add orange juice and stir. Add bananas and cook over low flame five to eight minutes on each side. Be sure not to let fruit become soupy. Raise flame to high, add Cognac and flame.

Lutèce has had the unswerving devotion of gourmets since it opened in February 1961 in a brownstone on East 50th Street with André Soltner, the Alsatian chef, in command of the kitchen. In 1972 he took over the business side as well from the original owner, André Surmain. Lutèce has continued to prosper, guarding the four stars conferred by influential food critics and turning away hundreds of requests for tables each day. André's wife, Simone, acts as maîtresse d'hôtel. The Soltners live above the restaurant.

Although some regulars prefer the upstairs or parlor floor, the special charm of Lutèce, particularly at lunch, is in the enclosed garden room at the rear of the ground floor with its trellised brick walls and potted palms.

The cuisine is pure classic French with such tours de force as mousse de pigeon in brioche, fresh asparagus in puff pastry, quail stuffed with foie gras, and frozen raspberry soufflé with fresh raspberries.

For dinner on Sundays at their house in the Catskills, André Soltner might prepare a specialty from his native Alsace, a simple dish made with the regional wine, Riesling. And for dessert, an open-faced apple pie, served hot.

COQ SAUTÉ AU RIESLING D'ALSACE
(Chicken Sautéed in Riesling)
Serves 4

Cut a chicken weighing four or more pounds into serving pieces. Salt and pepper the pieces and sauté them in two or three tablespoons butter in a broad saucepan over a medium fire until golden on all sides. Add one onion and one peeled clove of garlic, both chopped; one bay leaf; and two cloves. Add two cups Riesling, or any dry white wine of the Alsatian type, and one cup water. Simmer the chicken until the drumsticks are tender to the fork. Remove the chicken and keep hot. Reduce the pan juices for five to six minutes and strain.

In a second saucepan melt one generous tablespoon butter. Blend in one tablespoon flour, and gradually stir in the strained chicken bouillon. Add one cup heavy cream and a pinch of nutmeg and thicken the sauce by pouring it into three beaten egg yolks and re-heating gradually, stirring all the time with a whisk and never allowing it to boil.

Pour the sauce over the chicken and serve. The dish is greatly enhanced by a garniture of sliced and sautéed mushroom caps. Fine noodles are a perfect accompaniment.

TARTE AUX POMMES CHAUDES   *Serves 4*

½ pound *feuilletage**
2 pounds Golden Delicious apples
Juice of 1 lemon
4 ounces sweet butter
3 ounces sugar

---

* *Feuilletage* is the French puff pastry that consists of many layers of dough with very thin layers of butter in between. It requires a bit of skill to make, but it also can be bought at certain French bakeries and kept in the freezer to be thawed as needed. In the New York area, Voilà Bakeries, 140 Leonard Street, Brooklyn, N.Y., wholesale suppliers to hotels, restaurants and epicure grocers, sells both 5-lb. packages of dough and 20-lb. boxes containing sheets of dough ⅛ inch thick through such gourmet food shops as Dean and De Luca and Jefferson Market. Or telephone Voilà Bakeries (782-2700) for other retail outlets.

Line a ten-inch pie pan with the feuilletage and put in the refrigerator. Cut the apples in slices and mix with the lemon juice. Arrange the apple slices in the pie. Put the butter in little pieces on top of the apples, sprinkle half of the sugar on top. Bake in a 400 degree oven for 10 minutes. Add then the remaining sugar and bake for another 5 to 8 minutes, until sugar is slightly caramelized. Serve hot.

I met Jean-Jacques Rachou, chef/owner of La Côte Basque, when his friend and mine, Maurice Bonté, the pastry chef who was summoned to the Nixon White House to make Tricia Nixon's wedding cake and who now presides over one of the most elegant *patisseries* in New York, brought him to our countryside one weekend.

Rachou is one of the great artists of contemporary *haute cuisine*, famed both for the way in which he has lightened the French classics and for his extraordinary presentation of food.

A sixteenth-century man-of-war, its sails puffed with wind, is constructed entirely of bread. The crimson-edged white rose petals languidly gracing a plate of poached scallops and grapefruit slices turn out to be made of radishes. The sauces accompanying main courses of fish decorate the plates in which they are served with floral designs (achieved by squeezing two different sauces out of plastic bottles).

Rachou is probably the hardest-working restaurateur in New York, undoubtedly because he simultaneously operates two exceptional eating places, Le Lavandou at 134 East 61st Street, which he opened in 1975, and La Côte Basque at 5 East 55th Street. His day typically starts at 7:00 A.M. and ends at 2:00 A.M., and he follows this killer schedule six days a week.

When he rescued La Côte Basque from oblivion by buying it from the son of the late owner, Henriette Spalter, Rachou called in the artist Bernard Lamotte to freshen up the murals suggesting the port of Saint Jean-de-Luz that Lamotte had created when Henri Soulé opened the restaurant in 1958. Lest anyone overlook the new owner, Lamotte incorporated "J. J. Rachou" in the sign above the café at the right side of the mural above the bar.

Côte Basque is a haunt of fashion designers like Arnold Scaasi and high-powered financiers such as Herbert Anthony Allen, head of the investment banking firm of Allen & Company, Inc., and also chairman of Columbia Pictures, and his cousin Terry Allen Kramer.

To me it is not at all surprising that when Jean-Jacques Rachou descends from his Olympian heights on Sunday, his one day of leisure, he dines on an easy-to-prepare (and healthful) menu of grilled chicken, baked potatoes and a green salad.

In the recipe that follows, note that the marinade of oil, lemon and thyme is typically southern French, as one would expect from a native of

Toulouse. The combination of broiling and baking seals in the juices and ensures a moist, tender chicken.

POULET GRILLÉ AU CITRON

1 broiling chicken (3 pounds), split in half
1½ cups vegetable oil
Fresh thyme leaves (or 1 teaspoon ground thyme)
1 large lemon, cut in slices
Salt and pepper
1 onion peeled and sliced thin

Salt and pepper the chicken halves. Place in a baking pan or grill, bathe with one cup of the vegetable oil and sprinkle with the thyme. Leave for two hours in the marinade, to which the lemon slices have been added. Make a separate marinade of the remaining one-half cup oil and the onion. Preheat oven to 350°.

Remove the lemon and place the pan under the broiler for ten minutes on each side (basting the chicken with the marinade when you turn it) until the chicken acquires a blond color.

In a separate roasting pan, make a bed of the sliced onions, which have been removed from their marinade; place the chicken on the onions, cover with the lemon slices and bake in the oven for ten to fifteen minutes.

POMMES EN CHEMISE

4 large Idaho potatoes
3 ounces butter
1 cup sour cream
Salt and pepper
⅛ teaspoon nutmeg
1 tablespoon chopped chives
1 tablespoon chopped parsley
1 tablespoon grated Swiss cheese

Preheat oven to 350°. Wash the potatoes and bake for forty-five minutes or until well cooked, testing with a prick of a knife. Remove from oven and cut lengthwise in half; with a soup spoon, scoop out the pulp without breaking the skin. Mash the pulp with a fork, then work in the butter and the sour cream. Add salt, pepper, nutmeg, chives and parsley. Refill the skins with this composition, sprinkle grated cheese on top. Return to the oven until you have a nice glaze.

Sirio Maccioni says, "I'm Italian at heart, but the restaurant is French." The restaurant is Le Cirque, the hangout for the Reagan circle—Jerry Zipkin, the Buckleys, Betsy Bloomingdale and her California group when they are in town—as well as for the fashion press, former President Nixon, several heads of state and *le beau monde* from every continent when they are visiting New York. Since the restaurant is in the Mayfair Regent Hotel, one block from Monsieur Marc, I feel I am part of "The Circus."

Born in Montecatini in Tuscany, Sirio started at seventeen to learn the restaurant business from the bottom up—at Maxim's in Paris, on Italian cruise ships, and at the famous, now defunct, Colony restaurant where, as maître d'hôtel, he seated such regulars as the duke and duchess of Windsor, Aristotle Onassis and Frank Sinatra. President and Mrs. Reagan have dined in L'Orangerie, Le Cirque's room for private parties.

In 1975 Sirio went on a vacation trip to Nova Scotia with several restaurateurs and food critics. It was a busman's holiday and everyone was experimenting with dishes made from the wild boar and lobster that were the local specialties of the island on which they stayed. When someone called for pasta, he prepared this glorious example from the ingredients at hand: spaghetti, vegetables, basil and sweet cream. Craig Claiborne published the recipe in the *New York Times* and the dish achieved instant chic. It is one of the few Italian entrees on the primarily French menu of Le Cirque.

SPAGHETTI PRIMAVERA

1 bunch broccoli
2 small zucchini
4 asparagus spears, 5 inches long
1½ cups green beans, trimmed and cut to 1 inch
Salt
½ cup fresh or frozen peas
1 tablespoon peanut, vegetable or corn oil
2 cups thinly sliced mushrooms
Freshly ground pepper
1 teaspoon finely chopped hot, fresh, red or green chilies or about ½
    teaspoon dried red pepper flakes
¼ cup finely chopped parsley
6 tablespoons olive oil
1 teaspoon finely chopped garlic
3 cups red, ripe tomatoes cut into 1-inch cubes
6 fresh basil leaves, chopped, about ¼ cup, or about 1 teaspoon dried
    basil
1 pound spaghetti or spaghettini

2 tablespoons fresh or canned chicken broth
4 tablespoons butter
½ cup heavy cream, approximately
⅔ cup grated Parmesan cheese
⅓ cup toasted pine nuts

Trim the broccoli and break into bite-size flowerettes. Set aside.

Trim off and discard the ends of zucchini. Do not peel. Cut the zucchini into quarters. Cut each quarter into one-inch (or slightly longer) lengths. Should total one and a half cups. Set aside.

Cut each asparagus spear into thirds. Set aside.

Cook each of the green vegetables separately in boiling salted water until crisp but tender, about five minutes. Drain well, run cold water over them to chill, and drain again. Combine all vegetables in mixing bowl.

Cook peas and pea pods one minute if fresh, thirty seconds if frozen. Drain, chill with cold water, drain again. Combine with all other vegetables.

Heat peanut oil in a skillet and add mushrooms. Add salt and pepper to taste, shaking the skillet. Cook about two minutes. Add chopped chilies and parsley.

Heat three tablespoons olive oil in saucepan and add half the garlic. Add the tomatoes and salt and pepper to taste. Cook about four minutes, stirring gently so not to break up the tomatoes. Add the basil, stir and set aside.

Place the remaining three tablespoons of olive oil in a large skillet, also the remaining garlic and the vegetable mixture. Cook, stirring gently, just long enough to heat thoroughly.

Drop the spaghetti into boiling salted water. Cook until *al dente*. The spaghetti, when ready, must retain just a slight resilience in the center. Drain. Return spaghetti to the kettle.

Select a utensil large enough to hold the drained spaghetti and all the vegetables. Melt the butter in this utensil and then add the chicken broth, the cream and the cheese, stirring constantly. Cook gently on and off the heat until smooth. Add the spaghetti and toss quickly to blend. Add half the vegetables and pour in the liquid from the tomatoes, tossing and stirring over very low heat.

Add the remaining vegetables, and if the sauce seems too dry, add about one-quarter cup more cream. The sauce should not be soupy. Add the pine nuts and give the mixture one final tossing.

Serve equal portions of spaghetti mixture in four to eight hot soup or spaghetti bowls. Spoon equal amounts of tomatoes over each serving. Serve immediately. Four portions will serve as a main course; six to eight as an appetizer.

Sirio shared with me two of his favorite recipes, Chicken Diable, which is the simplest fare, and Escalope de Veau Vieille France, which could do for dinner *à deux* or for a black tie sit-down dinner.

CHICKEN DIABLE

1 3-pound chicken, split in two
1 tablespoon vegetable oil
2 tablespoons Dijon mustard
½ cup white bread crumbs
2 halves broiled tomatoes
2 tablespoons melted butter
1 small bunch watercress

Salt and pepper the two chicken halves according to taste, then cover skin with vegetable oil. Broil chicken on both sides for approximately fifteen minutes. Remove from broiler and cover the bird with a thin layer of mustard and sprinkle liberally with bread crumbs. Spoon the melted butter over the prepared chicken halves and put back in oven. Allow to cook at 350° until the bird turns golden brown. Garnish with broiled tomato halves and sprigs of watercress and serve very hot with your favorite barbecue sauce.

ESCALOPE DE VEAU VIEILLE FRANCE

3 slices of milk-fed veal (approximately 3 ounces each)
1 tablespoon flour
9 sliced mushrooms
1 teaspoon Cognac
½ cup heavy cream
few drops of lemon juice
1 cup cooked noodles
1 teaspoon oil
1 teaspoon butter

Dip veal in flour and sprinkle with salt and pepper. Heat oil in pan, sauté veal two minutes on each side and remove from pan. Add sliced mushrooms to pan and sauté. Add Cognac and flame, then add heavy cream and cook until reduced by half. Squeeze few drops of fresh lemon and correct the seasoning. Place veal back in sauce and cook about thirty seconds. Serve with piping-hot buttered noodles.

One of the joys of my youth in France was the stop we used to make on the way back from skiing at Val D'Isère at the three-star restaurant Pyramide owned by Ferdnand Point at Vienne near Lyon. A specialty *chez* Point was Truite Farcie Braisée au Porto, intriguing because the trout was braised in other than white wine, its usual partner. Point's recipe called for port, a fortified wine, but there are numerous other possibilities.

Pierre Theye, chef of the S.S. *France*, was an ardent fisherman. When he retired from the steamship company, he signed on as chef at Le Cygne, one of New York's gastronomic temples, which he left to go work for the shah of Iran. He now lives in France. While he was in New York, I used to pick him up at the restaurant on Friday evenings and drive him to the country for a weekend of trout fishing.

His recipe for stuffed salmon trout (so-called because of its pinkish flesh) calls for braising in red wine, a Bordeaux, hence its name, Chambord. If pike is not obtainable, a mousse of salmon for the stuffing is equally divine.

TRUITE FARCIE CHAMBORD

1 salmon trout, about 2½ pounds
mousseline of pike (see recipe below)
2 ribs celery, diced
1 large onion, sliced thin
6 sprigs parsley
¼ teaspoon dried thyme
1 bay leaf
fish stock (see recipe below)
1 bottle red wine
9 ounces butter
2 ounces flour
3 crayfish
4 mushrooms
1 truffle

Clean trout and slit open in back. Stuff with mousseline of pike. Stitch with needle and thread to close.

In a fish poacher, make a bed of the diced celery, sliced onion, two sprigs parsley, thyme and bay leaf. Place trout on the vegetables. Add fish stock to cover (about one inch) and two cups red wine. Bring to a simmer on top of the stove and cook for thirty-five minutes.

Remove fish from poacher, place on platter and keep warm. Remove thread. Strain liquid into saucepan and cook over high heat until reduced to two cups. Make a velouté by melting three ounces of butter in a saucepan, adding two ounces flour and cooking slowly until mixture bubbles. Remove from heat. Pour in reduced stock, stir with whisk to blend; simmer for five minutes. Add six ounces butter. Stir with whisk.

Decorate with crayfish, four fluted mushrooms, four slices truffle. Pour sauce over fish.

Mousseline of Pike

1 pound pike filet
1 egg white
1 cup heavy cream
¼ teaspoon cayenne
¼ teaspoon nutmeg
salt
freshly ground black pepper
½ ounce Cognac
2 ounces chopped truffle

Put pike and egg white in bowl of a food processor and process for two minutes. Add cream and process for one minute. Add Cognac, salt and pepper, cayenne, nutmeg and chopped truffle. Process for one minute.

Fish Stock

2 pounds fish bones (including head)
2 cups coarsely chopped celery
2 onions, sliced thin
1 carrot, sliced thin
1 bay leaf
¼ teaspoon dried thyme
4 sprigs parsley
2 quarts water
½ bottle red wine
salt and freshly ground pepper

Combine all ingredients, bring to a boil, simmer thirty minutes, and strain. What you don't use for this recipe may be frozen.

Gérard Reuther, chef at Tucano, the restaurant adjoining Club A, the New York branch of Richard Amaral's chic disco clubs of Rio de Janeiro and Paris, trained in his parents' restaurant in Lyon and with those three-star chef/owners the Troisgros Frères in Roanne and Roger Vergé at his Moulin de Mougins on the Côte d'Azur. Later, he worked with Pierre Theye on the S.S. *France* and at Le Cygne.

Passionate fisherman that he is, it follows that Gérard Reuther's specialty for friends is a hearty bouillabaisse, that chowder mixing numerous fruits of the sea.

BOUILLABAISSE DU VIEUX PORT   *Serves 6*

1 3-pound red snapper, fileted
3 small sea bass, heads and tails removed
1 3-pound striped bass, fileted
1 filet of whitefish
1 filet of codfish
1 dozen shrimp
24 mussels
24 littleneck clams
3 1-pound lobsters, steamed separately for 15 minutes
20 threads of saffron dissolved in 3 ounces water
2 ounces Ricard or other anise liqueur

Preparation for fish stock: Take out all the tiny bones from the whitefish and cod filets. Sauté fish in two tablespoons olive oil with one onion sliced thin, two ribs celery diced, one-quarter teaspoon dried thyme, one bay leaf, one strip lemon peel and one strip orange peel. Add one gallon of water and ten ounces tomato paste. Season with salt, black pepper and cayenne. Simmer thirty minutes, then strain.

Preparation for the rouille: Take the inside of two hard rolls (not the crust) and mix with five ounces of finished fish stock. In a food processor, puree ten ounces red pimiento, six cloves garlic (peeled), three egg yolks and the mixture of fish stock and bread. Gradually add fourteen ounces of olive oil until mixture is the consistency of mayonnaise. Finish with half the saffron.

Vegetable garnish: Sauté one chopped Spanish onion and four pieces white of leeks in two tablespoons olive oil for five minutes. Add four fresh, peeled, diced tomatoes and five cloves garlic, chopped. Season with salt and cayenne and cook for fifteen minutes.

Final preparation: Cut the fileted red snapper and striped bass into two-inch cubes. Mix with vegetables and remaining saffron. Place in a pot with the sea bass and all the shellfish with the exception of the lobster. Cover with stock. Simmer twelve minutes. Add Ricard. Add cooked lobster two minutes before serving. Serve rouille and croutons separately.

When Nancy Reagan checked in at the new Ritz-Carlton Hotel on Central Park South during her one-day visit to New York to attend the gala preview of the Vatican Collections at the Metropolitan Museum of Art in January 1983, it was a feather in the cap of John B. Coleman. The hotel was then barely two months old. First Families usually stay at the Waldorf Towers, although First Ladies on expeditions without their husbands have sometimes digressed, as Lady Bird Johnson used to do, to the Carlyle.

The Ritz-Carlton is one of the newest examples of a countertrend to the megahotel typically built in the heart of U.S. cities, the small, cozily luxurious hotel such as John Coleman has been developing since 1973. That year he bought the old Whitehall in Chicago, where he was engaged in real-estate development and other business enterprises and was married to the daughter of the columnist Ann Landers. They have since been divorced.

John Coleman restored the Whitehall, bought the Tremont and did the same, and in 1978 the down-at-the heels Fairfax in Washington, which was where the Reagan friends stayed during the inaugural festivities two and a half years later.

In 1980 he bought the Navarro in New York, which had outlived its heyday as a base for wealthy South Americans. He paid $15 million and spent $25 million to turn it into a 256-room hotel with the ambience of an English private house. In the meantime he had acquired, under a licensing agreement, the right from the Ritz-Carlton Hotel in his native Boston to use its name, the most elegant in American hotel history, in New York and Washington. He rechristened the Fairfax accordingly.

Sister Parish was hired to give the New York Ritz-Carlton her inimitable "undecorated look" with lots of chintz and reproductions of English country furniture. Eighteenth- and nineteenth-century sporting oil paintings collected by John Coleman hang in the public rooms. The bedrooms have four-poster beds, linen sheets and down pillows; there is a Jacuzzi and a telephone in every bathroom, and Nancy Reagan found the towels had her monogram on them.

The restaurant was named the Jockey Club after the dining room of the Washington hotel and furnished in a hunt-club style, with a long eighteenth-century English pine bar, burgundy leather tufted chairs, Spode china and fresh flowers at every table. The cuisine is a combination of French classic and *nouvelle cuisine* with a few all-American standbys such as the Jockey Club beefburger.

During the inauguration festivities, Jerry Zipkin was recommending Jockey Club crab cakes to everyone who stayed at the Fairfax Hotel, as it was then called. John Coleman gave me the recipe for this *specialité de la maison*.

JOCKEY CLUB CRAB CAKES   *Serves 4*

24 ounces fresh all-lump crabmeat, picked over
4 ounces fish velouté, cold (see recipe below)
3 egg yolks
1 tablespoon Dijon mustard
2 teaspoons Worcestershire sauce
1 cup freshly ground white bread crumbs (to bind)
1 tablespoon finely chopped parsley
1 tablespoon salt and freshly ground white pepper
4 ounces vegetable oil
4 ounces unsalted raw butter
4 parsley sprigs
tartar sauce (*optional*)

In a two-quart mixing bowl, combine the cooled fish velouté, egg yolks, Worcestershire sauce, mustard and parsley. Whisk until all ingredients are well blended. Add the crabmeat, mixing gently so as not to break up the chunks. Add the bread crumbs to bind the mixture so the patties may be formed. Divide mixture into eight balls. Shape the balls into round cakes, approximately four ounces each. Preheat oven to 350°. Put the vegetable oil in a large ovenproof sauté pan and heat. Carefully place the crab cakes in the pan. Brown on one side and turn, then put the pan in the oven for fifteen minutes. When ready, place the crab cakes on paper towels to absorb excess oil. To serve, place two on a plate and top each with a lemon slice. Put raw butter in a sauté pan and brown. Pour a portion of the butter on each crab cake. (Tartar sauce is also a fine accompaniment.) Garnish with boiled new potatoes and parsley sprigs.

Fish Essence (*for velouté*)

1 pound whitefish trimmings
1 ounce sliced onions
3 ounces mushrooms, sliced
¼ ounce parsley stems
1 bay leaf
1 sprig thyme
juice of ½ lemon
1 ounce butter
1 cup cold water
3 ounces dry white wine
pinch salt

In a one-and-half-quart saucepan, melt the butter. Add the onions, mushroom and parsley stems and cook without coloring. Add the fish, cover and allow to stew for fifteen minutes, turning the ingredients occasionally. Add the wine and reduce by half. Then add the water, lemon juice and spices. Bring to a boil, skim carefully and simmer gently for fifteen minutes. Pass through a fine strainer and use as required.

Fish Velouté

1 cup fish essence*
3 tablespoons melted butter
4 tablespoons flour

In a one-quart saucepan, melt the butter. Add the flour to form a roux. Mix well and cook slowly for five minutes until a sandy texture is obtained. Add the fish essence and bring to a boil. Reduce to a simmer and continue to cook for twenty minutes, all the while removing the scum that rises to the surface. The sauce should be of a fairly heavy consistency. Cool at room temperature and refrigerate.

Baroness Meriel de Posson, a Belgian and an accomplished sportswoman, lives in England and in Nassau and visits New York several times a year. We usually compare notes on hunting and the preparation of game. I told her that one of my all-time favorites was the specialty of the Restaurant Réal in Lichtenstein where I used to stop en route from the airport at Zürich to the Hotel Loruenser in Zurs. Three versions of venison were of-

---

* Commercially produced fish bouillon or clam juice may be used to shorten preparation time.

fered on one plate: a filet with chestnut sauce and rice, a filet with hot sauce, and a stew in sweet sauce.

On one visit to my salon after the baroness had been shooting in Austria, she told me she was planning to do some hunting in Virginia. "I found a new way to cook pheasant," she said, and gave me the following recipe.

In Belgium, they say that endive is good for the heart. I should add, "if not for the pocketbook." Here in the U.S., it is an expensive vegetable but an elegant one. In any event, chicken can be substituted for pheasant.

PHEASANT AND ENDIVE *Serves 4*

2 pheasant
16 endive
2½ sticks butter
¼ pound sliced bacon
salt
pepper
½ cup brown sugar
8 ounces heavy cream

Pat dry the pheasants, then clean off remaining feathers. Sprinkle with salt and pepper to taste. Put one-half stick butter in casserole with the bacon strips; add pheasants and roast in a 350° oven, basting constantly.

In separate pot, place very little water, one-half stick butter and all the endive. Cook until all the water has evaporated and the bottom of the pot turns *honey*-colored—not burned.

Drain, then cook again in melted brown sugar.

After pheasant has cooked, discard the grease. Place pheasant and endive in a serving dish to keep warm. If you wish, add cream to the casserole, a little at a time, stirring until it thickens. Pour over the pheasant and endive and serve.

I've always had a great weakness for Russian delights—ballet, music, caviar and dark-eyed brunette women—and so in February 1967 I gave myself a birthday present of a trip to the Soviet Union.

For a hairdresser, it was like stepping backward in time. The beauty salons—identified by numbers rather than names—were jammed with customers, who were subjected to the most primitive equipment: permanent-waving machines with electric cords; metal rollers; two shades of hair dye—black and red. Would-be blondes had only peroxide to give them a brassy look. I made my contribution to French-accented, Soviet-American friendship by presenting one salon with plastic rollers, metal hair clips, and several rolls of cellophane tape for anchoring the *guiches*, or cheek curls, that were then in style with artichoke-type haircuts.

I shall never forget the pretty young woman who followed me around the Hermitage Museum in Leningrad. She was lithe and skinny like a ballet dancer and she kept her eyes fastened on me as I studied the paintings and sculpture and listened to the explanations of the guide. Suddenly, she came close to me and slipped a piece of paper into my pocket. All I could make out from my meager acquaintance with the Russian alphabet was "Comrade Tatiana." I shrugged and put it back in my pocket.

When the tour was over, I went back to an unheated car with my guide and got inside. The windows were steamed over, and as I rubbed at them with my glove, thinking of a scene from the film *Doctor Zhivago*, which had just made a tremendous impact on fashion, I saw the girl on the steps. She smiled shyly and waved at me with her scarf as the car pulled away.

Recalling the piece of paper, I took it out of my pocket and gave it to the guide. She read it and a tear came to her eye. "Who gave it to you?" she asked.

I told her and she said, "Why didn't you talk to her?"

"Because I don't speak Russian," I said. "What did she say?"

She read it to me: " 'I don't know who you are but I want you to know I am your friend. The only thing I wish in this world is to hear the sound of your voice. Comrade Tatiana.' "

I'm still furious with myself. I would have turned Leningrad upside down to find her if only I could.

That trip was the first time I had my fill of caviar. For a foreign tourist, the cost was negligible. I had caviar with every meal and also gorged on caviar sandwiches for snacks, as nonchalantly as I might have had Croques Monsieur (grilled ham-and-cheese sandwiches) in Paris.

Fifteen years later, my friend Annik Klein, a Frenchwoman living in New York, took over the assignment of distributing Petrossian caviar and other epicurean products in the U.S. market.

Two Armenian-born Muscovites, Melkom and Moucheg Petrossian, are credited with introducing caviar to French society in the 1920s after they departed from Bolshevik Russia and settled in Paris, where they found a lively colony of fellow emigrés hungering for sturgeon-egg appetizers. The brothers managed to secure European sales rights from the Soviet authorities, who then controlled sturgeon fishing in the Caspian Sea including the Iranian side.

The Petrossian family still runs the shop on boulevard de Latour-Maubourg specializing in caviar, Norwegian smoked salmon, foie gras, truffles and other nourishment for *le grand monde*.

Annik invited some of her friends, among whom I was fortunate to be counted, for a caviar-tasting party the likes of which I never expect to attend again. Nor do I think it would be beneficial for my liver or my pocketbook to do this on a regular basis, considering that the highest grade costs about $23 an ounce and the one to be smeared on pancakes about $9 an ounce. But in the process, I learned some things about caviar I hadn't known before, and also about the serving of vodka, its preferred companion.

First, the vodka. One should start with two bottles of Russian Stolichnaya vodka, one of which has been previously emptied. Take a lemon, wash the skin and dry it, and then peel it in one continuous strip. (If you are not experienced at peeling apples and oranges as dessert fruits, this may take some practice.) Insert the strip in the full bottle of vodka and place it in the freezer for twenty-four hours. When you remove it, the vodka will have a pale yellow tinge, a zesty flavor and will pour with the consistency of oil. Serve it in silver cups if you have them (the metal retains cold and heat better than glass) or crystal cordial glasses. Transfer the remainder to the empty bottle and keep it in the freezer for future use.

As for the caviar—Annik offered three types for the first tasting: Beluga, which has the largest grayish beads and a light taste; Ossetra, which has a slightly smaller bead, a color range from yellow to brown, and a fruitier flavor; and Sevruga, with still smaller eggs of light to dark gray and a strong flavor.

The caviar was spread on triangles of lightly toasted bread brushed with a film of sweet butter. Dousing with lemon alters the taste of fine quality caviar, and such accompaniments as chopped onions and egg should be reserved for lesser grades.

The tins should be opened just before serving and placed on a bed of crushed ice rather than emptied onto a dish.

Annik then introduced us to pressed caviar, a concentrate made from more mature eggs. It has the strongest flavor and costs less than half the price of Beluga. She served it with hot blini. The small, round buckwheat cakes were sprinkled with melted butter, heaped with pressed caviar and topped with a spoonful of sour cream.

It became clear at this intensive gastronomic feast why vodka is better than champagne with caviar. Champagne is really too sweet and its sparkling quality somewhat distracting.

My profession has taken me into homes that few are privileged to see. The private quarters of the White House, which I have already described, heads the list. I have been to residences far grander but not necessarily more inviting, and some much less imposing but unforgettable. What interests me in someone's home is the degree to which it expresses the owner's personality, whether she arranged for furnishings herself or hired a decorator to carry out her wishes.

I have concluded that a woman who is truly elegant in her dress and appearance will live in compatible surroundings. Obviously, it takes money to live with fine furniture and art, but the same eye for line and color that is essential to develop a refined taste in dressing can help one create an appealing environment with relatively modest resources. I recall a living room in the Oscar de la Rentas' compound in La Romana in the Dominican Republic. Françoise de la Renta had covered the walls and cushions with inexpensive flower-printed squares to create a wonderfully airy yet voluptuous effect. This was before women's magazines were instructing their readers how to decorate with bed sheets.

For some reason I don't quite understand, the contrary is not the case. I have seen women whose homes were magnificent but who couldn't put themselves together with any distinction. It may be a question of interest, that they attach more importance to decorating their homes than to adorning themselves.

Often when I have been asked to a client's home to comb her hair, she has asked me to stay for a drink or a meal. Whenever possible, I have made my way to the kitchen, my favorite place in any house.

Mrs. Charles Wrightsman, wife of the oilman and art collector, divides her time between a house in Palm Beach and an apartment in New York that is a private museum of French eighteenth-century treasures. She and her husband were benefactors of the Metropolitan Museum of Art and in the process of collecting she became an art scholar.

A dark-haired woman with delicate features and a sprinkle of gray in her dark hair, Jayne Wrightsman is a perfectionist in every phase of her life, including temperature control. To protect the wood-paneled walls and the antique furniture, the temperature in the apartment is maintained at 72 degrees and the humidity at 55 percent. When I went to the apartment to comb her hair one afternoon in late spring, I heard her instructing a new maid to place the white wine to be served that night in the refrigerator no more than one hour before it was to be poured. White wines should be served slightly chilled, not iced.

"I make the best daiquiris," Mrs. Wrightsman told me, and when I tasted the one she offered me I couldn't wait to get the recipe.

JAYNE WRIGHTSMAN'S DAIQUIRI *Makes 3*

Mix four teaspoons of superfine sugar made into a syrup with three ounces of lime juice, freshly squeezed. Add 6 ounces of light Bacardi rum.

Run a slice of lime around the rim of each cocktail glass and dip rims into bowl of superfine sugar. Place in refrigerator one-half hour before using.

Pour contents of the mixture into cocktail shaker one-third filled with ice cubes. Shake well. Pour into chilled cocktail glass.

Do not leave any mix in shaker. Transfer to another container and refrigerate for use as second or third cocktail.

Terry Allen Kramer, the Broadway producer, entertains leading theatrical, financial and political figures in her Park Avenue apartment. Although she has competent staff in her homes in New York and Nassau, she likes to prepare some of the dishes if she has the time. She serves a brook-trout mousse with drinks and recommends it be made a day or two in advance.

TROUT MOUSSE

1 smoked brook trout, skin removed
3 ounces cream cheese
3 tablespoons fresh lemon juice
1 teaspoon chopped parsley
1 teaspoon chopped chives
1 small onion, grated fine, almost pureed

Puree all ingredients. Place in small oiled mold or bowl and chill overnight. Turn out on plate. Surround with crisp, thin crackers.

Terry Allen Kramer also likes this white-chocolate mousse because it is easy to make and looks so beautiful when arranged on a pure white china or crystal plate surrounded by green leaves and white buds or flower petals.

WHITE-CHOCOLATE MOUSSE WITH CHOCOLATE SAUCE

Mousse

½ cup cold milk
1⅛ teaspoons Knox gelatin
6 ounces white chocolate
1 teaspoon vanilla extract
1 cup heavy cream
¼ teaspoon lemon juice
Dash of salt
2 egg whites

Place milk in an unheated double boiler and sprinkle with gelatin; let gelatin soften. Put on heat; when gelatin is completely dissolved, stir carefully; add chocolate, and stir occasionally until melted. Remove from heat. Stir in vanilla and let cook to about 80 degrees.

Beat well-chilled cream to soft peaks and fold one-half at a time into chocolate mixture. Add lemon juice and salt to egg whites and beat until stiff but not dry. Fold into chocolate mixture one-half at a time. Chill.

Chocolate Sauce

2 tablespoons unsalted butter
½ cup sugar
½ cup Dutch chocolate
2 cups heavy cream

In a saucepan, melt butter over medium heat until bubbling. Add sugar, and whisk together. Add cocoa; whisk together. Add cream. Bring to just simmering. Remove from heat; strain; cool. Lay plastic wrap directly on surface of sauce to avoid skin formation.

Assembly

Cover surface of plate with sauce. Using large heated spoon, deftly scoop two ovals from bowl of mousse and position on plate.

Frances Munn Baker, whom I had known in New York and Paris, invited me to her villa in Grasse when I was visiting the French Riviera. She had restored three small buildings of an old monastery. Some of the kegs in which the monks had distilled their brandy were still on display.

In one of the buildings, which was shaped in the round, she had broken through the stone walls to create a bathroom with wide windows overlooking the hills. She called it "my 747," and it did remind one of the cockpit of a jumbo jet. It had an antique pewter bathtub set in marble.

Mrs. Baker was passionate about needlepoint, and the living-room sofas, chairs and stools were covered with her handiwork. To enter the room was like stepping into a field of flowers, the colors blending as in a Monet painting.

The kitchen was a typical French country kitchen with old wooden tables, clay pots for the vinegar, and a shelf of cookbooks. Mrs. Baker, a gourmet, planned the menus and did the marketing. My eye caught sight of vegetables the likes of which I have missed during all my years in America. "May I peel the asparagus?" I asked the cook.

She looked quizzically at Mrs. Baker, who said, "You don't have to do that."

"Ah, but I should love to," I replied, and when she saw that I meant it, she opened a bottle of white wine, which we sipped as I scraped away and then addressed myself to slicing the tomatoes.

Lunch was a beautiful local fish cooked with herbs and tomatoes and garlic as they do in the south of France, with fruit from the garden for dessert. We ate on the terrace beside the swimming pool with her guests, Elizabeth and Anastassios Fondaras of New York. Afterward, both women washed their hair inside the house and I set it outside, and gave Mr. Fondaras, an investment banker, a haircut, too. We sipped calvados as we talked. It was an afternoon in paradise.

The lunch inspired me, when I was back in New York, to prepare red snapper in the same provincial style.

FILET OF SNAPPER *Serves 4*

4 filets of red snapper (*or 2 whole fish*)
12 young red potatoes
1 bunch parsley, snipped
2 stalks celery, chopped
4 whole tomatoes, cut and remove seeds (or 1 16-ounce can peeled tomatoes)
1 large onion, finely chopped
1 clove garlic, crushed
1 bay leaf
1 pinch each of basil, marjoram, thyme
1 cup white wine
25 black olives (*from Nice preferred*)

Boil potatoes for fifteen minutes. After they have cooled, peel then slice. In a frying pan, sauté onion in two tablespoons butter and two tablespoons olive oil. Add tomatoes, crushed garlic, celery, parsley and spices. Add wine gradually and cook for about twenty minutes, stirring often, until sauce thickens.

In a separate pan (9 x 12 x 2), place a drop of oil. Rub fish on both sides with oil and sprinkle with salt and pepper. Add sauce, the olives and the potatoes. Bake in 350° oven for forty minutes, basting occasionally.

What impressed me about the various residences of Mr. and Mrs. John Hay Whitney was their comfort and cheerfulness. The rooms beckoned you; nothing made you afraid to touch, although so many of the furnishings and paintings were of museum quality. Every place they lived in was truly a home.

Despite the fortune he had inherited and the fortune he himself had made in various enterprises, Mr. Whitney was a modest man, generous and warmhearted. His French butler, Emile, used to tell me, "I work for a prince." At Christmastime, Mr. Whitney used to call together the staff at Greentree, his 500-acre estate in Manhasset, Long Island, so that he could personally wish them well and give them their presents. There were more than twenty people he chatted with in his genuinely interested manner. He always used to thank me for coming to do his wife's hair. Mrs. Whitney loved wildlife and nature, which made me feel very close to her. She used to bring me quail she had shot and sausage from their plantation in Thomasville, Georgia.

The Whitneys' house on East 63rd Street was a wonderful mixture of English and French taste. He had been ambassador to Britain in the Fifties and the house was filled with exquisite English furniture and part of his collection of French post-Impressionist paintings.

When Princess Margaret visited New York, the Whitneys entertained her at dinner. After I combed Mrs. Whitney's hair, the butler showed me, with considerable pride, the table set for the royal guest. The sheer flower-embroidered cloth by Porthault was so fine that it looked like a veil between the mahogany and the plates and stunning display of silver.

When construction was begun in the street for the Second Avenue subway, the Whitneys moved out of the house and into a duplex apartment on Beekman Place. By then, Mr. Whitney had come into possession of six Picassos from the Gertrude Stein collection. He and his brother-in-law, Mr. Paley, David and Nelson Rockefeller and André Meyer of Lazard Frères had put up $6 million to buy the collection, and those pictures were part of his share.

I had never seen a man's bedroom to equal Mr. Whitney's in the house on 63rd Street; the walls were of mahogany imported from England with green pleated moiré silk between the panels, and there was a huge bed made of the same wood. But that was before I saw the bedroom on Beekman Place, where he hung his Picassos. Mrs. Henry Parish II, the decorator, picked up the colors from the paintings for the walls and draperies and bedcover.

Sister Parish ran into a problem when it came to the sun-room overlooking the East River. Mrs. Whitney wanted a Henri Rousseau painting of a jungle scene brought from Greentree to hang in the room, but it turned out that it was too large. So Mrs. Parish reproduced it at one end of the room with a setting of plants and a palm tree with a black ceramic monkey nestled at the base of the trunk.

The Whitneys had a French cook who made a wonderful Boeuf Bour-

guignon they both enjoyed. And so have I when I have made it according
to her recipe.

BEEF BOURGUIGNON

3 pounds beef (from neck and shoulder), cut into 3-inch cubes
½ pint Burgundy
2 large onions, diced
2 bunches carrots, sliced
2 tablespoons oil
Butter
4 tablespoons brandy
3 cans beef stock
½ cup water
Juice of ½ lemon
1 pound mushrooms
20 small white onions
12 small young red potatoes
Bouquet garni

Put the Burgundy, diced onions, one bunch of carrots and the bouquet garni (made of fresh thyme, parsley and two bay leaves, all tied
together) in a deep dish. Add the beef, salt and pepper, and marinate,
covered, overnight.

Pour off the marinade and save it. Dry the pieces of beef and sauté
very quickly over hot fire using the oil and one tablespoon butter.
Brown on all sides but do not overcook, then put in a large heavy
casserole.

Sauté the onions and carrots from the marinade together, adding
more butter if needed. Put the meat back in the sauté pan with the
carrots, onions and bouquet garni. Get everything very hot, then
flame with four tablespoons of brandy, shaking the pan to keep the
flame going. Reduce the heat and cook for five minutes. Take out just
the meat and set it aside. Pour the marinade into the pan (with the
carrots and onions) and cook over medium heat for fifteen minutes to
evaporate the wine. Then put everything into the large casserole and
add the three cans of beef stock, being sure there is enough liquid to
cover the meat.

In a separate pot, cook mushrooms in butter to slightly brown
them, then add one-half cup water and the lemon juice. Remove
mushrooms and set aside. Pour the liquid into the casserole with all

the other things and simmer the mixture for two and a half hours. Strain everything into a large pot.

Take out the pieces of meat. Discard the carrots, onions and bouquet garni. Strain the sauce into a pot and place over medium heat, skimming the grease from the top. Bring to a boil and add just enough roux (about two tablespoons) to thicken. Boil for about ten minutes. Taste and add salt and pepper if needed. If not sweet enough, add one or two tablespoons of port or one teaspoon sugar.

Put in one tablespoon butter in water and boil together the white onions and the other bunch of carrots. Cook the small potatoes separately.

Put everything in a large pot—meat, carrots, onions, potatoes, mushrooms—bring to a boil and serve. Do not overcook.

Everything about Mrs. Paley was done to perfection. The notepaper matched the little vase by the telephone on her desk that contained pencils sharpened to flawless points. That was her refined taste and also her husband's. Mr. Paley was to have everything just so, whether in his business or his private life, his office or his home, and his haircut must be perfect, too. For years he was president of the Museum of Modern Art.

Mrs. Paley's was an artistic sensibility and she was very gifted at drawing. She liked to sketch hands, which, she told me, were the first thing she looked at in meeting an individual for the first time. She believed you could tell a lot about people by looking at their hands: whether they were honest, sensitive—lots of things. She also sketched her grandchild's face.

Drawing was her private hobby and she didn't want to advertise her talent. Only if she felt close to you would she show you her sketches. Although Russell Page, the English landscape designer, had laid out the scheme for much of the gardens at Kiluna Farm, Mrs. Paley loved to garden herself—she had a need to feel the earth with her fingers. She certainly had a magic touch. After I saw the vegetable garden she had planted, every bit as beautiful as her flowers, I could imagine her waving her wand and causing it to appear, a perfect harmony of line and color, with the red cabbages set just so next to the parsley.

She planted daffodils outside her bedroom window in Manhasset so that she could see them when she got up in the morning. But she was disappointed. "The daffodils are angry. They turned their backs to me," she reported one spring morning with a smile. She had overlooked the exposure of that side of the house and the flowers were facing the sun at that hour.

Mrs. Paley taught me how to naturalize a field or a border with daffodils. Dig up an area of soil, throw the bulbs down as though you were rolling a bowling ball, then make sure that each bulb is right side up before covering them with dirt.

For cut flowers inside the house, Mrs. Paley liked delicate blooms on long stalks—tall and slender like herself, I thought—and she preferred them to be white. Freesias and lilies were among her favorites. Nancy Reagan also likes white flowers, especially the scented variety.

Although I personally like colorful arrangements, naturally done with an air of *chic negligé* in a countrified manner, white flowers have a tradition of elegance, possibly because of the aesthetic purity they evoke.

At a cocktail party in New York for Givenchy honoring his thirtieth anniversary as a couturier, the room was filled with masses of white spring flowers: dogwood, lilacs, tulips, peonies, roses and freesias. The buffet was in keeping with the elegant backdrop—caviar, smoked salmon and pâté in one room, and an array of French cheeses in another, as waiters passed from one to the other with trays of champagne.

To what do we owe this chic of white flowers? Some trace it to the all-white drawing rooms that Syrie Maugham, the interior decorator, imposed on London society in the Twenties and Thirties. Cecil Beaton, the scenery designer, said they looked like "albino stage sets."

In Paris, the incomparable Antoine contributed to the mystique with his superstition about having white lilies around him when he started something new. He had himself photographed lying in a glass bed shaped like a coffin, flanked by white calla lilies, a flower that received its American endorsement from the young aristocrat Katharine Hepburn, in the 1932 film *Bill of Divorcement* ("the calla lilies are in bloom"). I must say that however many times I have seen those flowers in elegant settings, they always remind me of Easter church services.

The heavy fragrance of some white flowers—gardenias, lilies of the valley, tuberoses—and the somewhat lighter perfume of freesias, lilacs, narcissus, and lilies probably accounts for some of their popularity among the *beau monde*, which goes to great lengths to scent their rooms with Rigaud candles and Guerlain potpourri. There are two schools of thought about the latter. Personally, I find the custom rather inconsiderate of those who may be allergic to scent, somewhat along the order of the after-dinner cigar, which, however fine its aroma, may offend the person on the adjacent banquette at La Grenouille.

There is an emphasis on fragrant white flowers in the so-called moon gardens that are planted to be enjoyed in the evening. It's a very romantic idea to set a border of white flowering tobacco, four o'clocks, sweet alyssum and delphiniums within view of the living-room windows or the veranda of a country house, and to plant a moonvine to climb the trellised arch of the path leading to the border, and on which one can stroll in the moonlight with a beloved.

Cognoscenti who keep tabs on the social status of botanical species assure me that a blue garden competes with white in snob value. Each has its partisans, though some maintain blue is the Avis to white Hertz.

Georgianna Orsini, another devoted gardener who, like Mrs. Paley, is very private about her artistic gifts (she is an accomplished pianist and poet as well), showed me her blue garden on a midsummer afternoon we spent with mutual friends in Dutchess County, New York.

She and her husband, the owner of Orsini's restaurant, are a glamorous couple. Georgianna is willowy, a long-stemmed American beauty, as they used to say, with thick chestnut hair and lustrous brown eyes. Armando, a Roman by birth and handsome profile, was trained as a civil engineer but made his career as a restaurateur to fashion society and the jet set.

"This is my sadness garden," Mrs. Orsini said as we stood before a plot of blues, purples and mauves surrounding a burbling fountain. It was inspired by *Swan Lake*, "when the curtain goes up and the prince is lost in the woods." She added, "Something wonderful happens, but not forever."

Electric-blue delphiniums rose majestically around purple asters, pale blue phlox, mauve tree roses, white snapdragons and artemesia. The gray of the stone and the artemesia and the vertical thrust of the roses set the direction for the garden. "All it awaits is twilight," she said.

The temperature hit 98 degrees and we shifted position to escape the sun, sitting for a while in an arbor by the swimming pool listening to the cooing sound from the dovecote above; then moving to the gazebo a few yards from the house, where we sipped mint tea and munched on orange-peel cookies and chocolate-dipped strawberries while wind chimes tinkled. Wooden tablets inscribed with haiku—"I Sit Here Making the Coolness My Dwelling Place," "The Melons Look Cool Flecked with Mud from the Morning Dew"—are hung in the little circular pavilion. She attaches her own poems to the trees in the wooded area of their property, which is hidden at the end of a winding road on the border of Connecticut.

We moved to the terrace outside the weathered redwood house that looks like an enchanted cottage rising from a series of gardens and overlooking the Hudson Valley. There in the shade, surrounded by pots of orange, peach and red-toned tuberous begonias with ruffled petals, we continued our conversation while I cut her hair.

Georgianna Orsini grew up in Albany, New York, and considers herself a self-taught gardener. Living in Italy for a few years in the Seventies "under that benign climate" expanded her horizons with the confidence of knowledge and creative awareness.

She learned three "extremely basic things," she says. "One, we Americans don't use big enough pots. That was the generosity of the Italian people—give the plants more room. Two, the importance of good dirt. I go into the woods here to get it. Three, the importance of general fertilizer. There we had a wonderful mold from the chestnut trees, but here it's compost. And, oh, yes, a fourth—watering.

"The price I pay for all this," she said, indicating the gardens in midsummer bloom, "is daily vigilance. I'm like the nun making the rounds of the convent. From May to September, I stay here. I don't go to New York. I decided I can't do everything."

In whatever sphere, elegance is hard work and discipline.

Georgianna Orsini believes that a person who is sensitive to people, plants or animals is usually sensitive to all three. "It's creatureliness," she says. Certainly, as hosts, she and Armando are noted for the particular pleasures they bestow on their guests and their awareness of personal whims and foibles.

For a birthday celebration around the Fourth of July, just before the cake is placed on the table, Georgianna might appear with stalks of campanula (the flower known as cup-and-saucer or bellflower) just picked from the garden. She selects the most chalicelike florets and hands one to each guest for Armando to fill with champagne.

The Orsinis are far removed from the competitive, museum-type fetes of *le grand monde*. Georgianna believes in costume parties, and in small gatherings "like children's parties, where everyone can succeed. Ordinary parties are costly in terms of pressures and strains.

"Women don't have to be beautiful at my costume parties," she says. "The purpose is to take people out of themselves, beyond the masks they usually wear." Particularly with shy, sensitive people, she finds that getting them to put on costumes lets them achieve a spontaneity in their small talk and exchanges at the dinner table.

At a Halloween party, she and Armando dressed as a pair of dolls, Raggedy Ann and Andy, authentic in every detail from their red mop hairdos to their patterned socks. Two very reserved guests came as abominable snowmen, a financier as Charlie Chaplin's Little Tramp, and his wife as a flapper in lamé and pearls.

As the guests drove up to the gates in the blackness of an October night, they were greeted by ghostly wails and a phantom flapping over their heads. In the garden soil by the front door was a phalanx of tombstones with inscriptions from old New England graveyards.

More surprises were in store for them. The first course at dinner was carpaccio, the raw beef sliced paper-thin and lightly dressed with oil and vinegar. The round table was then cleared and a circular butcher block placed on top. Armando and the housekeeper appeared with a steaming copper pot, which they overturned on the block, the contents taking a free-form shape before the astonished eyes of the guests, who were given forks and told to begin. As each one made inroads on the concoction of polenta and sausages, it assumed the contours of an inkblot in a Rorschach psychological test.

Armando explained that soft polenta, Roman-style, was traditionally eaten by families in this manner off the marble tables in their kitchens. In restaurants it was served in wooden plates, as it must also be stirred in the pot with a wooden spoon, since the heat evaporates when the polenta is placed in ceramic. He had a three-inch butcher block made so that he could offer the dish to guests in their home, but ideally, he said, it should be made of lighter-weight cedar or oak.

Here is the recipe for polenta and sausages, which should be followed by a light dessert of sherbet or macédoine of fruits.

POLENTE E SALCICCIE *Serves 6*
(Polenta and Sausages)

1 package of instant polenta
4 sausage links, 5–6 inches long
1 cup white wine
1 medium onion, chopped
2 tablespoons olive oil
1 24-ounce can peeled tomatoes
6 tablespoons Parmesan cheese

Heat the olive oil in a large frying pan over a medium flame. When oil is warm, add onions. When onions are golden, add sausages and prick them with a fork. After ten minutes, add the wine. When the wine has evaporated, check to see that the sausages are cooked (try with a fork), then add the tomatoes. Cook for one to one and a quarter hours; until the sauce thickens and holds together.

In the meantime, boil water in a large pot and then add the polenta. Follow instructions on package. When cooked, pour it on a wooden board and spread it to a thickness of one inch. Cut the sausages into medallions and put them on the polenta. Then spread the sauce on all the polenta and sprinkle with Parmesan cheese.

If you do not have a board, scoop the polenta into individual wooden dishes and add the sausages, the sauce and the cheese.

Armando Orsini has certainly played a part in making New York aware that France no longer holds a monopoly on chic cuisine, any more than it does on fashion. His restaurant on West 56th Street is a stronghold of the Beautiful People. At lunchtime, the fashion crowd claims the upper floor with its tile-topped tables and sunny country-Italian atmosphere. The editors of *Women's Wear Daily*, *Vogue* and *Harper's Bazaar* are the regulars, along with Halston, Givenchy, Valentino and Jackie Onassis (conferring as an editor with an author), occupying the best tables by the windows. Businessmen looking for privacy and legroom congregate downstairs, which is windowless but cheered by a twenty-five-foot mural of an Italian garden.

At night, the upstairs/downstairs symbols are somewhat reversed, and the place to be is downstairs. There one is likely to see Burt Reynolds and other celebrities from the American film world, and ultrachic Nan Kempner. Sophia Loren and other European habitués ask to be seated upstairs because they prefer the high-ceilinged spaciousness.

Pasta, which has always been a staple of Orsini's menu, and which Armando personally consumes in its simplest forms, has traveled a long way to chic status. When Brooke Astor served spaghetti with mushrooms as a first course to President-elect and Mrs. Ronald Reagan at a dinner party in her New York apartment in December 1980, pasta was certified as "in."

On one of his frequent visits to his native Rome, Armando was served Rigatoni alla Vodka as a main course at a very elegant dinner party. Rigatoni is a Roman pasta, just as spaghetti is associated with Naples. "Vodka and pasta—it sounds terrible," he says, "but it's wonderful as long as you give the vodka a chance to burn off, so as to get rid of the bitter taste." The red peppers add a subtle taste of spice to the aesthetically pleasing sauce, which is turned pink by the combination of tomatoes and cream.

Armando Orsini further explains the chic of pasta in a weight-conscious society. If you don't want to get fat, don't serve it with meat. Serve it as the principal dish. "Look at Sophia Loren," he says. "She eats pasta like crazy." Pasta by itself, preceded by a light appetizer or salad and followed by a light dessert, such as fruit or sherbet can be good for you and elegant as well.

RIGATONI ALLA VODKA   *Serves 4*

1 6-ounce can peeled tomatoes
4 ounces vodka
1 espresso spoon of red pepper
1 pound rigatoni
½ pound butter
4 tablespoons heavy cream
4 tablespoons grated Parmesan cheese
Tomato sauce (approximately 10 tablespoons; more if necessary: to a dark pink)
8 leaves of fresh basil or 2 teaspoons dry basil

(For best results, put the pepper in the vodka and let sit overnight.)
In a frying pan put half of the butter and the peeled tomatoes and salt to taste (approximately one tablespoon). Cook on a low fire for half an hour and put aside. Cook in water the rigatoni; when *al dente*, drain *very, very* well! Put the rigatoni in a big pan over medium fire and stir a few moments to make the pasta really dry. Then add the vodka (with the pepper) and stir until the alcohol has evaporated. Add the remaining butter and the cream. Mix well. When the riga-

toni are well coated, add the tomato sauce and mix again. Add the Parmesan, toss and serve.

I suppose that the question I am asked more often than any other by clients from out of town is how they can get a reservation for lunch or dinner at one of the "in" restaurants—as defined either by a powerful food critic or by John Fairchild's W.

If the question is put on the spur of the moment—that is to say, they would like to go from Monsieur Marc to lunch at Le Cirque—the answer is simple: Forget it. And the answer would be the same, on short notice, for a three-star restaurant in Paris or the one restaurant in Philadelphia where the chic types supposedly congregate. You will forgive me if I don't give the name, because after the rude treatment I was accorded on the telephone, I blocked it from memory.

The owner of a notably chic dining place in New York feels the same way about the owner of a restaurant that has been awarded a fourth star by the *New York Times*. He was turned down in his request for a table on the evening of his wedding anniversary. Fraternity, if indeed there is such a thing in the restaurant business, didn't apply. "I'll never call him again," he said, unaware perhaps of how many people feel the same way about his own restaurant for the same reasons.

It's funny how much a part of the *beau monde* is this tyranny exercised by a few successful restaurant owners and their maître d'hôtels. To be denied a table—or to have a reservation accepted and then to be placed in the draft of the entrance or by the swinging door to the kitchen or the archway leading to the *toilettes*—is excruciating humiliation.

The editor of a fashion publication who always occupied the *premier rang* of tables at a French restaurant where his industry congregates was astounded to be escorted to Siberia, the table nearest the kitchen, the day after he was fired from his job.

Even Mrs. Paley was challenged by the late Henriette Spalter, owner of La Côte Basque, who set herself up as an arbiter of elegance in the late Sixties by refusing to admit women in pants. Mrs. Spalter was known in the trade as Madame Pipi because she had formerly presided over the checkroom at Le Pavillon in the days when that was the number one temple of *haute cuisine* in New York; her friendship with its *patron*, Henri Soulé, was responsible for her coming into possession of Côte Basque, a restaurant he had created for his overflow.

When Mrs. Paley arrived in a pantsuit, Spalter read her the edict, and rather than inconvenience the friend with whom she was to have lunch, "Babe" went into the ladies' room, removed the pants and came out in the tunic, which on her looked like a chic mini. But she never returned to the restaurant, and many of her friends joined her in staying away. Elegance had the last word, after all.

Restaurateurs don't feel they have to apologize for their conduct. They point out that their seating capacity is limited, that it is completely natural for them to favor their loyal clientele and to maintain the standards that made their restaurants so popular in the first place.

"If you're not famous, if your name is not immediately recognizable, then you must be known to the restaurant in some other way—as a regular client or by introduction from one," says one of the top restaurateurs, not mincing words. "We all have our hangouts, and people must accept that."

That's exactly the truth. Famous restaurants are more like private clubs than public accommodations for eating, although none of them would want to be heard admitting it to a state licensing agent. "Twenty-One" is where businessmen and entertainers go to see and be seen, and where their wives bask in the reflected glory. Lutèce is like a pension for an exclusive number of *fins becs* who can afford to gratify their palates, and in New York there is no shortage of those. Le Cirque and La Grenouille have bi-coastal society and the fashion crowd; Régine's, the nightclubbing jet set. And on an off-night, like Saturday in June, they still don't have any trouble filling their tables.

So, to answer the question posed at the beginning of this section: Telephone or write ahead for a reservation, and don't be surprised to learn that the restaurant is booked as much as two weeks, or even five weeks, ahead. If you have pull, and if it means that much to you to dine there, don't hesitate to use it, or any other means at your disposal. There are secretaries with *authoritaire* manners, backed by the powerful credentials of their bosses, who can extract a table from the most arrogant maître d'hôtel. And there are certain women who can turn on an accent—some say it's called "mid-Atlantic," but whatever it is, it carries an impression of English nannies and Swiss boarding schools in the background—and successfully outsnob a snobbish keeper of the restaurant door.

As a joke, I once identified myself on the telephone to the nameless Philadelphia restaurant as a representative of a French eating guide. It worked, though I don't think it would have in New York.

There are cases where a very attractive couple has appeared at a restaurant without a reservation and very charmingly begged for a table, even if they had to wait. It was their life's desire to dine there, they said. And they were seated. The crucial phrase is *very attractive*. Restaurants are conceived as stage sets by their owners. It is essential for them to have *beautiful people*, literally so, as well as celebrities, to dress up the appearance.

And so, the hard truth is that if you are physically pleasing and well dressed (polyester will not even get you a civil turndown), you will have better luck in obtaining a good table, and maybe even in getting a reservation to begin with.

Elegant manners never hurt either. Maître d'hôtels and owners are impressed by behavior as well as appearance. Address them with a "Good afternoon" or "Good evening." If you have a date to meet someone, say so, and ask if the person has arrived rather than plunging into the room to see for yourself.

If you see someone you know, just wave hello. That's all. Or if you pass their table on the way to yours, say, "How are you?" and pass on. Don't stop for a big conversation and don't scream across the room to get their attention.

What do you do when the maître d'hôtel ignores you? When he lets you stand at the entrance while he talks at length on the telephone or chats with customers already seated? Or looks through you to welcome a familiar face that arrived after you?

I don't think there is much you can do except put his behavior into your mental computer and act accordingly when it comes to deciding whether you wish to come back and how you will recommend the restaurant to your friends.

Which brings me to another anxiety-provoking subject: tipping. Will slipping the maître d'hôtel a $20 bill get you the table you want? Not in a good restaurant the first time. But if you want to build goodwill for the future or establish yourself as a regular, a discreet handshake with the bill pressed between your palm and his on a regular basis does have long-term results. It should be done on leaving, giving the impression of appreciation for service rendered rather than a bribe for admission.

I have heard it said that overtipping is inelegant, a sign of insecurity. That may be, but from personal knowledge I can say that some of those who occupy the best tables in the clubbiest restaurants are most lavish tippers. Of course, it's also true that they are celebrities for their wealth and accomplishment, and their patronage would be desired anyway on that score alone. There are other celebrities who are notoriously stingy and who are always led to the number one table; they think it is their due, and figure that the restaurant needs them as adornment anyway. And they are right.

So if you are a "nobody" by the arbitrary standards of a certain restaurant, you should not overtip, because it won't do you any good; but neither should you undertip, because that is not fair to those who served you.

You can't go wrong if you follow the general rule for U.S. restaurants where service is not included. (The European practice of calculating service charges and embedding them in the bill is gaining in some resorts.) Give 15 to 20 percent of the bill, depending on the service you have received. If there is a captain who does more than hand you a menu, divide the tip between him and the waiter: one-third for the captain, two-thirds for the waiter. Some people who are poor in arithmetic and don't want to whip out a pocket calculator use little tricks. In areas like New York City where the sales tax runs around 8 percent, they double the tax and add or subtract a bit.

If I am really pleased with the food, I send a bottle of wine to the chef to show my appreciation. It is customary to give a wine steward $2 for each bottle of wine served.

If the service is really poor, as has happened to me in some very well-known restaurants, I show my displeasure. I won't leave nothing, but I will cut the normal tip in half. Once after I did that, the waiter followed me to the checkroom and said, "You made a mistake." I replied, "*You* made the mistake. The food was cold. We had to ask repeatedly for bread, for butter. We had to beg for everything. I didn't come here to eat cold food after waiting an hour."

The usual tip for a checkroom attendant is $1 for one coat and 50 cents for each additional coat. Washroom attendants receive a minimum of 50 cents.

NOTES ON
ENTERTAINING

I think the cocktail party is an inelegant way of entertaining except for a business purpose, such as to honor a designer upon the introduction of his perfume, or a *vernissage* to celebrate an exhibition of paintings at a gallery, in which case the room may be filled with chic types, and the canapés and flowers can be elegantly presented.

On a private level of entertaining, though, have a few friends for drinks to meet a visitor from out of town, by all means, but a mob scene looks as though you wanted to satisfy all your social debts at once.

I prefer small groups. In the country where everyone can spill outside, I may go to forty.

Georgianna Orsini says, "Cocktail parties are dehumanizing experiences, a series of rejections, which is why I never give them and try to avoid going to them."

I agree, but since there are too many times we must go to them, for business or in order not to hurt a friend's feelings, there are a few rules for making it all civilized and even enjoyable.

• You must never engage in serious conversation. Talk small. Don't bring your business into it, and don't tell your personal problems. Just scatter a little sunshine and move on.

• Don't come too early unless you must have a serious word with the host or the guest of honor. Come about midway in the stated period when the room is warmed up for you, so to speak.

• Do say goodbye to the host and hostess. When people say to me, "They'll never know we're gone," I say, "They invited me and it's rude not to say both hello and goodbye."

In Paris, they sit down to dinner at 10:00 and go on to a disco afterward. Americans are more work-oriented, although the influx of foreigners into the New York scene is changing things. As a rule, Americans dine earlier;

how early depends on geography, how far the guests have to drive and how early the business leaders expect to be at their desks in the morning.

In New York, 8:00 P.M. is the chic hour to invite guests for dinner, because it gives everyone a chance to change and to drop into a cocktail party beforehand.

Elegant hostesses telephone personally to extend the invitation and then follow up with a card or note as a reminder.

Forty-five minutes from the time the first guest arrives is sufficient time for drinks before dinner, particularly if most of the guests have already been imbibing. It's chic to offer flutes of champagne or white wine but to have a setup of hard liquor somewhere on the side for those who prefer it.

It's acceptable to skip canapés entirely. If you feel you must offer them, do with two or three light things—smoked salmon, caviar, pâté. Crudités with a dip may look pretty but most guests don't really like them that much and they can be messy.

The wise and considerate hostess has a boiled chicken breast or some other neutral food in reserve for the guest who can't tolerate the main course. More and more people seem to have food allergies or to be on restricted diets, whether by choice or necessity. If they don't know the hostess very well, they probably won't tell her in advance.

The single flower in a crystal bud vase at each place setting is one of those chic ideas that happens to be better for conversation and economical as well in these days when a centerpiece for the dinner table from a fashionable florist costs a small fortune.

When You Are Invited

Don't bring flowers to your hostess. They are a nuisance at that point but most welcome the next day.

I always make mental notes about the taste of the hostess and host to guide me if I do send flowers and for use later on when the occasion may arise for a gift.

One owes it to one's hostess and host to dress as well as one can for their party. This doesn't mean satin and sequins, but even if one doesn't have time to change between the office and the dinner, a woman can choose clothes for the day that can be made a bit more festive with a scarf or jewelry, and a man can certainly take a clean shirt to the office.

INDEX